TRANSFORMING THE CHARACTER OF PUBLIC ORGANIZATIONS

Transforming the Character of Public Organizations

Techniques for Change Agents

A. Carol Rusaw

QUORUM BOOKS
Westport, Connecticut • London

Library of Congress Cataloging-in-Publication Data

Rusaw, A. Carol, 1946–
    Transforming the character of public organizations : techniques
for change agents / A. Carol Rusaw.
        p.   cm.
    Includes bibliographical references and index.
    ISBN 1–56720–103–2 (alk. paper)
    1. Organizational change.   2. Administrative agencies.   3. Public
administration.   I. Title.
JF1525.073R87   1998
352.3'67—dc21   97–20730

British Library Cataloguing in Publication Data is available.

Copyright © 1998 by A. Carol Rusaw

All rights reserved. No portion of this book may be
reproduced, by any process or technique, without
the express written consent of the publisher.

Library of Congress Catalog Card Number: 97–20730
ISBN: 1–56720–103–2

First published in 1998

Quorum Books, 88 Post Road West, Westport, CT 06881
An imprint of Greenwood Publishing Group, Inc.

Printed in the United States of America

The paper used in this book complies with the
Permanent Paper Standard issued by the National
Information Standards Organization (Z39.48–1984).

10 9 8 7 6 5 4 3 2 1

Contents

Illustrations

FIGURES

Acknowledgments

The book's contents, rooted as they are in human experiences, reflect the support, encouragement, teaching, and personal values of numerous transforming agents I have known. My particular thanks go to Bernardino Espinosa, my first supervisor who was also a model of spiritual leadership for me and for so many other faculty at the Defense Language Institute. I also thank Terry Newell, Jim Wolf, and Allan Drexler, who not only trained change agents in the Senior Managers Program at the Department of Education but inspired many of us when we most needed it.

I thank especially those exemplars who were willing to share their change agent experiences in order that we all might better serve public needs and inspire those who follow us, particularly Ruth Crone, Al Ilg, Lee Erdmann, and Gene Gavin.

I also appreciate the thoughful comments and suggestions from colleagues in the field of management, public administration, and organization development. Special thanks are due to Peter Vaill, Mike Harmon, Fred Luthans, Bob Goliembiewski, Jane Moosbruker, Peter Carleton, Alex Pattakos, and Dave Arnold.

Lastly, I wish to thank my husband Michael, who has given me a vision, a hope, and the determination to keep reaching.

Introduction

Like people, organizations have distinct characters that give them identity and purpose. Character includes personality traits, but it also involves underlying patterns of assumptions, motives, and preferences that provide meaning. Character influences what "makes sense" to us and directs our actions accordingly.

Character gives us our individual identities, but it evolves through learning in association with others. Sense-making comes from our abilities as well as from our social participation. We learn to value that which we have learned to trust, for example, and esteem those who act consistently trustworthily. We do not, on the other hand, normally like those whom we do not trust. The logic is based on our thinking about similar experiences involving trust. Character helps us align our mental, emotional, and affective states with action.

By this line of reasoning, illogical associations stem from misaligning inner states with actions. We may value untrustworthy people; we may feel anger toward someone but behave as if we do not have conflicting issues toward them; we may believe it is important to exercise honesty and fairness in making agreements, but we may keep important and accurate information from others to protect ourselves. The logical flaws suggest inconsistencies in character.

Flaws and inconsistencies develop unconsciously. We are not aware that what makes sense to us does not make the same sense to others. We may find this out only by comparing our logic and experiences with those of others and noting both congruities and gaps. Through negotiating similar-ities and differences in logic, we gain understanding of what is "true." When we make our knowledge and connections of logic with actions public through dialogue, we become aware of our own character.

Organizations, too, develop unconscious patterns of assumptions that they accept as true over time. To the extent that organization members can agree on the fit between what is commonly believed and valued and what is acted on, organizational character is logical. When gaps between beliefs and actions come to light, however, organizational character manifests itself.

Character flaws come from various combinations of genetic and social imperfections. Our human intelligences are limited, our perceptual apparatus cannot tell us all we know about any given experience, and our emotional states have undergone testing through numerous painful social situations. We have not coped as well as we could have with different problems, stresses, confrontations, and illnesses.

Organizations have genetic and social limitations as well, and their coping abilities depend on more complex social events and networks of others in organizational life histories. The genetic inheritance of organizations includes conditions such as reasons for coming into being; resources such as intelligence, ambition, capital, and robustness depend on the parents or "originators." In many instances, these include the owners or executors. Before birth and during early infancy, organizations have key decisions made for them, such as: What purpose will be served? Who will be the critical "others" in constituent networks? What are the environmental obstacles and how will they be met? Who will play support or nurturing roles? As organizations mature, the genetic inheritances unfold and predispose the organization to choose one course from among many. When organizations face difficulties, their characters confront opportunities for growth and redirection. Like people struggling with decisions to make during such times, organizations need the help of change agents.

For public organizations, such tests of character are more profound and complex. The "parents" are usually legislators who charter the organization from a series of compromised values and negotiated actions across political parties. Critical others in the organization's social network are numerous, diverse, and often conflicting: the public in general, interest groups, the courts, private sector organizations, lawmakers, regulatory agencies, and the media. Finding consensus among discordant voices is difficult and strains meaning-making. Instead of a nurturing community from which to take cues, public organizations face a myriad of contenders for services and entitlements. Even when organizations provide public needs, they do so with limited resources and discretionary power. This sparks widespread constituent dissatisfaction. Charges of "too much red tape" and "government waste and inefficiency" arise. Public organizations, in short, end up doing right things for all the wrong reasons, and the wrong things for the right ones.

Changing character flaws, particularly in government organizations, takes a reeducative and resocializing approach. First, because the logic is incongruent with action, change agents repair the gaps by reforming concepts, feelings, values, and beliefs. Second, change also involves creating new forums for analyzing the connections between inner states and actions from multiple participant viewpoints. Third, change integrates new principles of thought and action to create a more just and caring community for future social interactions. In brief, agents of change transform organizational character, the heart and soul of organizational thought, feeling, and action, through holistic, sense-making activities.

This book introduces individuals who wish to transform government organizations to ideas and tools for turning desires into realities. The overall plan of the book introduces the reader to the systems view of change: the integration of human logic in the planning, design, and structuring of organizations. The book shows readers how to analyze, diagnose, and reform the character of organizations. In addition, the book defines and describes specific competencies change agents need to confront obstacles, on one hand, and to build support through empathy, encouragement, learning, and community, on the other.

The book takes the view that the change agent's own character transformation is central to leading organizational transformation. Successful change is a process of continual self-reflection, remaining open to different viewpoints regarding problems or issues, creating and validating hypotheses about needs for change as additional data are analyzed, supporting and empowering those who share responsibilities for making change happen, and acting with integrity or wholeness in making decisions regarding change. Because perspectives guide actions, change agent perspectives, values, beliefs, and motives predispose certain choices. These inner states must be examined, compared with other viewpoints, and tested in action to assess their sense-making accuracy.

The role of the change agent is similar to the "sociotechnical" views in its use of the human self as an instrument to change complex technical systems. It differs, however, in its greater emphasis on collective and nonlinear change. Much of the sociotechnical change literature focuses on individual change agents who, through discussion with clients, determine a particular change strategy and carry it out with some degree of client involvement. In this book, change agents immerse themselves with a diverse set of others to create a shared vision of "truth" and sensible or logical principles by which they will enact it. The sense-making process proceeds from both conscious and unconscious levels of awareness; much of it is unquantifiable and is based on perceptions of phenomena. Unlike many books on organizational change, this one contends that "soft data" from consensus produce the "hard" or measurable data. Changing organizational systems stems from changing the human conceptions of the organization first.

To describe how change agents use an inside-out approach to leading change in public organizations, the book is divided into five parts and 16 chapters. Part I introduces the concept of organizations as humanly constructed entities and explains the need for using humans as the primary vehicles for bringing about change. It discusses a rationale and a methodology for undertaking change based on studying humans in their natural context. Chapter 1 provides a rationale and overview for using Greenleaf's change-agent-as-servant approach to transform public organizations. The central point is that successful change requires much from the inner self of the change agent in order to understand the human basis of organizations. Reflection of self in relation to higher principles produces guidelines for transforming mental models and practices. Chapter 2 depicts the interrelationships between people, organizations, and work. Change agents need skills for understanding how human ideas develop concrete systems, or interrelated, recurrent tasks that create products and services. Understanding the intertwining of people and processes from a holistic perspective yields accurate and valid data on which change agents can weave action strategies. Chapter 3 introduces techniques for gathering useful and valid data for change by using a naturalistic inquiry approach. It describes steps in holistic organization transformation, including identifying and defining the problem and the client system, contracting for change, and discussing action research as a means for data collection and analysis. Chapter 4 shows how change agents can effectively use their own selves to diagnose problems, interpret data, and develop collaborative strategies for intervening in organizations. Chapter 5 describes guidelines for implementing and evaluating change strategies. It highlights some essential elements in designing strategies and indicates some possible trouble spots during the change cycle. The chapter points out that evaluation, although seldom done following implementation, is a vital component in testing whether interventions have accomplished desired aims. The chapter also illustrates how an evaluation was done in one organization and how results were used in subsequent decision making.

Part II provides an in-depth view of the key roles change agents play in working with clients to transform organizations. The discussion rests on the assumption that the values, systems, perspectives, and experiential bases of knowledge influence how actual transformation comes about. With the understanding that organizational reality is a socially defined and negotiated process, change agents and clients need to take stock continually of their inner resources that affect change design and enactment. Chapter 6 shows how change agents can use their own selves to diagnose problems, interpret data, and develop collaborative strategies for intervening in organizations. The chapter includes a checklist of assessment questions that change agents may wish to use in working with client groups. Chapter 7 points out that before change agents can introduce interventions, they must heal often deep-rooted wounds in others. Clearing misperceptions of intentions, healing broken relationships, and preparing work climates for justice and humaneness are examples of essential tasks. Ways that change agents can alter the relationships between client perspectives and actions are examined in Chapter 8. The chapter offers step-by-step advice regarding how change agents may use a normative reeducative design to produce cognitive and behavioral skills changes. Perspective change, in particular, begins with identifying prevailing ideologies as they are used in dialogue. Following dialogue sessions, change agents may work with clients in small groups to align behaviors with perspective changes. Perhaps the most critical behavioral outcome of such sessions is learning how to share power among diverse interests in public organizations.

Part III examines how change agents can empower clients to share responsibility for change. Chapters 9, 10, and 11 provide in-depth ways in which change agents may develop empathy, encouragement, courage, compassion, and hope to enable clients to become more independent in directing change. Chapter 9 depicts how change agents used empathy and encouragement as tools. In particular, it describes how change agents used collaboration, active listening, and dialogue to handle sensitive issues that impeded organizational transformation. Chapter 10 discusses various forms of resistance to change. To meet resistance, change agents need to both name the obstacles and support clients. Promoting trust, sensitivity to client vulnerability, and relying on data is essential in overcoming resistance. In examining the use of empathy and encouragement in the strategies of the agency director, however, the chapter shows how change agents can transform despair into work satisfaction as well as motivation to produce high-quality services and goods. That change agents and clients require finding hope as a guide in the transformation journey is the message of Chapter 11. The chapter points out that this is difficult, however, because hope often appears in situations and conditions of emptiness, discouragement, and apparent helplessness. The chapter describes these paradoxical conditions as the beginning of a transformation cycle. To examine the characteristics of hope as a foundation for further change, the chapter indentifies several descriptive metaphors of hope.

Part IV illustrates the importantance of using skills to involve diverse interests and needs in public organization transformation. Because many public organizations involve unionized employees, change strategies require particular ways to ensure labor-management cooperation, according to Chapter 12. The chapter reviews many positive outcomes of labor-management cooperation and identifies some potential difficulties that can impede organizational change. The chapter illustrates the use of co-operative strategies in analyzing a quality-of-work-life case in state government. Chapter 13 describes a case example of how an intergovernmental organization created consensus and committed action to solve complex social, economic, and environmental problems facing a large metropolitan area. The chapter maintains that change agents need skills for developing shared visions and values among pluralistic public, private, and nonprofit organizations to tackle serious problems affecting public interests. Chapter 14, through a case example of a self-directed team structure in municipal government, exemplifies the integration of individual and organizational learning. Through the vision and leadership of a town manager, municipal workers eliminated hierarchical job boundaries and worked interdependently to manage their own functions.

Part V points out that change agents need to nurture wholeness of values and actions within themselves first. Personal integrity paves the way for leading organizational transformation holistically. Chapter 15 describes the origins of many typical ethical dilemmas change agents encounter and some useful ways they may resolve them. Finally, Chapter 16 maintains that change agent effectiveness depends a great deal on integrity, or the integration of principles, personal values, beliefs, and intervention strategies. Alignment is key to transforming oneself, others and organizations. Integrity signifies wholeness, the basis for service for the common good.

In brief, change agents prepare individuals and organizations to act from higher principles to create a more just and humane environment. Change agents model ethical principles by which individuals interact and carry out their organizations' purposes. Without learning to act with integrity or wholeness, people will allow character flaws to emerge and supplant change agent efforts.

TRANSFORMING THE
CHARACTER OF
PUBLIC ORGANIZATIONS

PART I

Getting Grounded in Organizational Transformation

CHAPTER 1

Leading Public Sector Change from the Inside Out

The greatest discovery of our generation is that human beings, by changing their inner attitudes of their minds, can change the outer aspects of their lives.
—William James (1890). *The Principles of Psychology*

The copy machine was out of order for the second time in a week. The machine usually jammed after the fiftieth copy, often lodging staples, paper, and globs of sticky jet ink in its belly. The university would probably offer the usual excuse—that continued underfunding and cutbacks in programs and services left it little choice but to keep the relic. Earlier that semester, I had taught graduate students about Weber's machine model and Taylor's efficiency methods; but the university trustees couldn't even understand that adding oil, tightening bolts, and dusting the bearings (like training, career development, and performance bonuses) would improve productivity. It felt uncomfortably similar to my 20 years in government.

Since beginning to work in government in 1975, I have heard plenty about changing government. Change has been phrased in several different ways, the most recent being "contracting out," "hollow government," and of course, "reinventing government." One politician after another has introduced programs to cut back and to do more with less. People barely recover from one initiative before they are hit with another one. As a human resource consultant in the federal government, I have witnessed terrifying work paralysis and human degeneration, casualties of misguided efforts to improve, reform, or reinvent government. The methods being used simply were not working, and I knew there had to be an alternative way to bring about organizational change.

I take the view that change involves transformation that has to start from within. Leading organizational change is a matter of understanding who one is: what is important, what motivates, what inspires, and what threatens. What goes on inside is the basis for working with and through others to attain shared goals.

CHANGE THROUGH MONOLOGUE

One incident still stays with me. I was a Presidential Management Intern at the U.S. Department of Education, working as a special assistant to the deputy undersecretary for management. The Reagan Revolution had swept through the Department, uprooting whole divisions and hanging swords over the careerists who remained. I remember one day when my boss called me into his office. He leaned back in his leather chair, chin in the palm of his hand, his leg cocked on the mahogany table.

"I want it hot and jazzy, hot and jazzy," he said with two rhythmic snaps of his fingers.

I scribbled the words on my notepad as I sat across from him.

In the then newly created Department of Education, he wanted to improve productivity and morale. His new initiative followed by about a year the department's politically designed merit pay and performance program. As a trainer on a cross-agency task force, I had the unenviable task of informing a group of managers and supervisors that they would lose pay for just performing satisfactorily. For a raise, there would have to be measurable improvement. In the middle of my briefing to over 100 managers in the headquarters auditorium, 2 or 3 jumped up, shook their fists, and blasted the administration.

Maybe he would be impressed with quality control circles (QCCs), I thought as the Undersecretary continued to describe his vision. I'd read about them as a graduate student in public administration and knew they had produced quick turnarounds—exactly what my boss wanted to see before his stint at the department ended.

I returned to my office and pulled together the latest QCC information from leading training and organization development journals and wrote a concept paper. The undersecretary liked it and was prepared to circulate it among his senior staff.

He wasn't quick enough, however. Within three months, the deputy undersecretary and the hot and jazzy QCC idea evaporated. The political appointee left, and his replacement decided that he wanted his own productivity improvement program. He had in mind something that would show taxpayers they were getting at least an eight-and-a-half-hour workday from the bureaucrats with fewer funds. This, of course, meant cuts in salaries and expenses, another round of hiring freezes, and staff reductions.

My office dissolved, and I ended up in management development, overseeing contracted-out programs. Life in the slow lane gave me time to reflect. No one but the deputy undersecretary wanted QCCs. No doubt the new deputy undersecretary would drive every bit as hard for productivity, then leave, frustrated, less than two years later. Meanwhile, the agency would continue downsizing, people would scoff at yet another "management initiative," and programs would, somehow, still get done.

Over the next ten years, I came to see the same scenario repeated many times; yet I had also seen a few cases that broke the mold. Some managers, invariably nonpolitical appointees, impassionately inspired, led and actually brought about serious changes. What made change successful in spite of the obstacles?

CHANGE FROM A DIFFERENT PERSPECTIVE

Before I left government in 1990 to work at the University of Connecticut, I was working for the Internal Revenue Service (IRS). In 1989 the Kansas City Service Center asked headquarters to send someone out to help them with their mentor training program. Because of my research in the area, I was given the assignment. My experiences had cooled my enthusiasm for the program, however, and I expected it to blow over soon.

The Internal Revenue Service has over 120,000 full-time employees. Every year, just before tax season starts in January, they hire hundreds of temporary data-entry staff. Usually working in three shifts around the clock, the employees key in taxpayer information in ten warehouselike service centers throughout the country.

Most are women; many are minorities. Supervisors and managers, however, are usually white males. The part-time status, complicated by racial, gender, and ethnic issues, frequently produces grievances. Established policies and procedures usually cover their resolution; but feelings of tension, fear, and hostility often remain. Subsequent episodes, which in many cases employees feel have been provoked by their supervisors, often explode into additional grievances. The part-time, temporary status of workers gives managers great leverage in firing. All of these factors contributed to a volatile workplace climate in spite of repeated efforts to change them.

But when I went to the IRS, the disaster I had expected, to my amazement, never happened. Instead, I witnessed a strong surge of excitement, enthusiasm, commitment, and expectancy among the program participants, the training and human resources staff, and management.

What went right? I wondered.

As I reflected more deeply, it occurred to me that the two officials took different approaches to viewing the "reality" of organizational change. This seemed particularly observable in the ways they acted toward themselves and others. The deputy undersecretary assumed that the reality of the department was tangible and fixed. Change was a matter of tinkering at the edges of the human resource system to produce a quantifiable leap in job satisfaction and results. Further, he saw himself as separate from the "problem" of motivation as he had defined it; other people were at fault for the low productivity. As a manipulator of change, however, he thought he could insert the "hot and jazzy" QCCs and results would suddenly and spectacularly pop up.

The Service Center director, in sharp contrast, aimed at a larger human purpose and saw himself as central to bringing it about. His actions said, "Human beings have been denied equal treatment in a number of personnel practices around here. This affects the productivity and morale of everyone. This problem needs to be resolved." By focusing on changing attitudes about others, reeducating managers and employees about the work contributions of women and minorities, and creating systems of rewards to support human resource policies and practices, the Service Center director rooted change in people rather than systems.

ORGANIZATIONAL CHANGE IN GOVERNMENT

The Service Center director's approach to change from the inside out rather than top-down had produced the changes envisioned. But what made this inside-out approach so effective? To find out, I thought about how government agencies are put together and managed in general. They are products of multiple committees and political compromises. Further, because their "enabling legislation" is usually broad and vague, over time their purposes evolve. As social and economic conditions change, government organizations take on new objectives and new programs, although the past is not buried.

This creates a dilemma. Because they depend heavily on legislative bodies for resources, organizations cannot discard outdated purposes and programs, which stay around like old luggage in an attic. For the same reason, however, agencies cannot initiate new programs. They are captives of legislative bodies which, in turn, are servants of a variety of public interest groups, political factions, lobbyists, and voters.

To survive continuous flux in organizational purposes and programs, career bureaucrats hang on to the status quo. They often resort to taking conservative views on issues and low-risk actions. In communication channels between career bureaucrats and political representatives, preserving the status quo often manifests itself as covering up, placing blame elsewhere, and ignoring problems.

This dependency may also lead career bureaucrats to go along with change grudgingly but not to embrace it wholeheartedly. Layers of suspicion from previous improvement initiatives have jaded people. The task of the change agent is to uncover these layers and allow careerists to heal: to take risks and create environments they can live in without fear and dishonesty.

GOVERNMENT AS HUMANLY DESIGNED AGENCIES

Because of attitudes, beliefs, and feelings that both define the parameters of change and direct how it is carried out, government organizations are human creations. They are not, as in Weber's classical sense, rationally constructed. This might be true if at least three conditions are met: People understand completely and explicitly define organizational problems, issues, and possible solutions; managers control inputs, resource levels, and outputs; and people make decisions without the influence of their own assumptions, beliefs, and feelings.

Government organizations are based on human purposes. One is to fill important social needs, such as the care of the indigent, the resolution of widespread socioeconomic problems, and mass unemployment in urban settings. Another is to correct sociopolitical problems that affect the well-being of the entire population, such as racism and classism. Third, public organizations provide essential services that would be too costly for citizens to finance with their own resources, such as schooling; postal services; clean and healthy air, soil, and water supplies; and public safety.

Public organizations are particularly grounded in human subjectivity. Reality, as Czarniawska-Joerges (1992, 34) points out, is not hidden "behind a wall of human distortion that must be overcome, but rather . . . where human perception is a part of it, a maker of it, and the only tool for its cognition." She goes on to define organizations as

nets of collective action, undertaken in an effort to shape the world and human lives. The contents of the action are meanings and things (artifacts). One net of collective action is distinguishable from another by the kind of meanings and products socially attributed to a given organization. (35)

INTEGRATING THE HUMAN ELEMENT IN CHANGING ORGANIZATIONS

If government organizations are nonrationally, humanly designed artifacts, how does the change agent go about defining, designing, and managing organizational change? The first step involves understanding the self as a primary instrument of change. This is coupled with an understanding of how the self relates to others within a social context, or reality. If the change agent regards reality as fixed or nonnegotiable, he or she sees others

as actors operating within a set of predesigned operating rules and procedures. Change becomes a matter of manipulating conditions. If the change
agent sees reality as open-ended and constructed by people to meet their
own purposes, however, change is participatory and driven by inner motives and feelings.

Change agents who lead from the inside out appear in four metaphors:
the change agent as a servant leader, the change agent as meaning-maker,
the change agent as a continuous learner, and the change agent as principled integrator.

Servant Leader and the Change Agent

The Service Center director's change strategy was successful in part because he exhibited empathy, willingness to listen, and the guts to take action. He brought about human changes because he himself had experienced
discriminatory treatment and understood the frustration of those who
could not rally support for change. As a change agent, the Service Center
director showed many of the characteristics of Greenleaf's (1977) "servant
leader," who initiates change from within and transforms convictions into
actions. In Greenleaf's leader-as-servant perspective, ten interpersonal qualities are critical:

1. *Listening.* Use of nonjudgmental, holistic understanding involving the mind,
   body, and spirit of both the speaker and hearer.

2. *Empathy.* Understanding and acceptance of uniqueness of the individual and
   feeling the other's pain or hurt.

3. *Healing.* Ability to recognize the brokenness in oneself and others and in organizations and to bring about wholeness of individuals and relationships.

4. *Awareness.* Sensitivity to need and commitment to act to resolve issues.

5. *Persuasion.* Ability to use influence to formulate and accomplish goals and
   objectives.

6. *Conceptualization.* Ability to motivate others to viewing reality in creative
   ways and to share visions of an improved future.

7. *Foresight.* Ability to understand history intuitively and realize key implications
   for the present and the future.

8. *Stewardship.* View of managers and employees as trustees of organizations;
   organizations exist for the greater benefit of society.

9. *Commitment to individual growth and development.* Willingness to expect the
   best in others and to help them achieve their own potential as human beings.

10. *Building community.* Belief that leaders share values, purposes, and objectives
    based on the leader's accepting responsibility for bringing about the best in self
    and in others.

Meaning Creator

The Service Center director's strategy of leading change from inside was also effective because it was anchored in human needs and concerns. The strategy opened doors for looking at issues that had been framed in unresolved complaints and short career ladders. He also cleared paths for sharing organizational resources and power that the white male managers had used to build and maintain mutual support.

Change leaders such as he feel, understand, and acknowledge the role of chaos and complexity in human relationships. To bring shared meaning from experiences is a chief goal (Schutz, 1970). Polanyi and Prosch (1975, 74–75) indicate that the change agent creates meaning by fashioning individuals' own perceptions of reality into a "visible embodiment": a symbolic concept that provides a wholeness of meaning:

Perception . . . is of things seen from the self as a center. The self is never carried away in indication; it is never surrendered or given to the focal object. . . . By contrast, symbols are self-giving. That is, the symbol as an object of our focal awareness is not merely established by an integration of subsidiary clues directed from the self to a focal object; it is also established by surrendering the memories and experiences of the self into this object, thus giving them a visible embodiment. This visible embodiment serves as a focal point for the integration of these diffuse aspects of the self into a felt unity.

Continuous Learners

The Service Center director created enduring changes because he corrected erroneous thinking habits and actions through reeducation. He worked toward changing operating philosophies about how work was organized and carried out. As Covey (1991) and Czarniawska-Joerges (1992) note, change agents view obstacles, past failures, gaps in understanding, and accomplishments as integral to their own, to others', and to the organization's abilities to grow and adapt.

Principled Integrators

The Service Center director used a particular set of values from which he evaluated strategies for working with others to accomplish his goals. These values guided his motivation to close the gap between what the organization said it valued and the records of people whose careers were thwarted. Stephen Covey (1991, 63) calls for an "inside-out" approach to change, "a continuing process of renewal, an upward spiral of growth that leads to progressively higher forms of responsible independence and effective interdependence." Covey maintains that renewal is possible only through integrity: a consistent adherence to values, principles, and actions. The coherence of actions, beliefs, and values enables followers to accept and develop commitment to what the change agent says and does.

INSIDE-OUT ORGANIZATIONAL DEVELOPMENT

The change agent in government organizations faces obstacles from the often choppy flow of information through fragmented legislative and judicial processes, multiple bases of power, and pluralistic public needs and expectations. Yet because of the human nature of government organizations, changing government from the inside out requires mastery of particular interpersonal competencies. From the four concepts described above, seven key competencies emerge, described in the following.

Using Self as an Instrument of Change

Change agents realize that change begins from within. From the inside, individuals construct the basis for interpreting experiences and for changing particular conditions. The most effective change agents cultivate a strong reputation for honesty, reliability, and responsibility. They periodically monitor themselves to make sure that their beliefs, values, and actions are in harmony. In doing so, they become aware of their own need to be healed. They seek continuous self-transformation because they know that inner well-being is the basis for helping others.

Empathy and Encouragement

Change agents respect others' rights to autonomous thoughts and feelings; consequently, they treat others with dignity. Sensitive to human needs but also wanting to share a better future, change agents seek out others. Through sharing thoughts and feelings, change agents work with others to reflect, discuss, and develop the commitment to act.

Compassionate Confrontation

Change agents recognize that unresolved problems cripple people and organizations. Confronting these problems before situations worsen, change agents are mediators. They broker ideas, resources, and influence to identify the causes of problems and strategies for resolution.

Creating Community through Dialogue

Understanding the linkage between inner views of reality and external actions, change agents seek as broad a construction of problem definitions and solutions as possible. They encourage multiple points of view from both people who desire change and those who oppose it. Through establishing wide-ranging parameters of perceived reality, change agents can fashion a shared vision of a possible future. This vision provides the basis for creating new symbols that animate people and bring them together.

Teachability and the Ability to Teach

Change agents sense the interrelatedness of people, jobs, knowledge, and organizational functioning. They understand that each affects the other in dynamic ways and that observable actions reflect ongoing change within the entire organization. Hence, change agents develop sensitivity to conditions that facilitate learning, events that trigger opportunities to gain new insights, beliefs that enhance possibilities for taking self-responsibility, and ideas that present new possibilities for exploring. Change agents also realize that errors are part of learning; through them, change agents find ways to discover meaning in what was not known before.

Integrity

Change agents periodically assess the strength and validity of their own assumptions, beliefs, and actions by soliciting feedback. This may involve seeking out information from trusted others, critical reflection and dialogue in small groups, or taking inventory of how others reacted to their proposals and the manner in which they made them.

To put ideas into effect, change agents also both know and respect their organization's own character. Character contributions include all the relevant stakeholders, the internal clientele, the dominant organizational culture (and relationships with subcultures), and the mission, purpose, and history of the organization.

Service

Change agents play a servant or catalytic role in leading change. They design, develop, and carry out strategies with the aim of improving the capabilities of people and organizations. They also commit their visions, hopes, and values to action by establishing networks of influence and support and by setting up task forces, focus groups, and training programs to create new opportunities.

REFERENCES

Covey, S. R. (1991). *Principle-centered leadership*. New York: Simon and Schuster.
Czarniawska-Joerges, B. (1992). *Exploring complex organizations*. Newbury Park, CA: Sage.

Greenleaf, R. K. (1977). *Servant leadership*. New York: Paulist Press.
James, W. (1890). *The principles of psychology*. New York: Holt.
Polanyi, M., and Prosch, H. (1975). *Meaning*. Chicago: University of Chicago Press.
Schutz, A. (1970). *On the phenomenology of social relations*. Chicago: University
    of Chicago Press.

CHAPTER 2

A Holistic View of Organization Change

> If truth comes to us primarily at a distance and from the outside, then
> our work too will reflect a distancing of ourselves from the objects of
> our work. Distance, not participation, will mark our work worlds. If,
> however, the universe best reveals itself through relationship and par-
> ticipation, then all work is about relation making or relation healing
> of some kind. And creativity must be integral to all human work as it
> is to all work in the universe.
> —Matthew Fox (1994). *The Reinvention of Work*

In a large government agency, the highest level of stress occurred not
around the holidays but on September 30—the dreaded day budget plans
had to be on the boss's desk. But it wasn't just the budget battles that raged
every year that sent managers to the brink of insanity; performance ap-
praisals were due, too.

In that agency, managers rated employees on a scale of one to five on
such characteristics as quality and timeliness, quality of work products, job
knowledge, persistence, adaptability, and resourcefulness. Managers rated
people in this system but lacked clear definitions, agreed-on standards, and
a systematic way of evaluating outcomes. They did not know for sure
whether performance had occurred or if it had even succeeded.

That all changed when the agency adopted the Integral Performance
Management System (IPMS). The IPMS examined and quantified work
processes and outputs over time, developed a standard or norm of produc-

tivity, and showed where individual employees performed in relation to the norm. The system promised higher motivation because employees could see exactly how they were doing at any given time and because supervisors could spot-check samples of work and take whatever actions were necessary. If work fell below the norm, the manager could counsel, retrain, or problem solve; if it was over the standard, the manager could give out rewards. Just the sheer satisfaction of doing a good job, however, was sufficient, the IPMS proclaimed.

In practice, it was another story. Managers complained even more about the excessive amount of paperwork they had to spin out, and the calculations of performance deviations took up most of the other time. In the meantime, employees complained because the system drove their performance. They had to make certain "goals" or risk losing their jobs. The union jumped in as well, and the numbers of grievances filed boiled over.

In introducing organizational change, change agents often overlook two important facts. Organizations derive life from human sources; people create organizations to serve their own needs, interests, and goals. In the IPMS example, the performance appraisal system came about to fulfill human goals of effectiveness and efficiency, control and order, accurate and timely feedback, and rewards based on quantifiable outputs. The problem, however, was that humans had little control over the system they created. Instead of working in harmony, people and the system resisted each other.

In addition, organizational systems overlap and influence each other, like gears in drives. For instance, training people affects technical capability. Instruction, as an input, produces abilities and skills as outputs. These, in turn, are inputs into the equipment people use. In general, the more advanced the skill inputs, the higher the quality and quantity of equipment output. In the IPMS example, changing the performance system affected not only the reward system but also interpersonal relationships, feelings about work effectiveness, management and coordinating functions, and even how the work outputs affected the ability of the organization to meet mission requirements.

This chapter introduces the concept of humanly designed organizational systems and a holistic process that change agents can use to transform them. The chapter provides a foundation for three core ideas: (1) human logic and design of organization must play an integral part in the process of change; (2) change agents need to use human relations skills in transforming organizations; and (3) methodologies of change must reflect a holistic approach, that is, examining the humanistic conception of organizational systems in light of actual practices. In particular, the chapter asserts that the human perspective is frequently ignored in government organizational changes because of the bias of rationality, as in the IPMS case. It also identifies eight central systems in government organizations and describes their purposes and functions from a subjective logic. Third, the chapter outlines a methodology for changing organizations from the inside out.

THE NEGLECTED HUMAN SIDE OF GOVERNMENT

Government organizations typically emphasize values of rationality: control, order, administrative neutrality, and accountability (Gerth and Mills, 1946). In American history in particular, Framers of the Constitution insisted on separating political from administrative power to discourage bias (Waldo, 1980). Yet the pyramid-shaped organizational structure, in which key administrative decisions rise, only increases the likelihood of bias. When decisions do reach managers, managers deal with only partial and distorted information. Moreover, because resources also diminish in proportion to the numbers and complexity of the decisions, only parts of original requests can be honored. Which parts and to what degree are subjective decisions managers must make.

Organizational change in public agencies has retained the rationality-based model and has ignored the real human framework of systems logic (Lincoln and Guba, 1985). Governments continue, for instance, to build hierarchical job structures with piecemeal responsibilities and limited discretionary power and to base rewards on quantifiable performance outputs. Organizational change frequently rearranges boxes on organizational charts but fails to address the frustration from lack of empowerment and meaning government workers feel.

WHO ARE CHANGE AGENTS?

Change agents are people who have an interest in transforming organizations and who use skills of thinking holistically, planning, coordinating, and facilitating to enable transformation to occur. Change agents may be people who work inside organizations, such as internal consultants, human resource professionals, managers, executives, and technical and clerical staff. They may also work as professionally trained external consultants, elected and appointed officials, or public interest groups.

Key is being concerned about making changes in cultural work processes. Change agents desire work that is easier, more effective and efficient, provides more self-control and self-actualization, and promotes community and commitment among workers. To bring desires into reality, change agents use influence and sometimes power as leverage. The aim is to create thinking and feeling in novel ways by using accurate and timely data from those involved in changes. Change agents also seek to foster collaboration in making decisions and commitments in carrying out agreed-on changes.

Change agents also learn skills of consulting, such as techniques for gathering, analyzing, and reporting data; eliciting useful and innovative ideas and strategies for change; managing resistance; and transforming ideas into operating structures in organizational systems.

Change agents are healers, visionaries, counselors, problem solvers, consultants, and action takers. They are people whose desires, thoughts, feelings, and energies attract others. Change agents find and create common threads of meaning as the foundation of a more inclusive social reality.

WHAT ARE SYSTEMS?

Systems reflect how tasks, functions, and "families" of jobs contribute to organizational performance. The personnel management system is an example. Specific tasks in personnel management include identifying required skills and abilities, recruiting and staffing positions with the best-qualified people, training and developing people to perform their jobs effectively and efficiently, developing policies and procedures for fair and equitable employment, and administering labor-management relations agreements.

Systems may be both formal and informal. Formal tasks are usually written, but informal tasks are learned from experience. In personnel management, formal tasks include collective-bargaining agreements and attendance policies, whereas informal tasks include how individual managers interpret and apply the written documents in actual situations.

Informal tasks reflect certain taken-for-granted beliefs and values in organizational culture. These tacit beliefs and values that influence actions account for more than two thirds of the formal tasks (Schein, 1985). For instance, a manager may hire a white male for an entry-level supervisory position in the belief that white males are easier to associate with than African-American males or white women. In an agency that values loyalty and minimizes conflict, it "makes sense" to hire white males. In the formal hiring process, such a manager may hire a white male in spite of the agency's affirmative action policies. The manager may find justification for the decision by saying that the white male candidate had superior technical qualifications to either women or minority candidates.

KEY SYSTEMS IN GOVERNMENT ORGANIZATIONS

Figure 2.1 shows eight interrelated systems that are common in public organizations. These systems include culture; power and influence; administrative/managerial; technological; resource acquisition and development; legal/regulatory; environmental interface; and incentives, inducements, and rewards.

Figure 2.1
Systems in Public Organizations

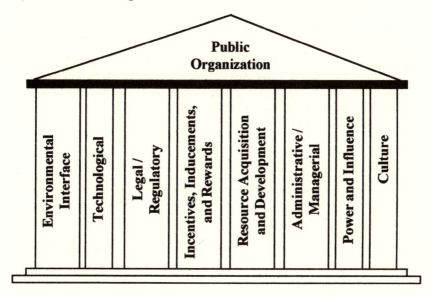

Cultural Systems

Organizations have unique identities that have emerged over their historical development. Cultures are archives that reveal patterns of thinking, feeling, and reacting people have commonly agreed and acted on as "the right ways."

Underlying cultures are sets of core beliefs and values. These indicate preferred ways to deal with such conditions as crises, threats to security, regard for people, achieving purposes, and dealing with pluralistic and competing interests. Cultural patterns vary according to several conditions. In public agencies, dominant political coalitions set the tone for deciding what values and beliefs are important. As administrations change, moreover, public organizations encounter crises that question these past values and beliefs. Over time, those values and beliefs that have enabled agencies to survive legislative transitions and adapt to new administrative priorities become significant and part of the archives. People learn these values and beliefs tacitly and teach them to groups that follow after them.

Power and Influence Systems

Public organizations derive power, or the ability to accomplish a goal or mission, from legal authority. The legal basis differs from private sector corporations in the sense that a single group of investors, stockholders, or owners do not control decisions. Public organizations belong to diverse constituents and perform services that benefit the public as a whole. In exercising power, public agencies have legal enforcement rights, regulatory responsibilities, and mediational jurisdiction.

Government agencies, however, use much influence to supplement their legal powers. They frequently use community task forces, agency liaisons, and interagency committees to generate constituent dialogue. Through exchanging ideas, discussing novel problem-solving strategies, and fostering positive climates for learning and growth, public agencies influence constituent compliance and commitment.

Administrative and Management Systems

Agency administrative and management systems regulate and coordinate internal and external resources. These resources include program funds; technological services; employee talents, skills, and abilities; and material properties. Administrative managers may have delegated authority for supervising programs, services, information, goods and products, and employees' work assignments.

Administrative and management systems are important components in creating a psychological climate. *Climate* is a general perception of how people feel about working in a particular organization (Poole and McPhee, 1983). It often stems from the ways people perceive managers performing their responsibilities and how they treat others. Employees may characterize climates as "open," "defensive," "anxious," or "warm," for example.

Technological Systems

To carry out legal purposes, public agencies use a variety of technical knowledge bases. Many agencies have a particular "business" to perform, such as enforcing building codes; regulating air traffic; providing federal grants to local public schools; or inspecting health standards in hospitals, restaurants, and hotels. Usually, professional "elites" perform the main functions in the particular agency business (Mosher, 1982).

Technological systems also include a mix of human expertise and automated information. Frequently, change agents enter technological systems, such as the IPMS discussed earlier, to create balance. In addition, the rapid spread of computerized administrative functions throughout government has eliminated thousands of permanent positions and has spawned even more contractual jobs in their places. Change agents not only help agencies deal with traumas of downsizing and contracting out; they also redesign jobs so that people's skills can be more effectively and efficiently used.

Resource Acquisition and Development Systems

Unlike private sector organizations that generate their own revenues, public agencies rely on the appropriations of popularly elected bodies. To prepare fund requests, allocate funds for operating components, and monitor resource use, agencies have various resource systems.

Over the past 25 years in particular, constituents have demanded high levels of accountability for spending publicly appropriated funds. Tax revolts across the country have enabled citizens to gain more direct control in budget decision making. Bypassing elected representatives, citizen groups have obtained more command over agency programs and funding. Because of widespread funds cuts, however, many public agencies cannot fulfill basic responsibilities. In one federal agency, for example, program managers used to fly to sites to check compliance with regulations. Because the agency was forced to slice travel funds, however, site visits now take place over the telephone.

Legal and Regulatory Systems

The law-based authority of public agencies establishes many systems. Agencies concern themselves with carrying out public laws, monitoring compliance, adjudicating and resolving disputes, and setting up regulatory policies and enforcement standards.

The subjective character of administration, however, often draws a thin line between "politics" and "administration" (Waldo, 1980). Frequently, administrators have only vague guidelines for interpreting laws. Moreover, because mandates do not necessarily guarantee sufficient funding or technical support, administrators have to garner support for programs. This becomes particularly precarious when administrators also become spokespersons or defenders of unpopular programs or rulings.

Environmental Interface Systems

Communicating interpersonally across systems and outside organizational boundaries is perhaps the most critical requirement of public agencies. The vaguely written laws, sparse resource allocations, and prevalent public mistrust have put great pressures on public administrators. Sharing information, staying in touch with constituent needs, and conveying openness, however, reduce the stress and enable administrators to gain some control.

Environmental interface systems work within organizations as well. Perhaps most important are the informal communications networks. Formal communications, such as memos, meetings, conferences, and newsletters, provide unequivocal and timely information to general audiences. But informal communications, such as luncheons and coffees, give employees a sense of inclusiveness. Change agents often build or improve informal communications channels to create team spirit. Developing face-to-face trust and involvement plays an important role.

Incentives, Inducements, and Rewards Systems

Chester Barnard (1938) and Herbert Simon (1947) maintained that organizations cannot expect employees to obtain satisfaction from financial rewards alone. They believed that organizations should use nonfinancial motivators to encourage employee satisfaction and productivity. The key, however, is finding motivators that satisfy from the employees' perspectives. Some factors that influence employee contributions are compatibility of goals with personality characteristics, quantity and diversity of available rewards, autonomy, and participation.

Organizations often create significant motivators through combinations of formal rewards systems, employee development opportunities, and job designs. In addition, organizations seek to improve employee satisfaction and opportunities for advancement through building supportive work climates. Many contributors to climates come from other systems, particularly the organizational culture, resource acquisition, technology, and interface systems. Hence, in changing organizations to produce such climates, change agents need to examine how other systems contribute to the formal rewards systems.

WAYS TO CHANGE SYSTEMS HOLISTICALLY

Aligning the systems involves developing an understanding of the uniqueness of the human perspective in creating particular organizations. Because each government organization has its own character, change must take uniqueness into account. This means that having a preset idea of what to change—even if that is what the change agent has been asked to do—may start the change process off badly. Change agents need to develop a feel for what makes *this* organization the way people define it.

To derive this understanding, change agents may use an eight-part methodology, as depicted in Figure 2.2. The rationale is to gather as much information as possible about the organization from the people who are "natives" and to articulate their perspectives throughout the change process. The change agent is like an anthropologist who enters a foreign culture and "soaks up" what people say, what they do, how they interact, and how they carry on everyday business (Geertz, 1983). From detailed descriptions, discussing observations and hunches with insiders, and soliciting ideas for possible change strategies, the change agent may create a design that will fit the particular character of the organization.

Figure 2.2
Steps in Holistic Systems Change

- Develop an understanding of the status quo
- Collect and analyze data
- Reflect on data and initiate dialogue
- Present data and elicit reactions
- Change the system collaboratively
- Intervene in the system
- Assess and evaluate interventions
- End relationships

Develop an Understanding of the Status Quo

The first step in changing organizations is to analyze how people define and carry out work (Van Manen, 1990). This involves suspending preconceived hypotheses about what might be "wrong" (Husserl, 1983). Usually, a client or person with whom the change agent works and who is ultimately responsible for changing conditions briefs the change agent on a problem situation. Block (1981) calls this the "presenting problem." Taking this description at face value, however, predisposes the change agent to find evidence for it. The presenting problem may not be "the way things really are."

In the IPMS example, the presenting problem was that people weren't working up to capacity. The client's solution was that the agency needed to implement a performance management system that included measurable standards, immediate feedback, and employee control over output. In this case, the agency "bought" the solution without checking out the employees' perspectives. Maybe the performance appraisal system worked in their view. What they would have liked to have had might have been more incentive bonuses, supervisors who gave them more autonomy in work hours, or more flexibility in assignments.

Collect and Analyze Data

Change agents gather information from various viewpoints using several data-gathering methods. Employee surveys and interviews are common. In addition, change agents observe and record interactions in different settings. Moreover, change agents examine archival information, such as key turning points in the organization's history. The records indicate what prominent beliefs and values enabled survival and adaptation and continue to influence present behavior and thinking. Archives also suggest how and why particular problem situations may have come to be.

Reflect on Data and Initiate Dialogue

Information from numerous data sources is perplexing. To make sense of what the data are saying, change agents often construct hypotheses of how events might be related or contribute to the situation at hand. They might use several analytical techniques suggested by Miles and Huberman (1984) to derive meaning from nonquantitative data. Central, however, is periodic reflecting on what the relationships signify to different interpreters. From diverse viewpoints of the same phenomena, change agents can detect a broader meaning and its implications for change. Hence, by integrating highly detailed observational notes with the change agent's own intuition, meaning emerges.

To verify working hypotheses and to obtain additional information, change agents discuss their intuitions, feelings, observations, and possible meanings with those experiencing the problem. Through discussion, change agents obtain valuable feedback. Moreover, they also ground their working hypotheses in actual situations. This makes the diagnosis more accurate as well as prepares people to participate in and support the changes suggested.

Present Data and Elicit Reactions

Change agents share data collected and analyzed with clients to obtain their insights. This often enlarges the framework of the client's idea of the problem, but it also frequently provokes resistance. Because things are not as the client had imagined or believed, the client may become defensive. This may take the form of denial, blaming individuals, rejecting claims of accuracy, and dismissing conclusions (and possibly the change agent as well). If the client refuses to "own" the data and refuses to act on them, the change agent may wish to suggest putting the project "on hold" or dropping it altogether.

Clients may resist change, however, because change exposes their fears and their vulnerabilities to error (Block, 1981). Change agents may wish to support the clients, however, as the clients think through ways to make changes. Change agents may offer interventions, or solution strategies, that will minimize the risk of failure but that will increase the likelihood of more control.

Change the System Collaboratively

After the client has decided to initiate change, the client and the change agent agree on specific ways to work together and what results each expects. The agreed-on action becomes a contract of mutual commitment to reaching specific goals over a definite period of time with adequate resources allocated. The change agent typically plays a variety of roles during this time (Lippitt, 1979), ranging from advocate to alternative identifier to reflector.

Intervene in the System

Argyris (1970, 15) defines interventions as entering "into an ongoing system of relationships, to come between or among persons, groups, or objects for the purpose of helping them." Interventions are a series of planned and programmed activities that clients and consultants engage in to bring about systemic changes. Interventions typically introduce new ways of doing tasks, new ways of improving organizational systems, and different ways of thinking and reacting (Etzioni, 1961). Some common examples include building teams, installing broader job responsibilities, writing policies, and developing performance indicators. Interventions may occur on individual, interpersonal, group, or organization system levels.

Assess and Evaluate Interventions

Throughout the intervention process, change agents monitor and assess progress. They use both quantitative indicators, such as indexes of increased technological outputs, and qualitative indicators, such as increased employee satisfaction with the new performance appraisal system. Change agents gather, analyze, and reflect on meanings of data, just as they did to understand the context in which the original issues emerged.

Often, interventions open additional issues that—although unforeseen in the beginning—present challenges. Because contingencies often occur in the intervention process, such as cuts in staffing or budget allocations or the leaving of key personnel, change agents need to build in contractual flexibility. This entails periodically returning to the action plan with the client and together determining what specific actions to take.

Change agents and clients also evaluate the short- and long-term effects of the interventions. Using both quantitative and qualitative data, they examine the extent to which interventions have achieved the original objectives. Usually, the change agent prepares a description of the outcomes immediately following the termination of the intervention. Sometimes, especially if the intervention has occurred over several years, has affected large numbers of people, and has involved several complex changes in many systems, follow-up evaluations occur periodically afterward. In many of these latter cases, change agents share results with external interests, such as the client's superior, political appointees, legislators, or funders (Patton, 1990).

End Relationships

Interventions result from planning, but the process of preparing for change and enacting it is often nonlinear. Planning often emerges after the fact, as in response to new data, a crisis, or discovery of a different technique. Change often is cyclical and, once begun, spins off other possibilities for change.

This creates a dilemma: The client may feel unprepared to handle new situations, and the change agent may feel he or she is expert in doing so. Using the change agent time after time, however, produces dependency. The goal of the change agent–client relationship is to enable the client to have the skills and abilities needed to carry on in the future independently. Hence, training the client in change agent skills is a critical part of the change agent relationship.

SUMMARY

Organizational change requires balancing the proportion of human relationship skills with technical systems expertise; both systems work cooperatively. But because organizations come from *human* rationality, achieve *human* purposes, and satisfy *human* needs, *human* skills should determine the character and direction of change.

Using human relations skills provides a holistic way to diagnose and intervene in interrelated organizational systems. Holistic methodology grounds diagnosing problems, generating solutions, preparing implementation goals, and evaluating interventions in human experience. It also provides for learning through reflection, experimentation, and dialogue. This not only enhances the quality and accuracy of the intervention process but also encourages personal involvement. Participation creates commitment to achieving shared purposes and facilitates continuing adaptation following the intervention.

Because human relations skills strongly influence change, change agents themselves play central roles in how change occurs. They provide such necessary elements as vision, encouragement, participation, and technical change skills. Change agents use the self as a tool for transforming people and organizational systems.

The remaining chapters discuss in greater depth the critical human element in organizational change. The chapters delineate particular competencies change agents need to fulfill roles and responsibilities. In particular, the chapters discuss use of self as an instrument of change, specific mediation roles, empathy and encouragement, confronting and supporting skills, participation, training and education, and integrity.

REFERENCES

Argyris, C. (1970). *Intervention theory and method: A behavioral science view.* Reading, MA: Addison-Wesley.

Barnard, C. (1938). *The functions of the executive.* Cambridge, MA: Harvard University Press.

Block, P. (1981). *Flawless consulting: A guide to getting your expertise used.* San Diego, CA: University Associates.

Etzioni, A. (1961). *A comparative analysis of complex organizations.* New York: Free Press.

Fox, M. (1994). *The reinvention of work: A new vision of livelihood for our time.* New York: HarperCollins.

Geertz, C. (1983). *Local knowledge.* New York: Basic Books.

Gerth, M., and Mills, C. W. (1946). *From Max Weber: Essays in sociology.* New York: Oxford University Press.

Husserl, E. (1983). *Ideas pertaining to a pure phenomenology and to a phenomenological philosophy.* (F. Kersten, Trans.) The Hague: M. Nijhoff.

Lincoln, Y. S., and Guba, E. G. (1985). *Naturalistic inquiry.* Beverly Hills, CA: Sage.

Lippitt, G. (1979). The trainer's role as an internal consultant. In C. R. Bell and L. Nadler (Eds.), *The client-consultant handbook* (56–66). Houston, TX: Gulf Publishing Company.

Miles, M. B., and Huberman, A. M. (1984). *Qualitative data analysis: A sourcebook of new methods.* Beverly Hills, CA: Sage.

Mosher, F. (1982). *Democracy and the public service.* New York: Oxford University Press.

Patton, M. Q. (1990). *Qualitative evaluation and research methodology.* Newbury Park, CA: Sage.

Poole, M. S., and McPhee, R. D. (1983). A structural analysis of organizational climate. In L. L. Putnam and M. E. Pacanowsky (Eds.), *Communication and organizations* (195–219). Beverly Hills, CA: Sage.

Schein, E. H. (1985). *Organizational culture and leadership.* San Francisco: Jossey-Bass.

Schutz, A. (1970). *On phenomenology and social relations* (H. R. Wagner, Trans.). Chicago: University of Chicago Press.

Simon, H. A. (1947). *Administrative behavior.* New York: Macmillan.

Van Manen, M. (1990). *Researching lived experience.* London: University of Western Ontario Press.

Waldo, D. (1980). *The enterprise of public administration.* Novato, CA: Chandler and Sharp.

CHAPTER 3

Techniques for Collecting and Analyzing Data

[W]e suggest that inquiry must be carried out in a "natural" setting because phenomena of study, whatever they may be—physical, chemical, biological, social, psychological—take their meaning as much from their contexts as they do from themselves.
—Y. S. Lincoln and E. G. Guba (1985). *Naturalistic Inquiry*

In the previous chapter, we saw that change agents lead transformation by working with interactive human and organizational systems. This chapter and the next take an in-depth look at the processes of change, from identifying problems and issues to implementing and assessing interventions. To provide detailed understanding, the processes have been divided roughly in half. This chapter examines organizational change beginning with identifying the initial problem, then communicating how the problem alters the present functioning of those affected by the problem or issue. Chapter 4 continues by outlining ways change agents and clients determine and implement solution strategies.

These chapters rest on the concepts of organizational change and the process consultation models that Lewin (1945) in particular developed. To understand how and why change agents use particular techniques for organizational change, it is helpful to examine briefly some key concepts of organizational change.

WHAT IS ORGANIZATIONAL CHANGE?

Planned and Systematic Transformation

Organizational change, broadly defined, refers to changes that organizations undergo as a result of careful problem diagnosis, strategy planning, solution implementation, and assessment and follow-up. Organizational change processes aim to improve an organization's functioning both in the present and in the future by correcting dysfunctional systems or processes. Organizational change, thus, is purposeful, as opposed to change that is involuntary and unplanned.

Based on Collective Involvement

Lewin believed that participation underscored change. He envisioned organizations as collectives of individuals working together to set up, accomplish, and monitor goals and objectives through specific tasks, work processes, or organized systems of processes. These common purposes, goals, interests, beliefs, and values provided frames of reference for thinking and practices.

Collectives develop their own particular symbols, thought patterns, and behaviors to define what to accomplish, how to govern relationships between themselves and others, and how mutual needs and interests will be met. Collectives may align their purposes with other collectives. Typically, however, their purposes vary, which is why a change agent needs to align purposes of different collectives with the central mission, purposes, and objectives of the larger organization.

Targets of Change

Burke (1987) states that organizational change uses data derived from behavioral science to transform one or more levels within organizations: individual, interpersonal, within-work unit, cross-departmental, or between an organization and its environment. Change may focus on any or all of the overlapping systems discussed earlier, including communications, culture, technology use, rewards, political interface, legal oversight, or administrative management.

STEPS IN ORGANIZATIONAL CHANGE

In general, changing organizational systems follow a particular pattern. As depicted in Figure 3.1, these include:

Figure 3.1
Steps in Organization Change

- Problem surfacing
- Client identification
- Contract negotiation
- Data collection and analysis
- Feedback
- Alternative solution generation and selection
- Selection of pilot project
- Implementation
- Evaluation and follow-up

---

1. *Problem surfacing.* Defining and locating a problem or an issue in its context.
2. *Client identification.* Determining who has both the responsibility and the authority for resolving a problem.
3. *Contract negotiation.* Working out roles and responsibilities for collecting and analyzing information concerning a problem, suggesting solution alternatives, deciding how to solve the problem or issue, and carrying out solution strategies.
4. *Data collection and analysis.* Examining data to identify problem causes, effects, and possible solutions.
5. *Feedback.* Communicating results of data analysis and making recommendations for resolving a problem or an issue.
6. *Alternative solution generation and selection.* Developing options for solving a problem and deciding on an alternative that meets identified need or purpose.
7. *Selection of pilot project.* Providing a simulation of conditions affecting a problem situation, trying out an alternative solution, assessing the fit between the solution and problem situation, and choosing the next steps.
8. *Implementation.* Putting the selected solution strategy into effect and observing the responses of people and technologies affected by changes.
9. *Evaluation and follow-up.* Judging the effectiveness of change strategy and making decisions regarding the next steps.

Problem Surfacing

People become aware that problems exist and interfere with their work lives in different ways. Perhaps the most poignant is crisis: A system breaks down. An organization has to lay off seasoned employees to cut expenses. An earthquake wipes out a large metropolitan area. Change disconnects abruptly.

Problems may erupt after long dormancy as well. People may express suppressed anger and even outrage several months or years after experiencing loss, abuse, or deprivation. Issues explode when people burst restraints.

In the public sector, change frequently occurs when a new political administration takes office and imposes a set agenda. Invariably, career employees have little chance to participate in planning for the changes, contribute valuable ideas concerning what will work, or offer feedback during implementation. Accordingly, employees have little motivation to commit their time and energies to helping change succeed, feel slighted, and may store up mounds of anger for future use. In imposed change, change often creates more problems than the designers intended.

Other organizations may initiate change based on a feeling that some things do not "make sense." Tired of routines, inundated with paper trails, and facing time pressures that never seem to disappear, frustrated employees may ask, "Why do we keep doing things the same way all the time?" Their interest may escalate, particularly after they have visited, observed, or read of similar organizations that have adopted a particular innovative technology. Exposure can create an unfavorable comparison that results in a change dilemma.

A few organizations, particularly those that realize the importance of constituent support for services and products, purposely search for problems that affect customer satisfaction. Although such environmental scanning is common in the private sector, more and more public organizations are becoming proactive about solving constituent problems before the issues become unmanageable. Customer surveys and small-group interviews, for instance, turn up conditions that may likely produce problems later.

Clients and the Client System

When people experience crises, frustrations, dilemmas, and opportunities for changing the status quo to achieve greater satisfaction and productivity, they often seek out change agent help. They look to change agents to help them solve their problems, to restore harmony in relationships, to create predictability and a sense of control in chaotic situations, and to explore innovative ways to enhance what is already working well. People who call for change agents have a high level of expectancy—a feeling of anxiety, on the one hand, and hope, on the other. They respect change agents because of their expertise, their records of success, their interpersonal skills, and their abilities to speak on their behalf to influence more powerful people. Such people begin the relationship with a great deal of dependency.

Change agents understand the dependency, but their goal is to turn the fear and sense of powerlessness into confidence and competence. To do so, change agents move the clients from dependence to independence through collaborative interventions. Change agents involve the clients in each step of the problem-solving process, from defining the problem, understanding the context that embeds and feeds it, to generating and finally implementing solutions.

Identifying "the client" is often tricky in public organizations. Because of the diversity of internal and external constituents, the layers of authority structures, and the legal limitations on discretionary decision making, change agents may find multiple clients. *Clients* refer to people who both experience the problem or issue affecting the quality of their work lives and are affected by the problem or issue itself. Manager A, for instance, may complain because of the paperwork bottleneck in his office; but a leading source of the backlog might be Manager B's understaffed office down the hall that receives the original request for service. Manager B then becomes a client. But Manager B blames her staffing shortage on last year's hiring freeze that the agency imposed in response to Congress's budget cuts. Fewer grantees receive services, but the volume of paper somehow escalates. Those who receive delayed service and wrong information on their approved grants also join the change agent clientele.

Contracting for Change

Although the person who contacts the change agent may initiate the relationship, the change agent may have to find the person who has the real authority and resources to change. Quite often this person may not have the same zeal as the initiator, and the change agent may have to use persuasion to convince him or her that the situation needs attention. Change agents then become advocates for the subclient's concerns.

To corroborate, change agents agree to collect, analyze, and interpret data with client assistance. Data are the levers of change. Data are not information, however. Information consists of facts, suppositions, stories, and records about phenomena. Data, however, have significance. Data are meanings that people from a variety of perspectives agree on and declare as important. Lippitt (1982) asserts that data achieve significance because they both are accepted as valid and have proven themselves fit for use over time. Their ability to describe situations accurately, as those who have experienced the situations can attest, verifies them.

Change agents investigate, analyze, diagnose, and illumine to build a database for change. The change agent typically provides expertise in data gathering and analysis, and the client system provides access to staff, informational, technological, and financial resources. From their agreement to work together, the change agent and client hope to resolve the problem, prevent or minimize future occurrences, and create a greater capacity for organizational productivity.

Data Collection and Analysis

In changing public organizations in particular, change agents need to develop a thorough knowledge of what the organization does, who it serves and why, who the key players are, and what have been significant events leading up to the problems or issues at hand. This is not easy. Every two years, top administrators leave office, and agendas with little connection to existing orders of business pop up. Public organizations are not only pluralistic in clientele and structures; they are virtual monopolies. One agency regulates air traffic; one collects all the nation's taxes; and until 1971, every piece of mail went through a single postal system. How does the change agent collect valid and useful data under shifting, multiple-headed, and one-of-a-kind bureaucracies?

Using Action Research. Because of the unique nature of public organizations, collecting and analyzing data need to take place as action research. Action research, as described by French and Bell (1990), is the process of systematically collecting research data about an ongoing system relative to some objective, goal, or need of that system. Action research incorporates feeding these data back into the system, taking actions by altering selected variables within the system based both on the data and on hypotheses, and evaluating the results of actions by collecting more data.

Action research enables the change agent to explore dimensions of a problem to uncover various possibilities for solving a given problem. As Block (1981) points out, the "presenting problem" a client describes may be only a symptom of a larger problem. Accepting the presenting problem as a given, however, may lead the change agent to form an erroneous diagnosis and recommend an ill-suited problem resolution strategy.

What to Examine. To develop as accurate an idea as possible of what the problem in its context consists of, the change agent may examine the problem situation in four main settings: structural, environmental, climate, and cultural.

Structural setting. Structures are recurring interactions that occur at any of the four levels of organizations described earlier. Structures, in other words, may refer to individual, intergroup, interorganizational, or intraorganizational levels of functioning. In many situations, particularly at the intraorganizational level, all others are somehow linked. Structural interactions help regulate and control tasks.

Structures, in addition, may be formal as well as informal. Formal structures, such as boxes on organization charts that specify reporting relationships, are usually proscribed by laws, regulations, or policies. Informal structures, on the other hand, emerge over time as ways to accomplish work effectively and efficiently. Informal structures, more plentiful than formal ones, are often constructed on the basis of experience and are governed by norms that people commonly accept in practice. Business lunch-eons, for example, are informal structures during which people often make important decisions.

Environmental setting. In public organizations in particular, environmental forces frequently determine how people transact work. An environmental setting includes individuals, groups, and entities having an interest in the organization mission and purposes. Public organizations have a high sensitivity to the needs and interests of clientele. Rainey (1997, 88) catalogs many of the leading stakeholders as chief executives, legislatures, courts, other government agencies and levels of government, interest groups, policy subsystems, the media, and individual citizens who seek out government services.

Climate setting. Climate refers to the ways people perceive how structures interact with working in the organization. Climate is actually a "psychological feeling" about how things are. If work structures provide few opportunities to exercise discretionary judgment—if, for instance, workers have to pass even routine decisions upward for approval—the climate may feel stifling. Such climates may produce workers who have little motivation to improve work conditions because they have virtually no involvement in them. Some possible effects might include worker passivity, complaining, mistrust of decisions handed down from the top, and boredom. Climate often results not only from the work structures themselves but also from the ways in which managers coordinate work flow (Weisbord, 1976).

Cultural setting. Organizational culture reflects the patterns of assumptions, beliefs, and practices that people in organizational settings have learned to do their work. Studying culture involves understanding the social anthropology that undergirds organizational operations. D'Andrade (1984) and Geertz (1973), for instance, define organizational culture as a pattern of symbols in discourse that are shared as common interpretations among people. Moreover, Hofstede (1980) sees organizational culture as a set of mental programs that predispose thinking and acting.

Edgar Schein (1992) notes that organizational culture has two main purposes: survival and adaptation to external environment and perpetuation of ability to survive and adapt through integration of internal processes. Organizational cultures serve several functions. Cultures of organizations provide frameworks of meaning that are shaped by collective ideas, experiences, and common worldviews. By studying organizational culture, change agents can understand the basis for how people develop agreement on shared values; the organization's core mission, primary tasks, and functions; the ways in which organizations make decisions and evaluate results; and how the organization directs members toward what goals to pursue.

Grounded Methodologies. One way of applying action research to a particular context is to use grounded methodologies. Lincoln and Guba (1985) perhaps best articulate the concept of "groundedness" in data collection and analysis. In their view, the change agent studies the problem in its natural context and from the analysis generates theories regarding how and why the problem came into existence. The theoretical explanation comes from a variety of data collection methods, including interviews and observations of people experiencing the problem, and from analysis of documents that provide a historical and cultural understanding of contributions. The change agent verifies the theoretical explanation by soliciting reactions from those from whom data have been collected and then inviting elaboration. This approach often produces additional areas of investigation and provides a rich or "thick" description of the problem in its context.

Grounded methodologies are particularly useful to public organizations because they can describe the unique features of agencies and their complex social, political, and economic relationships. They produce a blueprint for interventions based on human perspectives and experiences. Methodologies that use a quantitative approach frequently overlook key explanations for how and why public organizations operate as they do. Truth comes from multiple perspectives. To illustrate, Lincoln and Guba quote Bogdan and Taylor's (1975) case study of mental patients at a state hospital:

We have seen vivid scenes and behavior such as rocking and head-banging by residents interpreted in markedly disparate fashion. One attendant explained self-mutilation and head-banging as a direct result of severe mental retardation, while another claimed that a resident may bang his head against the wall as a response to sheer boredom and lack of programming. Similarly, one staff person remarked sadly, "These patients could really be helped if there were a program for them," while another praised the institution for its program: "I know I have the best recreation program in the country. We do everything for these kids." The staff's views of residents further exemplify the gross differences in perspectives. . . . Truth then emerges not as one objective view but rather as the composite picture of how people think about the institution and each other. Truth comprises the perspectives of administrators, line-level staff, professional workers, outsiders, volunteers, maintenance staff, residents and family. (Bogdan and Taylor, 1975, 10–11, as cited in Lincoln and Guba, 1985, 80)

Using Grounded Methodologies. To use grounded methodologies in collecting and analyzing data, change agents should follow particular procedures. In brief, these include:

1. Choosing widely representative populations as samples.
2. Conducting interviews and observations on-site over a period of time.
3. Analyzing statistical reports, documents, and records that bear upon the problem or issue at hand.

4. Reflecting on information individuals, observations, and documents have provided and determining additional areas to probe or questions to ask.

5. Providing summary reports of data for clarification and verification to people interviewed.

6. Conducting further research to provide additional explanations.

7. Asking respondents to provide further clarification or elaboration.

A CASE EXAMPLE

How might this methodology work in an actual case? One example occurred in an agency that had become aware of the relatively few numbers of women and minority employees who had been promoted into upper management. The problem surfaced as a result of employee complaints over several years, recommendations from personnel officers and affirmative action officials, and top-level administrators who had felt pressure from external oversight organizations. The 5,000-member agency had neither a formal policy for affirmative action nor programs to help qualify women and minority employees for managerial positions. To address the problem, the agency head appointed a task force consisting of the affirmative action officer (a minority female), the personnel director, the training director, personnel management specialists and trainers, and female and minority members in a variety of line positions.

Contracting for Change

The affirmative action officer, appointed as the task force chair, engineered most of the changes. As a first step, she oversaw the writing of a formal policy for training and promoting underrepresented staff members. She obtained a variety of statistical reports from the Office of Personnel Management and collected interview data, policy statements, and training program designs from other agencies that had highly successful policies and programs. After several discussions with top managers, the affirmative action officer obtained their written endorsement of the policy and a plan for action. Although the affirmative action officer pressed for a comprehensive training program for employees and a coaching program for their supervisors, she received approval only for an employee training program.

Collecting and Analyzing Data for Program Design

The affirmative action officer delegated the program design to personnel management and training specialists. Because regulations prohibited automatic promotions following training programs, program participants could only be trained to qualify for promotion; training would increase their competitiveness. To qualify them completely and accurately, the training program had to incorporate skills that participants would use in the future.

To determine particular needs, the personnel management specialists and trainers conducted in-office interviews with 25 women candidates and their managers. These respondents came from each of the agency's nine divisions. Among them were a handful of African-American and Hispanic women. Each interview was written and later given to the respondents to check for accuracy and for additional information. In addition, the change agents examined respondent job descriptions and compared them with what respondents said they actually did.

After a preliminary round of data collection, the change agents identified categories of information that helped them understand issues respondents faced. The categories also suggested topics that could be incorporated into the training program.

To examine the consistency of data across individual interviews, the change agents developed a coding system. Data categories pertaining to conflicts with field offices were labeled "conflict/field"; "conflict/role" related to the conflicts participants faced in fulfilling the responsibilities of regulators and service advisers. The categories appearing most often across cases became important as topics for training.

Further, as change agents identified relationships between categories, they could understand how certain conditions contributed to others. For instance, the scarcity of information respondents received from supervisors appeared to produce several forms of conflict. Conflict, in turn, affected relationships between respondents, their supervisors, and field personnel. The patterns of relationships gave course designers ideas on related skills areas to include in the training. In the case of conflict management, for example, participants would require competence in assertiveness, listening, and problem solving.

The process was not straightforward, however. After additional information was collected, new categories emerged, whereas some existing categories had to be expanded or reduced in importance; others were eliminated.

The simultaneous data collection and data analysis process indicated several potential problems beyond program design. Some problems had roots in the informal organizational structures, and changing the structures was beyond the charter of the intervention. For instance, agency managers had had little formal training in supervisory skills. This meant that there were few normative models for the training program to use. In addition, the skills most managers used were highly technical; they had obtained them through many years of working in field offices as specialists. Not only were the managers expected to know the "how-to's" of the particular business; they were also expected to understand the unique interests and roles of external industry clientele and to communicate effectively with them. Women did not have opportunities to gain industry knowledge, however, because the largely all-white male supervisory cadre had denied the women opportunities. For instance, women seldom attended client meetings with their superiors. If they did, the supervisors ignored them or belittled their contributions. Some respondents believed their managers would support training, but many others believed the managers would resent it.

Findings

The initial data collection and analysis revealed that respondents' managers required some degree of training if the program were to be successful. The communications needs, moreover, suggested that training include follow-up opportunities to attend clientele meetings and practice skills of assertiveness, active listening, and problem solving. Because the top agency officials had rejected the coupling of training with a subsequent project, however, the change agents' options were limited.

To overcome this barrier, the designers prepared an orientation checklist for participant supervisors along with suggestions for helping participants apply skills following training. In addition, the designers incorporated supervisory relationship skills throughout the training, which included not only skills for working with recalcitrant supervisors and clientele but also skills for enhancing self-esteem, confidence, and assertiveness.

INTERPRETING DATA

From a Native's Point of View

The goal of grounded methodologies of action research is to provide a comprehensive view of "what it is like" from the viewpoint of those experiencing some phenomenon. Change agents collect and analyze data in order to uncover what that viewpoint is. They know they have reached this goal when data become redundant or "saturated" (Glaser and Strauss, 1967; Miles and Huberman, 1984)—that is, subsequent rounds of interviewing, observing, and document analysis keep saying the same things.

Conditions Affecting Data Collection and Analysis

Using grounded methodologies to research actual work problems requires care. The close relationship of the researcher to the subjects poses a critical dilemma: On the one hand, the change agent/researcher becomes involved with the ongoing situation to the point of gaining a native's understanding; on the other hand, the change agent/researcher may introject any number of biases into the data collection and analysis. Miles and Huberman (1994, 438) list some of the leading forms of bias:

1. data overload in the field, leading to the analysts' missing important information, overweighting some findings, skewing the analysis;
2. salience of first impressions or observations of highly concrete or dramatic incidents;
3. selectivity, overconfidence in some data, especially when trying to confirm a key finding;
4. co-occurrences taken as correlations, or even as causal relationships;
5. false base-rate proportions; extrapolations of the number of total instances from those observed;
6. unreliability of information from some sources; and
7. overaccommodation to information that questions a tentative hypothesis.

To maintain a balance between subjective and objective involvement in the research, Miles and Huberman (438–439) recommend documenting and reviewing frequently what actions were taken, what codes were used to label and categorize information, and how hypotheses can be substantiated with actual data. Keeping an accurate and up-to-date "audit trail" is essential. At a minimum, Miles and Huberman recommend describing sampling decisions made; how data were collected and analyzed; sample population and basis on which they were selected; analytic strategies used; and data display methods.

In relation to the case study, one of the chief biases change agents found was their tendency to insert their own interpretations of the technical language respondents used. The change agents often translate the jargon into words and phrases that made sense to them. But in so doing, they analyzed their own interpretations. To reduce this bias, the change agents recorded verbatim vocabulary that respondents used in later interviews.

Validating Data

To validate data, change agents present observations, insights, and possible explanations they develop to respondents. Clarification and elaboration of the data respondents furnish become the basis for subsequent rounds of simultaneous data collection and analysis and feedback.

The use of respondents in action research not only gives change agents an idea of how respondents themselves use different mental models to define and interpret reality; action research also involves respondents in the design and use of possible interventions. In testing theoretical explanations of researched phenomena, change agents can develop interventions that are both accurate and usable among similar populations elsewhere.

SUMMARY

Organizational change is a comprehensive and carefully planned process of improving present and future operations. It examines individuals, groups, interorganizational systems and processes, and between-organization relationships. Changing organizations holistically assumes that altering one part changes all others associated with it. The holistic character of organization transformation also recognizes the connection between objective forms, such as organizational charts, job descriptions, and policy statements, and human interpretation processes.

To account for the richness of objective and subjective relationships, an action research format allows understanding dynamics and prepares for accurate and valid diagnosis for organization change. Action research blends the objective and subjective components in using a grounded methodology, which allows the theoretical explanations of phenomena under study to have linkages with experiences, perspectives, and beliefs that people share. Further, action research permits respondents to participate in designing interventions. This helps create data that are not only valid but also useful.

In the following chapter, we will examine how change agents may use data from grounded methodologies to design strategies cooperatively. The collaboration between change agents and the client system, however, rests on the degree of perceived, mutual trust. To enable clients to understand data and to make necessary changes, change agents need to help clients overcome many fears and doubts. Clients, on the other hand, need to learn to trust the expertise and guiding visions of change agents to reach goals.

REFERENCES

Block, P. (1981). *Flawless consulting: A guide to getting your expertise used*. San Diego, CA: University Associates.

Bogdan, R., and Taylor, S. J. (1975). *Introduction to qualitative research methods*. New York: John Wiley.

Burke, W. W. (1987). *Organization development: A normative view*. Reading, MA: Addison-Wesley.

D'Andrade, R. G. (1984). Cultural meaning systems. In R. A. Shweder and R. A. LeVine (Eds.), *Culture theory*. Cambridge: Cambridge University Press.

French, W. L., and Bell, C. H., Jr. (1990). *Organization development* (4th ed., 99–106). Englewood Cliffs, NJ: Prentice-Hall.

Geertz, C. (1973). *The interpretation of cultures*. New York: Basic Books.

Glaser, B. G., and Strauss, A. L. (1967). *The discovery of grounded theory*. Chicago: Aldine.

Hofstede, G. (1980). *Culture's consequences: International differences in work-related values*. Beverly Hills, CA: Sage.

Lewin, K. (1945). Research center for group dynamics. *Sociometry, 8*(2), 9.

Lincoln, Y. S. and Guba, E. G. (1985). *Naturalistic inquiry*. Beverly Hills, CA: Sage.

Lippitt, G. L. (1982). *Organizational renewal* (2nd ed.). Englewood Cliffs, NJ: Prentice-Hall.

Miles, M. B., and Huberman, A. M. (1984). *Qualitative data analysis: A sourcebook of new methods*. Beverly Hills, CA: Sage.

Miles, M. B., and Huberman, A. M. (1994). Data management and analysis methods. In N. K. Denzin and Y. S. Lincoln (Eds.), *Handbook of qualitative research* (428–444). Thousand Oaks, CA: Sage.

Rainey, H. G. (1997). *Understanding and managing public organizations* (2nd ed.). San Francisco: Jossey-Bass.

Schein, E. H. (1992). *Organizational culture and leadership* (2nd ed.). San Francisco: Jossey-Bass.

Weisbord, M. (1976). Organizational diagnosis: Six places to look for trouble with or without a theory. *Group and Organizational Studies, 1*(4), 430–447.

CHAPTER 4

Building Trust and Preparing
for Change

I create my own environment and can change it in any way I wish. I
am limited only by my fear, and need not be limited by that.
—Jack Gibb (1991). *Trust: A New Vision of Human Relationships
for Businesses, Education, Family, and Personal Living*

Changing organizations is paradoxical. It's like taking your children to a
roller-skating rink and having them pressure you to join them. On the one
hand, you think of the times you were a kid and thought nothing of whirl-
ing around on skates, going as fast as you could, and not minding it at all
when you fell. But then reality crashes in. You're afraid of looking foolish,
especially in front of your children and their friends. You hear messages in
your head about middle-aged people like yourself, and somehow your feet
freeze inside your shoes. Change is a possibility. Perhaps with practice, you
could succeed. Fear, however, keeps you from trying.

Change pushes us toward relieving tension and pain, but it also defies
us to find ways to rid ourselves of it. Change invites us to explore uncharted
areas, but it doesn't promise us they'll be as idyllic as we'd expected them
to be.

Change agents help clients take the first step. They listen to their fears
and concerns about failing and about looking bad to important people.
They also, however, provide options in situations that appear to have limited alternatives. Change agents find and even create resources. They sub-

due fear and replace it with courage. Clients learn to trust them and then change.

This chapter discusses the processes of using data for developing and implementing organizational change. It emphasizes the importance of building client trust as the basis for introducing and sustaining interventions. It also describes the role of the change agent in empowering the client during and after the decision to transform organizations.

GIVING CLIENT FEEDBACK

In the previous chapter, we looked at the cycle of change that change agents typically follow in organizations. We observed that clients, or people who call in change agents for help, often become aware of problems interfering with effective and efficient organizational operations in various ways. Change agents discuss the problem and receive permission as well as resources to investigate and diagnose the problem in relation to its setting. Through a variety of action research techniques, the change agent collects and analyzes data and verifies their accuracy from people whom the change agents interviewed or observed, or from scanned records. After data collection and analysis, the change agent presents a summary of findings, implications, and recommendations for change. We are now ready to look more closely at the feedback stage—when the change agent gives both a written and an oral report of findings.

The Importance of Trust

Cultivating trust is important throughout the change process but most especially after data have been collected and analyzed. Not only does the client fear what the data may say, but people from whom the data were taken may suspect something is wrong. Before data are fed back to the client, tension is perhaps at its peak.

To deal with the uncertainty, fear, and possible loss of face, clients may develop several forms of defensiveness. Some more common defenses might include questioning the change agent's methodology, wanting to know who said what, and threatening to fire people interviewed.

In a state agency a change agent team interviewed senior officials and top career managers regarding their perceptions of mission, goal clarity, and interpersonal trust. The team presented its interview findings to the agency head, noting the high degree of cooperativeness the client system had exhibited. Although the interviews revealed a clear need for team building, the change agent team indicated their confidence in its success; the client system seemed to be sanguine—a factor that increased the likelihood of success.

After the change agent team had presented its recommendations, however, the apparent trust unraveled. Several managers asked the agency head where he had heard of the change agents, what their credentials were in working with sensitive issues, and how reliable they would be if their home office were out of state. One manager refused to attend the six-day retreat the change agents had planned. Another said he didn't accept "all that touchy-feely stuff"; they never solve "the real problems," he believed. Still other participants complained about attending, citing needs for transportation to and from the retreat facility, problems finding child care, vacation plans that had to be terminated, the fact that additional funds spent on the retreat were needed to pay overhead expenses, and concerns about what staff members would say about their managers' leadership styles.

The 15-member retreat group was particularly nervous, however. The state had recently asked each agency to reduce its programming by 10 percent. Some members feared they would have to lay off staff members, whereas some even thought the agency head was using the retreat as a "hatchet job" on themselves.

Although it is important to understand possible reasons for client resistance to change, it is more important for the change agent to create conditions that produce trust. Unless bonds of trust can be established, implementing change will be precarious. Lack of trust produces "games," as we observed in the case example. The client and the client system battle attempts to change. In wars such as these, no party wins completely; rather, the furor leaves behind seeds of future conflicts.

ELEMENTS OF TRUST BUILDING

In giving feedback, the change agent needs to polish credibility—the feeling that what is said is true and honest, has depth, and is helpful. Change agents can work toward optimal credibility by exhibiting six central behaviors: being honest, listening nonjudgmentally, keeping information confidential, cocreating a vision of hope, showing high self-regard, and expressing confidence in the client's abilities to change—with help (see Figure 4.1).

Honesty

Change agents need to scrutinize their own feelings and values about what clients ask them to do. Similarly, if the change agent suspects lack of congruence between what the client says and his or her actions, the change agent should articulate the feeling and probe where it comes from. The change agent should express feelings and substantiate them with evidence. In addition, the change agent should ask for comments or clarification to test the intuition. By opening the door to sharing feelings, concerns, and

Figure 4.1
Elements of Trust Building

- Honesty
- Nonjudgmental listening
- Keeping confidences
- Cocreating vision
- Believe in yourself
- Express confidence in client ability

---

fears, the change agent allows the client to let out concealed emotions and perhaps reveal blindspots that may interfere later.

Nonjudgmental Listening

Because of the heightened emotional arousal in feedback, the change agent should expect the client to "dump" feelings. The change agent should not feel intimidated, belittled, or threatened but should listen to the barrage and realize it paves the way for the client's listening. Clients who do not verbalize their feelings during the feedback stage may indicate that they have other agendas for the data use; change agents should proceed cautiously. When this happens, the change agent should attempt to determine the reasons for the unexpected, low-key responses.

Keeping Confidences

The change agent has a responsibility both to the client and to the respondents furnishing data to prevent the information from being abused. Violating the confidentiality and the anonymity of the data destroys the change agent's trustworthiness. The change agent may take several steps to keep the data confidential and anonymous:

1. Replace names with numbers.
2. Eliminate all references to actual names of people, organizational titles and designations, or any other possible identifiers.
3. Allow respondents to double-check reports before they are submitted to the client.
4. Destroy original notes of interviews, observations, and document analyses after the final data collection and analysis report has been written.
5. Provide written and signed guarantees of confidentiality and anonymity to each respondent before data are collected and analyzed.

Cocreate Vision

During the feedback stage, clients may set themselves up for expecting the worst and listen for cues that confirm their suspicions. It is important that no matter how difficult the data may be to present, the change agent find patterns that offer potential rebuilding. Within such reports, particularly when people and systems appear at their worst, change agents can discover opportunities to chart new directions, construct new relationships, and build stronger and more efficient work flow processes. Hope provides a vision and begins to recirculate energy and excitement. It also offers workable options.

Believe in Yourself

Change agents inspire clients by radiating a certain exuberance. Their strength comes from within. Change agents are sure of themselves because they have spent much time finding out who they are and what they value. Change agents are effective instruments of change by believing and practicing that which they know as true. Having a base of strength from inside not only enables the change agent to withstand the traumas of intervening in human organizations but also brings healing and hope to others.

Express Confidence in Client Ability

Clients, not change agents, ultimately have to do the hard work of transforming organizations. Change agents can provide the vision, the skills, and the plan, but clients have the responsibility for making differences. To support the client, the change agent can point to qualities the client has that are important in bringing about change. The change agent might also point out the resources the client already has, such as knowledge and skills, external support systems, technological help, and past successes in related areas. Finally, the change agent can express his or her own support, particularly in contributing expertise, in solving the organizational problem or issue.

PREPARING THE CLIENT SYSTEM FOR CHANGE

Once the client has accepted the feedback and has decided to proceed with making changes, the change agent can help the client system get ready. The preparations include assessing readiness for certain types of interventions, selecting the appropriateness of design to the problem or issue defined, analyzing key stakeholders and cultivating their support for change, and setting up a flexible plan of desired outcomes, milestones, and costs.

Mapping the Client System

In initiating change, the change agent needs to know the extent and configuration of the client system. The *client system* refers not only to the immediate person or hierarchy of persons that ask for help initially but also to the systems the problem or issue affects elsewhere in the organization. Figure 4.2 shows an example of a client system map for a Medicaid program within a state Department of Social Services.

To map out the client system, the change agent can examine the formal organizational chart, which will indicate the flow of political power and reporting relationships. It will also suggest the amount of discretionary power available to decision makers. For instance, if the organization is a large, multilayered, pyramidic structure, it is not likely that the top manager has much detailed knowledge about the intervention. Getting top-level support and resources will be difficult in this case because authority and accountability are dispersed and vaguely defined. The steeper the organizational structure, the more likely resource decisions are passed upward.

The organizational chart may offer clues to the informal power and influence systems and, to an extent, the resource acquisition and development systems. But observing and interviewing people at work in the client system will give more useful information regarding readiness for change. In particular, looking at informal communications patterns reveals much about the client system culture, management, technology, and environmental interface. Who talks with whom? What topics do they discuss? How frequently? Where do discussions take place?

The informal scan also turns up potential "informants"—knowledgeable and articulate persons in the client system who can give information about who the key players are. Informants can also provide an understanding of some of the leading interests, concerns, and even possible barriers the key players might offer. To develop a graphic idea of the configuration, the change agent can ask the informants to draw a diagram of the organization showing where the key players are located. The informants can also specify their feelings and attitudes as well as perspectives about the players.

SURVEYING READINESS FOR CHANGE

Having a general map of how extensive the client system is and how it is arranged, the change agent can assess how prepared it is to undertake interventions. Figure 4.3 shows some of the information the change agent needs: trust levels, previous experiences with change, levels of technical knowledge, attitudes toward change, willingness to participate in change, extent to which information is shared currently, and depth of interventions needed.

Figure 4.2
Example of Client Map

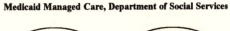

Medicaid Managed Care, Department of Social Services

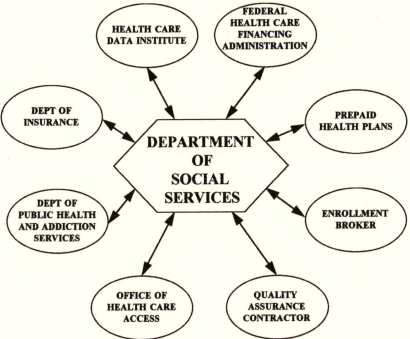

Trust Level

To begin change, change agents need to establish a baseline of client system trust. This baseline gives the change agent an idea about the depth of interventions that can be tried out. Trust is an essential foundation not only of change management but also of effective organizational operations.

The change agent can gauge the level of trust through administering a validated survey questionnaire, followed by a series of interviews regarding critical events in the client system. The change agent can also examine historical documents that furnish additional information. Finally, change agents can observe people at meetings, during breaks, and in their natural office settings.

Previous Experiences with Change

The client system may have undergone successful change programs in the past and may have favorable dispositions toward the one being planned;

Figure 4.3
Elements in Readiness for Change

- Trust levels
- Previous experiences with change
- Levels of technical knowledge
- Attitudes toward change
- Willingness to participate in change
- Extent to which information is shared currently
- Depth of interventions needed

---

on the other hand, particularly "bad experiences" may present obstacles. Past failed change efforts may have left people feeling anger, resentment, mistrust, and cynicism. The change agent should study the histories of such changes and observe possible reasons for their failures. For instance, were changes initiated, as in the opening case example, for personal reasons? Were people informed in advance regarding the changes? Did they have opportunities to participate in the design? Answers can give clues to potential minefields. If the change agent cannot avoid them, he or she can defuse them. Listening nonjudgmentally to "horror stories" people have experienced goes a long way toward decreasing tensions.

Levels of Technical Knowledge

Many organizations experience problems because people lack the technical know-how required for their jobs. They may have had education and training before they entered public service but have had little or none after. With widespread cuts in public organizations' budgets, funds set aside for employee development are often trimmed first. Moreover, with many professional and technical fields changing rapidly because of the onslaught of the information age, many employees cannot keep up with the latest developments. Thus, change agents often have to provide extensive amounts of training and development both in technical job specialties as well as in ways to become proficient in using new tools and technologies.

Attitudes toward Change

Differences in individual attitudes toward change can also account for how people will respond. Some people are adept at adjusting to changes, whereas others lose perspective quite easily and fall apart. People who have a high tolerance for ambiguity and who have a fairly high level of self-confidence usually adjust well; others need to have a precisely defined plan of action that presents no surprises and deviations to feel "in control." Change agents need to assess the adaptability and tolerance styles of individuals in the client system and provide detailed plans to all. By doing so, those needing in-depth information will feel satisfied.

Willingness to Participate in Change

People in the client system vary in the degree to which they are willing to participate in change. Some prefer quite active roles, such as volunteering for task forces and committees, serving as group spokespeople to communicate with clientele, receiving all pertinent memos regarding the intervention, and contributing their expertise to the planning and implementation. Others prefer to receive periodic informational notices. Still others do not wish to participate at all; they prefer others to make key decisions for them. The change agent should respect preferences but offer opportunities to all who wish to contribute. The main point is to not exclude anyone who wants to participate.

Change agents can stimulate willingness to participate, however, through building in a range of incentives. These can include such rewards as plaques and certificates, letters of thanks from the top official, and formal recognition of contributions. At a minimum, the change agent should create participation opportunities that provide for additional learning, particularly about organizational management. Opportunities should also include potentials for career advancement. Lastly, all voluntary participation should be enjoyable—people perform better if they are having fun.

Extent to Which Information Is Shared Currently

To a large degree, the flow of information through the client organization influences the level of trust and also the degree of involvement. People who have access to timely and relevant information are more informed about the problems and issues the organization is facing. The knowledge enables them to seek out additional information, particularly from those who are in positions to change conditions. This produces an exchange that gives people more potential influence than those left "out of the loop." Those excluded from information networks often resist change and may become suspicious and even sabotage attempts.

Depth of Interventions Needed

Harrison (1970) points out that levels of tasks and feelings are two chief gauges for determining the depth of interventions. Task levels are concerned with work behaviors and relationships and are measured by instruments that describe degrees of satisfaction. Interventions resolve gaps between work and satisfaction through negotiations and bargaining among work groups.

Personal-level interventions, which are based on quality of human relationships, vary in depth. Each intervention aims at producing openness. At the surface levels, change agents work with feelings, attitudes, and perceptions. On a deeper level, they use perspective changes to build better relationships between individuals and groups. At the deepest level, change agents work with individual values and attitudes that affect functioning, identity, and existence.

PLANNING INTERVENTIONS COLLABORATIVELY

Having conducted a readiness audit, the change agent can plan with the client a strategy for change. This usually involves several meetings with the client and key players in the client system. Change agents need to ensure that the client and the client system are clear about the purposes of the intervention, the objectives or goals, what their roles and relationships are, and some immediate and long-range results they can expect.

To accomplish these requirements, the change agent should promote collaboration throughout the planning and implementation stages. The change agent can use several types of participatory problem-solving and decision-making techniques. The planning meetings often use variants of "brainstorming" processes. In these, participants generate lists of all the possible causes and effects of problems and issues that they can think of. The change agent works as a facilitator, recording the ideas on a large wall chart without comment or judgment. After all ideas have been listed, the change agent directs the group to ask questions for clarity or elaboration; in addition, the group may combine similar ideas or eliminate duplicates. The change agent then asks group members to rank their top three to five choices and vote on them. The leading choices represent the group's consensus, or alternatives they can support (Delbeq, Van de Ven, and Gustafson, 1975; Hart, Boroush, Enk, and Hornick, 1985.)

The type of intervention chosen depends on several factors: (1) the targets of change, or who or what will receive the interventions; (2) the organizational level, whether individual, group, interorganization, or between organizations; (3) the depth of intervention in relation to objectives of change; and (4) the amount of time, financial and technical resources, and support the client is willing to devote.

Types of Typical Interventions

Although it is not possible to list *all* of the possible interventions and combinations change agents and clients may decide on, it is possible to describe some of the more common ones used in public organizations by level.

Individual level. Many of the individually based interventions center around job-related issues. Career advancement and job satisfaction are often candidates. In career advancement, jobs may be redesigned to permit broader ranges of responsibilities (Hackman and Oldham, 1980) and incorporate intrinsic rewards (Herzberg, 1983). In addition, individuals who show promise for attaining high leadership positions may benefit from an agency mentor training and development program (Kram, 1983). Individuals also receive training and development to enhance their present levels of professional and technical skills as well as prepare for future responsibilities (Schein, 1978).

Group level. By far, team building is one of the most widely used interventions. In team building, the change agent establishes trust among leaders and participants and enables the team to accomplish purposes more effectively and efficiently. Common uses of teams are to produce innovative solutions to problems, carry out top-down policies, and serve as forums for discussions of critical agency issues.

Teams are becoming more prevalent in organizations, particularly in the public sector. Many agencies have adopted forms of total quality management (TQM) and use quality improvement teams to generate ideas and solutions for solving productivity problems (Crosby, 1979; Juran, 1989). Teams require large amounts of training to function effectively. Typically, change agents teach them skills in problem solving and decision making, conflict management, group dynamics, productivity improvement, and organizational and interpersonal communications.

Interorganizational level. Across organization division boundaries, interventions often focus on improving communications and large-scale productivity improvement processes. Frequently, interventions involve the entire organization. Total quality management programs, for example, succeed only if the organization as a whole adopts them. Adopting the changes of TQM not only involves training in work improvement strategies and interpersonal relationships; it also involves changing the cultural dynamics of organizations. This includes the ways in which power is distributed, the rewards structures, the technological linkages, and informal communications networks. Implementing TQM programs or variants of them involves radical transformation of all organizational systems and their relationships with internal and external clientele.

At the organization-wide level, moreover, change interventions often entail installing new management systems. Performance management, linking rewards with organizational objectives and individual and team performance, is a typical example. Executive and management training programs, in addition, provide competencies for leading a variety of changes throughout agencies.

Intraorganizational level. Skills for collaboration among a diversity of interests and needs are perhaps most critical when change agents work with a cluster of organizations, individuals, and associations. Quite often, the collaboration takes the form of team problem solving and decision making, but finding consensus and developing shared meaning are difficult. Members often have divergent interests and loyalties; conflict among members is frequent, and atrophy is common.

On the positive side, however, intraorganizational interventions may produce a number of innovative solutions to problems that many different organizations face together. Resources can be shared to benefit common well-being. In addition, intraorganizational interventions can develop a "big picture" of problems and issues that individuals and singular organizations may not understand completely. This creates a synergistic movement: a widespread desire to take collective action to resolve perplexities.

Finding and Cultivating Change Champions

In planning implementation, change agents need to cultivate the support of several change champions. Champions are people who can advocate changes to top-level officials, influence people to adopt, bring a variety of resources to bear, and provide for continuity of leadership throughout the change process. In the public sector in particular, champions play key roles. Because of the political leadership at the top of organizational hierarchies, career personnel are the mainstays of day-to-day management. They not only know the organization's history, policies, and practices, but they also know the formal and informal structures of how work gets done. In fact, careerists often train their politically appointed superiors—a condition that often creates interdependence and fosters collaboration.

The readiness audit discussed earlier may reveal who some of the most likely candidates for champion roles are. In deciding to enlist them, however, the change agent should have some idea of desirable characteristics. Among the important qualities are:

1. *Positions of visibility.* Champions should be fairly high up the organizational ladder to enable them to exert a great deal of influence. Their central positions in informal networks are important in getting people who may not be otherwise committed to change interested and involved.

2. *High levels of credibility.* Champions should have reputations for trustworthiness. They should have many of the qualities that foster trust discussed earlier in this chapter.

3. *Openness to new ideas.* Champions are innovative people who are not afraid to take risks. They also convert ideas into practical applications and train others to take responsibility for seeing the ideas through. Champions tend to be well educated and models of lifelong learning.

4. *Understanding of organizational "games."* Champions have an intuitive understanding of the informal power and influence structures and processes in organizations. They have usually learned them from many years of experience. They also realize the limitations of such processes, however, and know when to forego them. They know when games will end up crippling organizational processes and harming people, and they refuse to join in them.

5. *Respect for people's integrity.* Champions help others develop their own abilities. They provide opportunities for personal as well as career growth and link opportunities to improving the organization as a whole. They usually look for the best qualities in others and find them.

Selecting a Pilot Project

Before initiating change, it is essential to try out a strategy and assess its overall effectiveness in achieving objectives. Pilot projects are small-scale demonstrations of how interventions can be expected to work. To determine the appropriateness of an intervention, the change agent should set up criteria for selecting pilots. In general, the pilot project should contain qualities that will enhance the probabilities of success. If the pilot fails, the event overshadows later implementation attempts.

Some of the important characteristics that will likely produce successful pilots are the following:

1. *Select a pilot area that has a fairly well working organization.* Organizations that have a reputation for having "problems" may live up to such expectations.

2. *Consider multiple pilots.* Having more than one unit testing the intervention will provide a basis for comparing what works under what conditions. Multiple pilots might be selected on the basis of their diversity; selecting pilots that are representative of a particular population, geographical location, profession, or technology, for instance, will provide a "thick" basis on which to make assessments (Yin, 1984).

3. *Develop effectiveness criteria.* Criteria for evaluating pilots should be developed with respect to the objectives they are designed to achieve. Moreover, change agents should include a balance of quantitative and qualitative assessments to provide a more adequate assessment. Some examples of assessment indicators include amount of time, money, and scrap saved; degree of user satisfaction with processes; and amount of resources required as inputs in relation to numbers of products or services as outputs.

The change agent and the client system should develop criteria and agree on how they should be assessed. The change agent should record the observations and share them with the client system so that the change agent and client can make adjustments.

SUMMARY

Beginning any form of change creates tension. Uncertainty about what data might reveal, fear of failing, and even fear of succeeding may provoke client resistance. To help clients understand their own concerns, and yet develop confidence in their own abilities to manage organizational transformation, change agents can build relationships of trust. The relief of worries and doubts and the confidence in the change agent's expertise can enable the client to make key decisions and resolve problems associated with intervening in human systems.

This chapter has provided change agents with tips on strengthening the client's resolution and commitment to change. Central to trust building is practicing nonjudgmental listening, exuding self-confidence, helping the client visualize an improved future, and finding ways to reinforce the client's abilities to believe in himself or herself.

To increase the likelihood that envisioned goals will bear fruit, the change agent can prepare the client system. Some particular techniques include a carefully crafted readiness audit. The audit should assess such key variables of success as existing trust levels, previous change experiences, abilities as well as willingness to contribute to planned changes, and depth of technological and human systems required.

Based on an assessment of client hopes and desires for change as well as system capacities for turning change plans into reality, the change agent and the client can decide on appropriate interventions. Optimally, the decision rests on the collaboration of the client and those internal and external stakeholders having interests in, or processes associated with, the contemplated changes. From the network of stakeholders, the change agent can identify and develop change champions to facilitate smooth intervention. Moreover, the change agent and client can decide on ways to test the change strategy selected under conditions similar to those where the solution will be introduced. Pilot projects further ensure success in that they permit bugs to surface and be fixed before launching the final design and strategy.

Building trust prepares the client mentally and emotionally for undertaking change. Because of the human subjective basis of organizational systems and relationships, having high levels of confidence that change will succeed is a vital precursor to success.

In the following chapter, we will examine ways the change agent can reinforce preparation through implementation procedures. The chapter details some ways to enable the outcomes of change to match their high expectations.

REFERENCES

Crosby, P. B. (1979). *Quality is free*. New York: New American Library.

Delbeq, A. L., Van de Ven, A. H., and Gustafson, D. H. (1975). *Group techniques for program planning: A guide to Nominal and Delphi processes*. Glenview, IL: Scott, Foresman.

Gibb, J. (1991). *Trust*. North Hollywood, CA: Newcastle Publishing Co., Inc.

Hackman, J. R. and Oldham, G. (1980). *Work redesign*. Reading, MA: Addison-Wesley.

Harrison, M. I. (1970). Choosing the depth of organizational intervention. *Journal of Applied Behavioral Science, 6*, 181–202.

Hart, S., Boroush, M., Enk, G., and Hornick, W. (1985). Managing complexity through consensus mapping: Technology for the structuring of small group decisions. *Academy of Management Review, 10*, 587–600.

Herzberg, F. (1983). One more time: How do you motivate employees? *Harvard Business Review, 46*(1), 53–62.

Juran, J. M. (1989). *Juran on leadership for quality: An executive handbook*. New York: Free Press.

Kram, K. (1983). Phases of the mentor relationship. *Academy of Management Journal, 26*(4), 608–624.

Schein, E. H. (1978). *Career dynamics: Matching individual and organizational needs*. Reading, MA: Addison-Wesley.

Yin, R. K. (1984). *Case study research: Design and methods*. Beverly Hills, CA: Sage.

CHAPTER 5

Implementation and Evaluation Guidelines

There will always be the feedback session in which, having spent a year of one's life gathering data, pouring over it, and writing a rigorous and conscientious final report, some decision maker says: "Well now, I know that you put a lot of work into this. I'm anxious to hear all about what you've learned. I've got about ten minutes before my next appointment."
—Michael Quinn Patton (1980). *Qualitative Evaluation Methods*

Intervening in public organizations is inherently political. Choices made to change ongoing structures and processes require the approvals and the commitment from ever-widening circles of career managers, political officials, and a vast network of stakeholders. The diversity of interests and goals can complicate interventions.

Interventions in public organizations often become tools of clout, particularly if outcomes reflect positively on high-level officials. The high visibility of interventions and their utilitarian character call for using patience at each phase. It is often not enough to obtain the go-ahead to make change happen; implementation in the public sector entails continuing rounds of approval getting, negotiations, and filtering. Typically, the client system grants approval to proceed after months of deliberation and bargaining, presses for visible and quick wins, and wants to hear good results only. The pressure for the change agent to deliver intensifies.

This chapter examines ways the change agent can navigate the rapids of implementation. In particular, it discusses the importance of keeping open channels of communications not only to strengthen client support but to maintain flexibility if the current changes suddenly. The chapter also describes an evaluation rationale for using case studies for public sector programs. It shows how this rationale works by depicting a training evaluation process in a large federal organization.

The artistry with which the change agent implements programs in public organizations, the chapter maintains, results not only from mastering complex technical skills but even more so from using highly polished interpersonal relationship competencies. Dealing with varieties of political actors in organization transformation dramas requires understanding of both their interests and their behaviors. The interactions also test the change agent's own reservoir of coping skills. The chapters in Part II begin to build that base of interpersonal relationship skills.

NOW TO BEGIN

After pilot testing a strategy and assessing its feasibility, the change agent and the client should plan for implementing the strategy on a larger scale. To do so, the change agent should prepare the targets of change, whether they are people or technologies or both. Because organizational systems are interconnected, changes in one system will ultimately affect changes in related systems. Accordingly, change agents need to envision what systems will be most directly affected and how.

Introducing a new automated information system, for instance, produces a variety of changes. The information flow will change as fewer people will handle stacks of reports, for example. Because the volume of work will decrease for some people, other forms of work will have to take its place. Does this involve retraining? Does it involve doing more parts of the "whole" task? If so, does this affect people's job responsibilities and pay scale? How will these changes affect performance management and financial resource systems?

In one organization that implemented such a system, technicians changed their roles from information collectors to customer service representatives. When other divisions of the organization adopted the information system, people called on the technicians to provide information on using the new equipment, specialized help for resolving problems, and questions regarding additional work applications. To meet the challenge, the change agent provided the technicians skills in customer service, such as listening, providing feedback, problem solving, and quality improvement techniques.

ESTABLISHING COMMUNICATIONS

Feedforward Loops

Because introducing change affects multiple systems at once, the change agent needs to set up ways to assess continuously the fit of the strategy with actual conditions in the client system. Setting up feedforward loops is an important way the change agent can manage this. Feedback loops help change agents foresee problems that can develop and take action before the problems occur. Feedforward loops operate like sensors in heating systems: They signal changes in the air temperature and activate devices to adjust the heat automatically.

Change agents establish feedforward loops in the effectiveness criteria they agree on with the client before implementation. The feedforward loops contain standards that indicate that performance is within the range of "success." When the standards indicate that performance is less than expected, the change agent intervenes.

In the women-in-management development program discussed in Chapter 3, the pilot session assessed whether the communications objectives, in particular, were being met. One of the objectives, for example, was to determine from the participants' viewpoints what the barriers to building effective communications networks were. The preliminary needs analysis had indicated that the barriers were related to three areas: (1) lack of previous management training; (2) unequal treatment; and (3) inadequacy of financial and technical resources in their organizational units. To check this, one of the trainers set up an observation checklist and recorded informal discussions of participants during small-group activities. She coded the interactions by each of the three categories during the weeklong training program. When the observation data were analyzed, however, the trainer discovered two additional barriers: headquarters and field communications were strained; in addition, participants experienced conflict in their roles as both legal enforcement officials and providers of effective customer service to those whom they served. Based on the observational data, the three trainers addressed headquarters-field relationships and role conflicts in the final program design.

Maintaining Open Client Discussions

During implementation, the change agent should hold frequent and informal discussions with the client. One purpose is to keep the client up to date and to assure him or her that the project is meeting its objectives. Another is to bring up problems or concerns or even new information relevant to the project for resolution. Lastly, frequent contacts enable the client to articulate suppressed conflicts or continuing doubts and fears. Building trust continues throughout the implementation phase of change.

Building in Flexibility

In public organizations, much can change quickly. A change in top administration can signal a new agenda for the organization. Further, cuts in allocated funds may force postponing or even canceling an important component of the intervention. In addition, because public employees receive high levels of media and public interest scrutiny, interventions that may appear to private sector organizations as "average" may come off as "extravagant" in public agencies. A seminar at a Florida vacation spot at a high-priced hotel may stir up a swarm of objections.

To prepare for contingencies in the public sector, change agents need to keep costs low and written information reports upbeat; sharing summaries with interested constituents, in addition, may save criticism later. At a minimum, change agents require a backup plan.

In a federal organization, a trio of change agents ran into a political quagmire when they initiated a particular intervention in their own organization. Their client was their second-level supervisor, a political appointee who had given the change agents his unqualified support. Three months after the change agents had begun their project, however, the political appointee was removed abruptly. The change agent team briefed his replacement on the project. The new client, however, delayed the project for months; after a while, he stated he did not want the project continued. Although the consultant team lost the new client, they found other career managers in the organization who were willing to try the project out in their units.

Knowing What Can Go Wrong

Understanding some frequent problems that occur in intervening in organizational systems can help prevent them. Ten of the more common reasons are listed in Figure 5.1:

1. The purposes of the interventions are not clear.
2. The people affected by change are not involved in planning.
3. Change agents ignore the informal work habits of people in the client system.
4. People fear losing their jobs if change succeeds.
5. Organizations have experienced too many unsuccessful interventions in the past.
6. Resource levels are inadequate.
7. The client system expects a quick and visible turnaround.

Figure 5.1
Some Potential Areas of Implementation Failure

- Unclear purposes
- People not involved
- Informal system ignored
- Fear of job loss
- Too many past failures
- Inadequate resources
- Quick turnaround expected
- Content with status quo
- No evaluation
- Failure to understand unique business

---

8. People see little reason for changing, especially if processes appear to be working properly.
9. The client gives little attention to evaluating the intervention.
10. The change agent does not understand the unique nature of the organization.

BUILDING CLIENT SUPPORT SYSTEMS

Change agents can prevent many interventions from collapsing and the client from reverting to former ineffectiveness levels by adding support structures. Chief are training and development programs. Without training individuals in the new systems, the change agent provides the client system with tools but not information on how to use them.

In addition to training programs, the change agent can model behaviors the client system needs. One way to do this is through coaching individuals. The change agent, for instance, can give one-on-one instruction in such areas as listening, giving constructive feedback, using assertiveness techniques, and other forms of interpersonal relationship skills.

Moreover, the change agent can extend the skills development by training trainers within the client system. After the change agent terminates the client relationship, for instance, individuals can conduct a variety of courses. Perhaps most vital are technologically based programs that highly adept individuals in the client unit may lead. Other examples are training programs for key players in the client system. In one agency, the change agent taught skills for managing labor union issues to personnel management specialists, who, in turn, trained all the agency's managers and supervisors.

In addition to training, change agents can strengthen existing rewards systems or create ones that are more efficient. Job-enrichment programs, which seek to incorporate rewards for enriching self-esteem and meaning of work, often provide intrinsic value (Hackman and Oldham, 1980). In changing work flow systems, change agents should be aware of possibilities for finding ways the new work patterns themselves can increase motivation and satisfaction.

Finally, change agents need to maintain positive relationships with key players in the client system and the change champions, in particular. Often, the change agent can sustain the relationships by short, informal visits from time to time, luncheons, and telephone calls. The more visible the change agent becomes *after* the intervention, the more likely the client system will maintain the momentum.

EVALUATING THE INTERVENTIONS

In evaluating interventions, it is important to gather data that will present a holistic view. The evaluation design and strategy may incorporate quantitatively based measurements to examine how variables have contributed to the overall outcomes. Quantitative strategies can ascertain how well certain predicted outcomes *did* occur. In addition, the design should feature a grounded approach based on interviews, observations, and analysis of reports that users of the implementation have produced. The purposes of the grounded methodologies are to discover how well the outcomes are occurring and to verify tentative hypotheses constructed during the data collection and analyses phases (Patton, 1980).

Who Evaluates and Why

The change agent usually prepares evaluation reports for the client and the client system. Ideally, the evaluators should share summary reports with those who had a role in developing the decision to intervene. Change agents should also send summary copies of outcomes to pilot project participants.

The client should oversee the distribution process, however, particularly if the implementation raised some confidential or organizationally sensitive issues. In addition, the client may wish to share evaluation outcomes with others in the organization who may be thinking about beginning a similar type of intervention, with the client's superior to show how the intervention improved certain conditions or solved a particular problem, and with staff personnel who may wish to develop organizational policies and procedures (Rist, 1994).

Scriven (1991) describes two forms of evaluation. *Formative* evaluations occur as programs are being implemented. Their purpose is to provide accurate and timely feedback about the quality of the program. Formative evaluations frequently use grounded methodologies to provide comprehensive understanding of how well a particular strategy is working. *Summative* evaluations, on the other hand, are long term. They assess the extent to which certain program strategies have or have not met the original objectives. Summative evaluations are frequently used for determining whether to continue a program, to make significant changes in its design, or to abandon it (Guba and Lincoln, 1981; Weiss, 1972).

What Is Evaluated

Evaluations examine leading indicators of program activities. Both tangible and measurable as well as subjective and speculative processes become evaluative grist. Some of the more common areas evaluated are:

1. Program impacts—overall changes produced in relation to organizational effectiveness.
2. Goals and objectives in relation to the impacts.
3. Resources used in relation to returns on investments.
4. Appropriateness of methodology in relation to type of intervention.
5. Degree of user satisfaction with interventions.

Purposes of Evaluation

In reality, clients do not evaluate interventions to a great extent. Often, evaluation reports go on a client's shelf and collect dust. One of the most common reasons is that clients have little time to read and take action on the recommendations change agents produce. In the public sector in particular, clients expect change agents to produce results in a relatively short period of time (Rehfuss, 1979). As noted (Weiss, 1970), results may be used for political purposes, such as to defend certain positions or to kill politically unpopular programs.

CASE STUDY EVALUATIONS

Case studies are perhaps the most fruitful methodologies for evaluating complex interventions. Case studies are especially useful in probing programs and projects to determine their utility. Because case studies provide a thick description of phenomena, they can produce information for answering a variety of evaluation questions. Further, they offer additional perspectives of causality; they show patterns of meaning that users of the implementation developed.

Case Study Rationales

Typically, case studies are forms of action research that investigate a "contemporary phenomenon within its real-life context when the boundaries between phenomenon and context are not clearly evident" (Yin, 1984, 23). Case studies as research methodologies have three main purposes: (1) to explore a particular "what" question; (2) to describe the incidence or the prevalence of a particular phenomenon; and (3) to explain "how" and "why" certain phenomena are causally or inferentially related, such as why bystanders fail to report emergencies under certain conditions. Exploratory case studies record observed occurrences and structures, whereas descriptive case studies show relationships between what is observed and what is recorded. Explanatory case studies, on the other hand, offer possible theoretical rationales for why certain phenomena are linked.

Case Study Methodologies

The change agent may develop case studies from data that he or she collects and analyzes simultaneously. Frequently, the change agent uses a variety of collection and analysis methods, including the following:

1. *Surveys.* Structured questionnaires of what people say they do, how they influence the workings of organization structures and processes, and how they view such processes affecting their behavior.
2. *Individual interviews.* Structured and unstructured questionnaires to understand particular individuals' insights, values, fears, reactions, solutions, and experiences.
3. *Focus groups.* A meeting of users of the interventions to assess reactions, suggestions, and comments.
4. *Document analysis.* Examining the history or background of a particular program, policy, or issue to analyze key concepts and ideas related to the problem or issue at hand and to verify inferences.
5. *Observational checklists.* Guidelines for what to look for; some common examples include how group members interact, how individuals respond to a particular phenomenon, and how environmental artifacts (such as room layout, furniture, and proximity of individuals) affect the climate in which the problem or issue is situated.

CASE STUDY EXAMPLE

The administrator of a small component within the U.S. Department of Agriculture (USDA) had requested a summative evaluation of a program that had trained newly appointed supervisors. The purposes of the program were to provide newly appointed supervisors with the skills needed to perform their roles effectively and efficiently and to accomplish the agency's technical mission. The agency head requested the evaluation because of possible agency funding cuts; it was necessary to know whether the program was meeting its objectives to justify its continued funding.

Agency Overview

The agency of about 6,000 employees was responsible for grading and inspecting a variety of agricultural products stored in warehouses across the country. Some examples of the types of products included fruits, vegetables, dairy, poultry, livestock, cotton, and tobacco. Employees graded each product they inspected (for instance, USDA Grade A eggs), and the grade, in turn, played in the determination of the market price producers received. Producers paid "user fees" for the employees' services, and these fees constituted over 80 percent of the agency's total funding sources.

Establishing Supervisory Training

Because of funding cuts in the mid-1970s, the agency discontinued its supervisory training program for approximately ten years. By 1983, however, the dearth of supervisory training had produced several problems in the organization: high rates of conflict; inadequate communications between employees and supervisors; conflict between producers and employees; and high grievance and attrition rates. The top administrator and the ten division directors realized that supervisory training needed to be reinstituted to correct problems identified. Therefore, in 1984, they chartered the agency training institute and specified that basic supervisory training was to be the first priority for action. The program was called the "Basics of Supervisory Success" course, or "BOSS."

In response, the first BOSS course was created two months later to foster several changes: to see the agency as a complete entity rather than as a conglomeration of loosely connected divisions; to develop supervisors with no formal training into a skilled cadre of leaders; to introduce participative problem-solving techniques to supervisors to correct the prevalent, top-down style; and to respond to interpersonal conflicts using a "win/win" strategy rather than forcing issues upward or handling them defensively.

Constraints

Agency officials wanted a quick turnaround of the investment in entry-level supervisor training. To accomplish the expected results, the agency had hired a training director and only one support staff member: a secretary who would coordinate program logistics, maintain participant contact, and pay program expenses. The training director was responsible for developing specific program goals and objectives, designing learning experiences, hiring qualified instructors, arranging for meeting facilities, contacting eligible participants, and scheduling training programs. The training director also arranged to have various personnel management specialists discuss tips and techniques for handling recruitment, staffing, hiring, equal employment opportunity, and labor-management relations issues.

The training director identified names of eligible participants from personnel documents and interviewed them in their offices or by telephone. Because of staffing shortages, time pressures to implement the program quickly, geographical separation of headquarters and field offices, and limited start-up funds, the training director based the needs assessment largely on critical incidents respondents described in interviews. He also obtained through personnel officers a baseline status of numbers of grievances filed against first-level supervisors for a three-year interval and turnover rates for newly appointed supervisors. There were no cost data available on how much the lack of training affected meeting the agency's mission. The training director, however, calculated a rough estimate of the costs of not training through using grievance and turnover rates.

Limitations in the data collection and analysis prevented detailed descriptions of program objectives. In addition, this information failed to clarify specific course content, problems to be addressed, and specific and measurable outcomes to be achieved. There were few logical connections between the problems training set out to solve, the effectiveness of training interventions, and results achieved.

In spite of support from top administrators, many of the operating managers did not support training as a means of changing either individual skills levels or organizational effectiveness. Most of the managers had spent their entire careers in the agency and had learned skills of supervision from their own managers—in a sort of craft and guild arrangement. This was the most effective—and inexpensive—way to learn a particular division's way of doing business with the producers, many managers felt. Accordingly, many managers failed to send eligible employees to the program. Those who did attend had special characteristics, such as high individual motivations to learn or supportive managers, which skewed the results of training because only a certain population tended to come.

Evaluating BOSS

To begin a summative evaluation of BOSS, the change agent gathered as much existing data as possible. These were usually documents that listed dates of programs; participant names, locations, and titles; and demographic information. There were also records of costs, such as instructor fees, meeting facilities, transportation, and meals. In addition, the change agent gathered available evaluations, such as summaries of end-of-course reactions and the training director's end-of-year reports to the personnel director and the agency head.

The change agent also looked at "unobtrusive" measurements (Spradley, 1979) to develop ideas on how the program might have reduced agency costs or enhanced agency productivity. The unobtrusive measurements were indicators that the training director had looked at in the needs assessment: personnel files, rough estimates of costs of not training, and grievance and turnover rates. The unobtrusive measurements enabled the change agent to understand what some of the problems in the agency had been and also to gain an understanding of what to look for when interviewing program participants and their managers.

The evaluation strategy had three goals: to conduct a series of interviews with the client; to conduct interviews with a sample of participants and their managers; and to examine available records of actual program outcomes.

Data Feedback Meeting

Participant interview data indicated that managers had observed numerous changes in the participants' attitudes and behaviors. In particular, the participants overwhelmingly took steps to solve work-related problems on their own, they were more likely to communicate program information with staff, and they showed more willingness to involve staff in decisions. In addition, although there were few "hard data," a rough estimate of costs versus benefits of the program revealed that the expenses involved in conducting the program did increase the returns the agency realized through fewer numbers of grievances filed and lower turnover rates among the sample population.

Client Responses

Although there were little objective data on which to base the decision, the qualitative data indicated the positive impact of the BOSS program (Wholey, 1979). The deciding variable was, however, the client's own value system. The administrator confided that if the BOSS program were to be disbanded, the general climate would likely deteriorate to the way it was before the training program. Because he remembered the "bad old days" before the training, the success stories passed on to him "made sense." He decided the program would continue running.

SUMMARY

Implementing change programs seldom follows an ideal path. In the best of conditions, program evaluations would have complete, accurate, and measurable criteria on which to base decisions; and decisions would be carefully weighed, their logic would be impeccable, and their outcomes would be lucid. People would decide based on uncompromised values in the best interests of all concerned.

Change agents know differently. Their realism, based on experience, tells them to prepare to encounter paradoxes, to have trouble reading clients' intentions, to not be surprised when clients rip up data and throw out the project. Being a change agent takes a toll, especially on the primary instrument of data collection and analysis: the self. In the following chapter, we will look more closely at what this instrument consists of and at the care and feeding of it.

REFERENCES

Guba, E. G., and Lincoln, Y. S. (1981). *Effective evaluation*. San Francisco: Jossey-Bass.

Hackman, J. R., and Oldham, G. (1980). *Work redesign*. Reading, MA: Addison-Wesley.

Patton, M. Q. (1980). *Qualitative evaluation methods*. Beverly Hills, CA: Sage.

Rehfuss, J. (1979, May–June). Managing the consultantship process. *Public Administration Review, 39*(3), 211–214.

Rist, R. C. (1994). Influencing the policy process with qualitative research. In N. K. Denzin and Y. S. Lincoln (Eds.), *Handbook of qualitative research* (545–557). Thousand Oaks, CA: Sage.

Scriven, M. (1991). Beyond formative and summative evaluations. In M. W. McLaughlin and D. C. Phillips (Eds.), *Evaluation and education: At quarter century* (19–64). Chicago: University of Chicago Press.

Spradley, J. P. (1979). *The ethnographic interview*. New York: Holt, Rinehart and Winston.

Weiss, C. H. (1970). The politicization of evaluation research. *Journal of Social Issues, 26*, 57–68.

Weiss, C. H. (Ed.). (1972). *Using social research in public policy making*. Lexington, MA: Lexington Press.

Wholey, J. S. (1979). *Evaluation: Promise and performance*. Washington, D.C.: Urban Institute.

Yin, R. K. (1984). *Case study research: Design and methods*. Beverly Hills, CA: Sage.

PART II

The Art of
Change Agentry

CHAPTER 6

Using Self as a Change Instrument

Through the Thou a man becomes I. That which confronts him comes and disappears, relational events condense, then are scattered, and in the change consciousness of the unchanging partner, of the I, grows clear, and each time stronger.

—Martin Buber (1958). *I and Thou*

One problem change agents face in public bureaucracies is the common belief that governments lack a human touch. In many cases, the perception is true. Art Buchwald (1983) recalled a painful incident after airline deregulation resulted in fewer roomy seats. Buchwald's seatmate, after sliding his briefcase under the seat in front of him before takeoff, had nowhere to put his knees.

"Could I put my knees in the overhead rack?" he asked a stewardess who was passing by.

"No," she answered. "That would be against regulations. It would present a safety hazard in case we hit turbulence."

When the exasperated passenger continued to ask where he should put his knees, the stewardess finally told him to take his complaints to management. The desperate man and Buchwald decided to solve the problem by putting their knees on each other's laps for the flight—providing, of course, neither put wrinkles in the other's pant legs.

People who have had to wait an hour in line to renew their driver's licenses only to find they were in the wrong line and had to fill out yet another form can share this man's frustration. But how easily we forget that the people behind the counters have their own problems as well.

During the early 1980s, the federal government shut down for a day while Congress and the president quibbled over budget projections. Employees who came to work in the morning left by 11 A.M. on that October day. Washington quickly turned into rush-hour gridlock as thousands crammed into available buses, subways, and long-delayed van pools to get to the suburbs. Some others, however, stopped at the District of Columbia unemployment office to file a claim. When the government reopened the next day, however, those who had to close the government found it more expensive to pay for the layoffs than to stay open!

The public's esteem of civil servants plummeted. Morale slid below zero; people joked about the psychologist who ended up in the mailroom of the Office of Personnel Management and the "riffed" senior official who bumped out a typist to save his benefits.

Like all rule-bound bureaucracies, governments often operate as if people did not matter. The goal of the change agent is to change that perception by helping governments manage *through* human beings. Valuing them—both those who serve and those who use the government's goods and services—is crucial for agencies to learn. Thus, to change organizations, change agents must begin by addressing how people have come to think of governments.

Organizations reflect assumptions people share and have inherited from predecessors. They are like webs that some spiders start, but others finish. The change agent needs to untangle the webs, look at mental models that people have had and continue to have, and interpret how these models affect current issues and problems.

This chapter discusses some central ways the change agent can understand the use of the self to analyze models of meaning and create the basis for changing organizations. It examines how the self develops knowledge, how knowledge can err, and how change agents can correct faulty assumptions. Because the change agent's self plays an important role in understanding how other people define and respond to organizational issues, the change agent's understanding of his or her own beliefs and values regarding change is essential. To assess what the change agent believes and esteems, the chapter includes a list of questions for reflection.

ORGANIZATIONS AS LIVING PHENOMENA

Organizations are built up from what Schutz (1970) describes as "common stocks of knowledge." People identify recurring patterns of events as cues for making sense of situations. Further, people label the cues in terms of familiar language, or language they have learned from growing up in certain social cultures. This reality is part of the everyday experiences of an individual's "lifeworld."

For example, a four-wheeled, boxlike object into which a baby is placed may be referred to as a "baby carriage," a "baby coach," a "baby buggy," or a "stroller," depending on particular geographical and socioeconomic communities. In England, people often refer to the object as a "pram." A member of the social group sees the object, recognizes it, and usually does not question what it "is." Meanings of recurrent, everyday events stem from "typifications," or what Schutz (1970) says are recipes for interpreting and acting.

The observer expects to see someone wheel the object with an infant inside. He or she takes the object and its label for granted unless something strange happens, such as seeing a monkey or a load of bricks inside the object. Unusual events or those for which people have had different experiences trigger needs to establish meaning.

Out-of-the-ordinary situations activate what Weick (1995) calls "sense-making" strategies. When events do not make sense, people invent explanations. As people accept these explanations as fact, people act on subsequent situations that are similar, without thinking.

"Troublemaker employees" are an example. An employee who reports late for work three days out of five comes to the attention of the supervisor. The supervisor also notices what appears to be an "attitude problem": a carelessness that appears in unfinished, erroneous, and late projects. The clues suggest a "problem employee," the supervisor threatens the person accordingly, and the employee does, in fact, live up to the label. Eventually, the supervisor transfers the employee to the agency "dumping ground" because the employee cannot be fired.

In diagnosing problems that dumping grounds inherit and contend with, change agents should fathom what Perrow (1986) calls "premise controls": those premises people use in interpreting and acting on organizational conditions. Understanding how individuals frame problematic situations shapes the way they react to them. Thus, rather than work on the symptoms, the change agent should examine the ideas that preceded those symptoms.

To understand this relationship requires two skills. First, the change agent should avoid accepting explanations for problems as "givens." Considering that explanations may be based on inferences taken as facts, the change agent should investigate the origins and outcomes of the explanations. He or she can accomplish this through "bracketing" (Husserl, 1983), or suspending judgment and observing the patterns of relations over time. Second, the change agent derives understanding by observing relationships carefully and thinking about what they mean. By comparing interpretations with what others have described, the change agent establishes a broader basis for understanding. Through comparisons of interpretations, change agents can raise new questions, examine how feelings have contributed to interpretations, and find alternative possibilities for change. Hence, the change agent can develop a more complete idea of what organizational events mean from looking at organizational events from different vantage points (Van Manen, 1990).

An Example

A broader basis for interpreting meanings and changing prevailing mental models and habitual responses developed in a medium-sized municipal government. Employees commonly referred to citizens who came to them for services as "pains in the neck." They looked at citizens who demanded immediate resolutions to problems, such as repairing potholes, plowing their streets first during snowstorms, and carrying their trash from homes to municipal trucks, as bothersome. The employees responded to the citizens defensively, often with curt words, not looking at people directly, and hurrying them through processing forms. Citizens, in turn, interpreted their treatment as rudeness and complained to the town manager. After he had investigated the complaints, the town manager criticized the employees. The cycle of complaints satisfied no one.

The town manager, however, attended a training program in which municipal employees in other communities practiced treating citizens not as "pains" but rather as "partners": as resources in solving recurrent service delivery problems. Through the training program, the town manager began to reflect on his own situation; he was able to bracket what he saw and understand more clearly how both employees and citizens interpreted a common "complaint" situation.

Following the training, the town manager hired a consultant to teach customer service skills so that employees and citizens solved problems cooperatively. Doing so, however, posed problems. A plethora of laws, regulations, and ordinances required town employees to provide services with neutrality, objectivity, and equality. There seemed to be a danger that giving citizens the services they demanded would inevitably lead to charges of favoritism. But when the consultant taught them to involve citizens in finding ways to look at problems differently and to find creative solutions, employees began to see citizens as allies. This not only reduced the stress that overly "legalistic" compliance had created but also helped employees find excitement in making long-overdue changes in how they handled citizen requests.

LEARNING ORGANIZATIONALLY

To introduce new mental models as a basis for changing actions requires two key understandings: how people learn and how what we learn influ-

Figure 6.1
Four Types of Learning

- Goal-directed
- Incidental
- Tacit
- Intuitive

---

ences behavioral change. If one defines learning as merely acquiring knowledge, learning may not necessarily result in different behavior. If learning actually transforms the prevailing thinking of an organization, however, change almost inevitably follows. What we think is inseparable from what we do; so learning that changes the way people view others also changes how they react to different situations.

Argyris and Schon (1978) refer to learning that transforms actions through changing underlying assumptions as "double loop learning." Double loop, or transformative, learning occurs when people use information from critical reflection or feedback from others on how their views and behaviors affect social encounters. The actions that result lead to maturity in thoughts and feelings (Fuller, 1990). Change agents can foster such maturity and promote overall organizational change.

Levels of Learning

Learning takes place on four levels of awareness: *goal-directed learning* occurs as deliberate, purposeful, and conscious efforts to acquire information, such as in learning to drive a car; *incidental learning* happens as people perform a specific task and later think about some particular aspect of doing it, such as reviewing agreed-on next steps after solving a recent customer service problem; *tacit learning* occurs subconsciously and involves cultural conditioning, such as eating with chopsticks; and *intuitive learning* springs from unconscious levels and appears as creative solutions to problems (see Figure 6.1).

Transformative Learning

Learning that changes mental models transforms actions. For instance, if a personnel director notices an increase in the numbers of sexual harassment complaints, he or she may realize that providing information alone will not reduce incidences. To change this, he or she may write policies that increase enforcement or may change work conditions that foster a climate of mutual respect for persons. In this case, he or she might augment

Figure 6.2
Common Sources of Erroneous Thinking

- Ineffective cause maps
- Inadequate fit with changed conditions
- Claims of allness
- Insensitivity to human needs

---

the policies with employee training programs and supervisory coaching programs. Using information from all four levels reinforces the goal of changing how people think of others.

Transformative learning often begins when data raise questions, doubts, or enigmas. Opportunities for sense-making are often opportunities to change fundamental assumptions. Sense-making occurs through social situations. Not long ago, a group of employees were talking during an office coffee break. They all felt that conflict between them and the managers was unbearable. Most of them believed that steps should be taken to reduce the conflict. One of them, however, suggested that instead of trying to get rid of conflict, they use conflicts as opportunities to learn more about what the managers wanted. This helped the employees see conflict as potentially positive. Looking at conflict differently, to find reasons instead of placing blame, also helped them learn how to manage conflict with their managers in the future.

Errors in Learning

Unfortunately, learning can sometimes lead to error, particularly if people do not use knowledge to change behaviors. Vital information can be missed for a variety of reasons. They may not hear accurately, their concentration might be distracted, or others may not provide complete and unbiased information. In addition, people often listen only to information that reinforces what they already know, that fits in with their existing mental models, or that reflects only optimistic situations. People may also mislabel information, such as when stereotypes prevent fresh understanding of phenomena, downplay information that seems preposterous, or change information that embarrasses them.

Learning that does not make use of complete and accurate information to change mental models shows up in four principal errors: ineffective cause maps; inadequate fit with changed conditions; claims of allness; and insensitivity to human needs (see Figure 6.2).

Cause Maps. Cause maps, like blueprints, are socially developed explanations for how and why things are put together as they are. Cause maps err whenever they mistake the uncommon for the typical, most commonly by ignoring critical differences. Senge (1990) notes:

We all find comfort applying familiar solutions to problems, sticking to what we know best. Sometimes the keys are indeed under the street lamp; but very often they are off in the darkness. After all, if the solution *were* easy to see or obvious to everyone, it probably would already have been found. Pushing harder and harder on familiar solutions, while fundamental problems persist or worsen, is a reliable indicator of nonsystemic thinking—what we often call the "what we need here is a bigger hammer" syndrome. (61)

One example is a client's assumption that training was equivalent to work. If people were to attend a weeklong training program and be paid for it, they should, he reasoned, be as productive as when they worked their "normal" 40-plus hours. Accordingly, he insisted workshops begin promptly at 8:00 A.M. and conclude at 5:00 P.M. The workshops began on Wednesdays and included "homework" assignments to be completed by Monday morning. The program failed, predictably, because of the client's failure to differentiate "learning" work from the regular work that people do every day. The demands of learning new habits, new rationales for actions, new skills, and of course, new ways to interact required participants to put out much more energy than what they would for the more routine tasks they were familiar with. Training is work, but it is a special sort.

Outdated Assumptions. Conditions in situations are in continual flux; what is assumed true in one set of circumstances may not be true in the future. One of the most difficult topics in the management training programs that I conduct is downsizing. The idea that government workers can lose their jobs because of competition was unthinkable 15 years ago. Reorganizations did take place, but usually no one was laid off. People came to expect that their longevity entitled them to permanent jobs in spite of economic downturns.

In a recent management training program, the facilitator, a former mayor and business executive, told participants that within five years most of the jobs in local government would be posted. If incumbents lacked credentials for filling them, the jobs would go to the best-qualified applicants. Many in the program were stunned. But when others described increases in contracting out coupled with widespread downsizing, the skeptics began to change their minds.

Imposing Allness. An unfortunate but common mistake is the assumption that what has worked for one person will work for everyone. Change agents compound the problem when they impose their own ideas (of what works) on others.

In a large federal agency, top officials had wholeheartedly "bought" a

TQM program fresh off the Deming (1982) shelf. According to the suggested procedures for installing it, top corporate leaders had to define and communicate organization culture clearly downward to the lowest employee echelons. This, Deming says, flows from a concise and concrete organization mission statement. One problem: None existed in the agency. The top officials met as a committee and—after debating for nearly two years what the agency was responsible for doing, to whom it really reported, and who the exact stakeholders or beneficiaries were—produced a glib, incomprehensible statement.

During the two-year hiatus, employees joked about the program; and the cynicism worsened as the committee videotaped a half-hour "discussion" of the organization's culture. Silent employees sat through the mandatory "training" that followed. The top officials, however, enjoyed talking about what the agency stood for, what it was doing to help its customers, the citizens, and how employees felt about working in such an innovative, pace-setting organization. The officials assumed that employees were as enthusiastic about the change as they were; but had they asked for ideas from the shop floor through discussions and debates, they would have received more accurate ideas.

Insensitivity. Argyris and Schon (1978) point out that the change agent needs to assess continually the match between information-taken-to-be-true and its practice. Unexamined "theories in use," they note, may produce actions that others view as insensitive. Not only does the inability to take the view of others inhibit effective interpersonal relations and the well-being of community, but it also discourages information sharing, critical to understanding perceived reality.

Often, the human resources people are brought in only after top management has already decided what should be changed, developed plans, and hired high-priced consultants to carry out their strategies. Training, if done at all, is typically limited to managers. Staff, especially administrative and clerical personnel, rarely know about the changes or understand how their jobs and their lives will change as a result. All the latter may know is that some new computers showed up on their desks one morning. No one told them how to turn the machines on, what they were to be used for, and what was expected from them. Managers simply assume that the employees will know what to do once the technology is in place. Such an assumption can prove disastrous.

MATURITY IN KNOWING AND ACTING

As people become aware of these four common errors in thinking and reacting, they open up new possibilities for growing as individuals and in relationships with others. Learning helps the self to mature. As people in organizations see themselves and others differently, organizations as extensions of people's beliefs and values mature accordingly.

In the maturation process, change agents play critical roles. Change agents can teach organizational members new ways to do work, opportunities to derive greater meaning and importance in service, and greater commitment to serving the public. They can also teach by showing examples of mature thinking and behaving.

To help change agents teach others, change agents need to nurture their own selves as instruments of change. Leading others involves leading oneself first. How can the change agent stay healthy?

Change agents face threats to their own maturity and well-being. These threats influence both thinking and actions. Seven types of threats are common: identity with the problem; erroneous thinking habits; inability to detect warning signals; no time for training; taking the self seriously; "do-it-all" syndrome; and working without vision.

Identity with the Problem

Change agents work closely with people having problems. To develop bridges of understanding and to encourage others to take responsibility for solving the problems, change agents require skills of empathy. Identifying too closely with a client, though, can turn counterproductive. Empathetic identification may entrap thinking. The change agent comes to accept problematic situations solely through the client's eyes and develops frustration and cynicism in trying to find fair, appropriate solutions.

Erroneous Thinking Habits

Similar to identifying too closely with the client's problem, the change agent may unwittingly adopt flawed thinking habits. These may appear as inadequate cause maps of situations, imposing ready-made solutions, or showing insensitivity to the abilities of people to think through options for solving problems. Moreover, change agents may accept certain assumptions about reality uncritically, often because of thinking habits ingrained in them from as far back as childhood.

Inability to Detect Warning Signals

Working with problems continually carries with it a great deal of pressure. Change agents may not become aware of pressures until physical or emotional symptoms send some painful messages. Working 12 hours on projects, meeting with client A on Wednesday, conducting a team-building session for next weekend, and doing an interpersonal communications skills training program for client B Monday through Friday are exhausting.

Added to that, change agents have to market their services, pay bills, and write end-of-project reports. If Susan has to go to her orthodontist on Wednesday afternoon and Jason has an important football game on Friday night, time pressures become even more acute. Headaches, stomach pains, and snap judgments flare up.

No Time for Training

In their zeal to help others, to make informed decisions, and to set workable schedules, change agents often forego what they recommend to others: taking time out to learn a new technique for a familiar job, solving a long-standing problem, or finding new challenges in routine tasks. Curiosity dims; sunsets with their variegated hues of gold and crimson pass unnoticed; and ideas that could lead to innovations drop like rain in lagoons. Change agents stagnate, lose interest in their work and in other people, and become increasingly lackadaisical.

Taking the Self Seriously

The pressures of change come with high expectations. Clients expect problem solutions to take care of recurrent issues for all times; they expect their staffs to work harmoniously at all times; they expect the new computer system to reduce all of their overhead expenses. Clients leave change agents little room for error and have low tolerance for mistakes. When things do happen differently than expected, clients blame change agents. The tendency, however, is for the change agent to accept the criticism personally. This adds to pressures and reduces the optimism necessary to try things differently next time.

Do-It-All Syndrome

Because clients—and change agents themselves—expect so much from change, change agents may feel they have to take on all the responsibility for designing, introducing, and carrying out organizational change. Saying no to clients is difficult because clients could question both credibility and reputation. Further, the expectation that some clients hold that change agents work magic on complex problems that are tied up with larger organizational issues casts the change agent in an omnipotent role. To live up to the expected role, change agents believe they have to be all things to all people.

Working Without Vision

Change agents, like others caught up in the pressures and expectations of solving organizational problems, may perish professionally because they cannot see a larger purpose for what they do. Working with people in the trenches, so to speak, change agents may fail to find light. Change agents need a vision that carries with it the optimism to think that people can manage their own problems; they need hope. And hope, like water and food, sustains the change agent's efforts.

NURTURING THE SELF

Helping others to see themselves as unique, valuable, and free to choose requires maintaining independent thoughts and interpersonal sensitivity on the change agent's part. This helps to cultivate learning opportunities. To nurture the self as an instrument for change, change agents require continual personal and emotional renewal. Practicing skills of reflection promotes self-maturity and revitalizes the soul.

Practicing Reflection

Reflection involves becoming aware of what conditions are contributing to sensitivity and determining how to change any conditions that are not. Reflection occurs best when the change agent is alone—able to bracket the stream of events, gain perspective, and plan for changes.

Through reflection, change agents can identify those conditions that are of critical importance to correct. This process leads to developing sensitivity to gaps between ideas, beliefs, and values and actions. Reflection that produces sensitivity leads to concern for changing mental models. Through reflection, change agents can integrate ideas with actions. This not only strengthens the relationship between the change agent and people he or she works with; it also promotes personal integrity and provides release from stressful commitments.

Change agents can practice reflection in three ways. First is listening critically to the self. What things are causing discomfort? What relationships and commitments are interfering with more important priorities? What needs to be omitted? Added? Who needs to be involved?

To obtain additional information about issues that are getting in the way, the change agent may talk about them with others he or she trusts. Colleagues may suggest additional conditions that are contributing to discomfort and some possible strategies to try out. Working with colleagues who are willing to provide constructive criticism and recommendations, in addition, will provide additional feedback, suggestions, and support. The technique is important to adopting the perspective of "the other" in identifying and testing ideas for change (Weitman, 1978). These colleagues can also offer emotional support and encouragement as the change agent adjusts thinking, believing, and acting patterns.

A third way that reflection may aid in choosing possible solutions is visualization. Imagining how those with whom the change agent works might respond if the change agent were to select a particular strategy is a great opportunity. It provides a way to understand how the solution will affect all of the elements of an entire problem.

A BRIEF SELF-ASSESSMENT

Because reflection plays an important role in the change agent's personal and professional health, it is helpful to practice it often. To help you begin this process, you may wish to ask yourself the questions about your beliefs, your values, and your current commitments to change. Practice the reflection exercise when you can listen to yourself—what that inner voice is saying about you and how you feel. If ideas come to mind, think about them in greater depth. Talk them over with people who know you well and whom you trust. Visualize changes you want to make and observe, in your imagination, how others will respond and how things will be different.

1. Think back to the last time someone mentioned the need to change something in yourself or in your organization. How did you react? Did you ask for specific information? Did you listen empathetically to what the other said, trying to determine the expectations and intentions from the other's viewpoint? What obstacles came to mind? How did you respond to them?

2. Are you willing to trust other people to help you change? Were there any people in your past who come to mind in particular? In what ways did they contribute to your feelings?

3. How do you express your own feelings with others, particularly when there is disagreement? uncertainty? mistrust? How do others respond to you? How do you react to them?

4. How do you communicate with a group of people who do not share your point of view about a particular issue? What were some specific issues and concerns that you felt during the communication process? How did you manage them? How were feelings dealt with?

5. Where do you usually get feedback? How do you use it? What results have you experienced?

6. What are some significant moments in your role as a change agent? What factors led to these being significant for you? Consider:

   - People involved
   - Past relationships
   - Meanings that you did or could not share
   - Expectations for the future

- What turned out differently from what you expected
- What changed in your social relationships
- What new insights you gained

7. How did you react to this reflection exercise? What did you learn? What were you reluctant to think about? What does this suggest?

SELF AS A TOOL FOR INNER CHANGE

For organizations to change, people have to change from the inside out. Because organizations' ideas are based on what is in people's minds and hearts, to change an organization means changing subjective ideas, attitudes, beliefs, and values. In bureaucratic organizations, in which legal constraints often impede human service encounters, the concept of self as a change instrument can lose effectiveness. But because the human instrument is most useful in changing humanly constructed organizations, the self requires nourishing. To help others mature in their perspectives and in their interpersonal relationships, the change agent also has to mature. Maturity comes through examining beliefs and actions, correcting errors in self-derived knowledge, and taking the perspective of others in making decisions. Self-assessment fosters critical sensitivity to issues that affect maturity. Reflection, discussion, and visualization bring renewed personal commitment to others and, with renewal, new competence in seeing one's self as an instrument of change.

REFERENCES

Argyris, C., and Schon, D. A. (1978). *Organizational learning*. Reading, MA: Addison-Wesley.

Buber, M. (1958). *I and thou*. New York: Charles Scribner's Sons.

Buchwald, A. (1983). *While Reagan slept*. New York: G. P. Putnam's Sons.

Deming, W. E. (1982). *Quality, productivity, and competitive position*. Cambridge, MA: MIT Press.

Fuller, A. (1990). *Insight into value*. Albany: State University of New York Press.

Husserl, E. (1983). *Ideas pertaining to a pure phenomenology and to a phenomenological philosophy* (F. Kersten, Trans.). The Hague: M. Nijhoff.

Perrow, C. (1986). *Complex organizations: A critical essay* (3rd ed.). New York: Random House.

Schutz, A. (1970). *On phenomenology and social relations* (H. R. Wagner, Trans.). Chicago: University of Chicago Press.

Senge, P. (1990). *The fifth discipline: The art and practice of the learning organization*. New York: Doubleday/Currency.

Van Manen, M. (1990). *Researching lived experience*. London: University of Western Ontario Press.

Weick, K. E. (1995). *Sensemaking in organizations.* Newbury Park, CA: Sage.

Weitman, S. (1978). Prosocial behavior and its discontent. In L. Wispe (Ed.), *Altruism, sympathy, and helping: Psychological and sociological principles* (239–246). New York: Academic Press.

CHAPTER 7

Mediation Roles of Public Organizational Change Agents

Imagination helps us sort out what comes to us. Its healing power consists in this receiving and turning over and looking through all the images and fantasy elaborations of experience in our bodies, in relationship to others, in our world, in our attempts to reach to the center of life. We receive and turn over, rather than repress. Thus handled, even terrible agonies of body or disintegrating anxieties of mind and soul can be lived with. Healing is sorting through and linking up. It means finding and connecting to symbols that bring and knit together the disparate elements of experience.
—Ann and Barry Ulanov (1991). *The Healing Imagination*

When Sarah and Angelina Grimke were growing up on a South Carolina plantation in 1817, no one ever questioned whether slaves had rights. People took it for granted that slaves really weren't human but were merely property. But when 12-year-old Angelina saw a young black boy collapse at her school from back and leg wounds from his master's whip, it stirred up her spirit. She told her older sister, Sarah, that beatings not only violated human dignity, but they also flew in the face of her Christian beliefs concerning compassion. From then on until their deaths in the 1870s, both sisters were ardent abolitionists and very active in the women's suffrage movement. Their outspoken convictions naturally provoked a great deal of opposition. Their efforts to help people with less status and power, however, called attention to injustice and inequality in the American democratic system. Over a hundred years later, the Emancipation Proclamation, the

Sixteenth and Nineteenth Amendments, and the Civil Rights Law of 1964 brought the vision closer to reality.

The Grimkes' struggle to change the predominant paradigms of the worth of persons foreshadowed the mediational roles contemporary change agents play in public settings. In mediating or influencing change, change agents enter into an arena that is often overwhelming. Long-held, unquestioned assumptions about oneself, others, and work relationships harden over time. Moreover, because no two people see situations identically, it's quite difficult to build the consensus required for initiating true and lasting change. Like the Grimkes, the public sector change agent holding on to a vision of a more humane and just future relies on inspiration, dedication of the self, and courage.

To mediate change effectively, public sector change agents play several facilitative roles. By creating shared understanding and commitment to action, change agents can move people away from the status quo. They function as bridges that allow people to transform working conditions from ineffective and inefficient to satisfying and productive.

In mediating change in public organizations, change agents help organization members find common answers to three important questions:

1. What main purposes does the organization serve? What purposes should it serve?

2. What or who does this service or product benefit?

3. How does my job and work relationship contribute to what the organization does? How does this help improve society in general?

Working with organizational members to elicit responses, change agents play five central roles (Figure 7.1).

This chapter describes and illustrates these mediational roles and identifies key behaviors that allow change agents to fill them. This chapter also reveals how actual public change agents successfully played each one of these roles in sample situations.

CREATORS OF VISIONS

Vision is the contemplation of a desired future based on actual possibilities in the present. It is a longing for something that gives completeness to difficult or unresolved issues, and it interprets present circumstances in light of what they might become.

Without a clearly understood vision, an organization's mission is almost impossible to achieve. Vision shapes identity and points toward particular goals. It also establishes the framework for preparing a step-by-step plan for attaining these goals. Further, vision creates an energy for accomplishing daily tasks because it relates the tasks to a larger purpose.

Figure 7.1
Roles of Change Agents

- Creators of visions
- Healers of broken relationships
- Advocates for justice and equality in public agencies
- Equippers of skills
- Architects of self-correcting systems

Public agencies are vulnerable to losing vision. For one thing, their missions are so vague and abstract that they seldom connect vision with practice. Public schools, for example, may have a vision of producing educated citizens, promoting economic growth, and fostering community development; they may have a mission to educate each child to reach the fullest capacity he or she possesses. In practice, however, many schools struggle with outmoded texts, underqualified teachers, overcrowded classrooms, and inadequate libraries. The mission that should theoretically enable schools to fulfill their vision in reality ends up producing students badly prepared to compete in a market-driven economy.

The problems caused by vague visions, unclear missions, and inadequate resources are exacerbated in organizations that have political leadership. Officials elected to two-year terms have a chance to develop long-range goals and strategies to attain them. To succeed, these officials find that they must compromise their goals to accommodate majority support. Financing also drives the goal-setting process. Bringing about change entails expenses that may be higher than simple operational systems maintenance. Hence, elected officials too often have to settle for partial and inadequate support.

In practice, many agencies have no vision or mission statement. A municipality recently changed from a weak mayor/council form of government to a town manager setup. The new town manager wanted her employees to upgrade their professional skills to provide improved services to the town's community. The first step was developing a statement of "corporate philosophy": a way to capture the underlying values that the managers and employees felt were worthwhile. Following several meetings of the town council, managers, and employees, the town manager facilitated developing a statement that reflected common desires for the municipality and also spelled out the relationships of major departmental functions in achieving the desired ends.

The lack of agreed-on mission affects both work performance and satisfaction. Because public employees usually don't have a stable sense of what their jobs involve and how they are related to others in a particular agency, they do not perform optimally. Further, because work is not connected to a broader social purpose, employees are seldom motivated to perform above what their job descriptions prescribe. This often leads to employees who interpret regulations literally, who watch clocks, and who demand pay raises on a par with what they believe the private sector pays people in comparable positions. Lacking intrinsic motivation to perform, such public employees may even become dissatisfied when they gain the tangible benefits they want.

Change agents help public organizations construct a vision of what they would like to become and flexible steps toward achieving that vision. The recent focus on total quality management principles applied to government has helped to clarify missions. The TQM movement has also changed typical superior-subordinate relationships into team-based problem-solving units. In addition, the growth in city manager forms of government, in which full-time, professionally trained persons administer operating units, has alleviated many of the short-focused practices of the mayor-council form.

Change agents also help employees who have lost sight of a vision. Often, these change agents are mentors or guides. Mentors identify talents or characteristics in others to improve present performance and future career development. Mentors not only suggest ways to bring out and hone these characteristics; they also provide opportunities for encouraging their growth.

Terry Parker, now the assistant city manager of Sacramento, California, was a mentor to a young man who had no clear idea of where he was going, who was having financial and marital problems, and who had become disillusioned about his own self-worth. Twenty years before coming to Sacramento, Terry had supervised a training section of air force police. In supervising the young man, Terry sensed that the problems were internal—only the young man could solve them.

To help him find possible solutions, Terry worked with the young man over several weeks. Terry asked him to define specific problems at home, in his finances, in his educational goals, in his career, and in his marriage and to write them down as succinctly as possible. Terry then asked the young man what he envisioned in one, two, five, and ten years. After he wrote the lists, Terry asked him what would help the vision become real. Terry also helped him determine which goals he could attain and which he could not, and together they prepared a career map to reach milestone goals. After the man accomplished the goals, he retrained. He completed his degree, straightened out his finances, and sought marital counseling.

Another way that change agents connect the desired future with the present is through symbolic imagery. Often, they depict a greater purpose to present conditions. President John Kennedy accomplished this in a university commencement speech eight months after the Cuban missile crisis, calling for peace through a new public understanding of America's relationship with the Soviet Union. The president maintained that lasting peace resulted from a mutual concern for well-being. This peace was "not merely a peace for Americans, but a peace for all men; not merely peace in our time, but peace for all time." Such peace would occur, he declared, not by thinking of the Soviets as "desperate and distorted" but by "conducting our affairs in such a way that it becomes in the Communists' best interests to agree on a genuine peace." He added:

If we cannot now end our differences, at least we can help make the world safe for diversity. For in the final analysis, our most common basic link is the fact that we all inhabit this planet. We all breathe the same air. We all cherish our children's future. And we are all mortal. (Quoted in Manchester, 1983, 205)

HEALER OF BROKEN RELATIONSHIPS

Bureaucratic organizations have built-in conflicts. Battles for scarce resources, bids for controlling program budgets, and claims among professional elites to decision-making rights touch off "turf wars." Some of these conflicts are cyclical because of the type of work the agencies do. For instance, every April 15, antitax organizations protest in front of the Internal Revenue Service headquarters. Budget hearings, negotiations with legislators over cuts in services, and reducing operating costs plague administrators every year. Moreover, agencies having concurrent jurisdiction for particular projects invariably light fireworks.

Additionally, government agencies have to contend with a number of interpersonally based conflicts. These may include superior-subordinate disagreements and grievances, conflicts between "difficult" coworkers, and wars of power and status differences between professional, career, and political factions. Additional flare-ups result from differences of race, gender, religion, and socioeconomic class.

Change agents heal rifts by uncovering hidden conflicts, helping people understand the ramifications of conflict management, and training them in more effective techniques for resolving issues that divide them. The healing process involves identifying and naming problems; gathering, analyzing, and sharing data; inviting reactions from people involved in the conflicts; and developing a strategy for eliminating anything counterproductive over which people have control.

One example involved a headquarters and a field training facility. Organizations geographically separate often feel they know the needs and interests of their constituents better than do headquarters officials. Thus, one field training office received a management training plan and program outline from headquarters staff but filed it away; instead, the field office developed its own program. When headquarters staff discovered this, they wrote letters, sent out staff to the field, and convened meetings. When it was over, however, the field office continued to conduct training in its own way.

The headquarters training director, responsible for both headquarters and field operations, decided to bring both groups together—outside the Washington, D.C. headquarters office—and begin building a team. Under the direction of a facilitator, the two groups identified their common interest in providing programs that constituents found useful and that reflected high-quality learning. Both groups became aware of the assets of the other and used them in creating a stronger process of program design and management. The "we" versus "they" stance dissolved as each group found goals, benefits, and strengths through participatory planning.

ADVOCATES FOR JUSTICE AND EQUALITY IN PUBLIC AGENCIES

Rationality and laws underlie the American governance system. Elected officials, acting on behalf of constituents, debate, decide, and enact legislation, and those who are responsible to the wishes of the electorate carry out the laws fairly and equitably. The governance system aims to provide an orderly and explicit process for attaining justice and equality for citizens.

In practice, however, the ends overshadow the means. Preoccupation with legal rulings in administration ironically creates injustice and inequality. In a governance system designed to minimize personal biases in administration, legality instead fuels them. In trying to accommodate diverse and often competing interests in deciding who gets what, administrators compromise personal values for political expediencies. When some disaffected group believes the administrators acted arbitrarily, administrators often resort to "gamesmanship" tactics of cover-up, obfuscation, or indecision.

Injustice and inequality are perhaps most visible in agency personnel management practices. Underqualified individuals, friends and former associates, and powerful white males, for instance, may fill vacant positions. The "glass ceiling" phenomenon continues to block talented women and minority members from attaining high-level agency posts.

In one state government, legislators created a sick-leave policy they thought would prevent abuse; instead, the policy created much harm. The policy allows clerical staff six days per year paid sick time. If they use it, however, their supervisors must attribute it to performance. The policy states: "Attendance at the level of good or better is a basic performance standard at [name of agency]. People who routinely exceed this expectation should be commended on an annual basis, with appropriate documentation placed in Personnel files." It further states:

Two or more occasions of sick leave within a three month period requires that the supervisor and the employee meet and discuss the reasons for the absences. Under the guidelines for progressive discipline, this should be considered as counseling. This is not punitive, but should serve to advise the employee of the importance placed on dependable attendance while providing the supervisor with an understanding of the factors impacting the employee.

Individuals using the full six days receive unsatisfactory performance ratings. Thus, clerical personnel may report to work ill, leave sick children home alone, or bring family members to work to avoid unsatisfactory performance ratings.

Change agents mediate principles of justice and equality with practices that achieve just the opposite. Mediation involves finding ways to reconnect agency missions with operating goals and renewing commitment to fairness and equality. But it also entails gathering, analyzing, and presenting for open discussion data from dysfunctional management and technical systems. In the process, change agents alter taken-for-granted paradigms in the agency culture and create new patterns of thinking and acting. Hence, combinations of persuasion and influence, data collection and feedback, and education enable the change agent to rekindle order.

EQUIPPERS OF SKILLS

Public agencies seldom have adequate resources to function effectively and efficiently. Unlike private sector organizations that can generate revenue to compete in markets, public agencies rely on legislative appropriations. Rather than being used for program administration, appropriated funds often reflect political interests. Budgets become footballs that are passed between opposing teams to score election wins. Often playing to the antitax and fiscally conservative crowds, legislators frequently underfund important programs but demand high returns. Over time, management, employee, and organization improvement programs collapse like decaying bridges.

Persistent budget cuts provoke hard management choices. Instead of sending people to training in conflict reduction techniques, mentoring, even customer service, many managers put their limited money into fixing immediate problems. If they have a choice between buying new computers and training people in using existing models, managers probably purchase equipment simply to keep up with current system demands.

Training public employees, even when training programs receive adequate funding, presents problems. Because they have had minimal training, and that badly outdated, trainers find they have to condense basic skills programs into many of their courses. The dearth of training and development for employees contributes to decimated productivity and morale. Even worse, it leads to an inability to develop innovative ways to solve problems and make decisions, not to mention impoverished relationships with internal and external constituents.

Change agents provide skills updates as well as teach people better ways to solve the problems confronting them. They instill motivation to learn on the job continuously, as they try out new ideas and create improved channels of information between departments and greater confidence in their own abilities to handle difficult situations. Through education and training, change agents foster holistic improvements both in individuals and in organizations.

ARCHITECTS OF SELF-CORRECTING SYSTEMS

Change agents rarely come into organizations to do "wellness checks." Frequently, they respond to crisis situations, typically problems that defy known solutions, such as organizational cultures that simulate warfare. However, such a crisis provides opportunities for change agents to build in safeguards for the new changes while at the same time preventing future conflicts. Change agents mediate problems by installing self-correcting systems.

For systems to self-correct, change agents rely on a combination of training and information production. Often, the two occur together. Change agents teach people how to identify potential problems before they become unmanageable. They also show them how to set up linkages with users of goods or services so that problems become joint ventures; constituents become partners in problem solving and resources for producing optimal services.

Organizations that have adapted forms of quality management have created many forward-feeding systems. Providing quality customer service, for example, rests on accurate, timely, and ongoing data from people using goods and services. In the town of Wethersfield, Connecticut, for instance, employees and managers in nine departments regularly meet with groups of citizens to discuss common problems, identify workable solutions, and prepare plans to implement innovative ideas. Employees having direct contact with customers implement the ideas incrementally; this usually does not require additional approvals or allocations of funds, technology, or staff.

In the police department, for instance, several officers provided training programs to help citizens prevent crime; recent half-day workshops were conducted for bankers, realtors, the chamber of commerce, the Greater Hartford visiting Day Care Providers Association, and residents of a public housing project.

We deal on a daily basis with people who call us about matters that aren't police work," explained Chief John Karangekis. "We try to listen and to see things from the viewpoint of people presenting problems to us. It creates networks and opens lines of communications; people see us as more than people you call 911 for.

He described several situations in which the police involve citizens in planning and carrying out improvement projects. In one example, the police department, the state highway engineers, and a citizens group created a plan to better control a busy, dangerous intersection. In another instance, police now bring completed copies of accident reports to residents who were involved in automobile accidents.

In playing the five roles, change agents exhibit various types of helping behaviors. In this chapter, several important ones have emerged and are summarized below.

Recapture Moments of Vision

Change agents foresee a new order of relationships between the organization and its internal and external stakeholders. Change agents not only clarify purposes but also establish guidelines for achieving specific and measurable goals. In doing so, they connect what is with what should, and can, be.

Express Anxieties as Well as Hopes

In public sector organizations, abstract missions and unclear operating goals may produce fear and reduced motivation among employees. Change agents understand that moving away from uncertainty paradoxically creates even more fear; unless people can identify specific and attainable goals, their anxieties will escalate. Thus, to reduce barriers of fear and despair, change agents encourage employees to describe their vision of what they believe important and how they can achieve it over time. By articulating problems as well as dreams, change agents enable people to move from uncertainty to purpose.

Bridge Diverse Viewpoints

Change agents recognize and value the diversity of group decision making. Without the ability to see problems from different viewpoints, change agents cannot identify potential barriers nor possible points of agreement. By encouraging individuals to articulate their ideas, change agents can fashion a strategy for change that encompasses what people collectively value and are willing to defend. The common strategy becomes a blueprint for taking collective action.

Remove Barriers to Self-Responsibility

Change agents realize that lasting change comes from people who develop responsibility for seeing it through. To help people gain self-responsibility for changing conditions, change agents use performance data to enable people to identify barriers to reaching goals. In addition, they encourage people to develop strengths through training and mentoring to remove obstacles.

Encourage Action Taking

Although change agents create sanguine future vistas, they also impel action. Change agents realize that unless people act on what they believe is desirable, change remains only an illusion. Change agents connect reflection with commitment in several ways. Some examples are helping organization members translate broad goals into action steps that affect their own interests; involving individuals in designing plans in concert with a broader segment of the organization membership; and associating mundane work with such broader social issues as justice, equality, and peace.

Restore Personal Relationships

Change agents reconcile organizational disconnections with internal and external stakeholders. Conflict over means and ends can create operational paralysis and leave lingering sparks of distrust, anger, and revenge. Change agents diffuse conflicts through discussion, finding common sources of agreement, and creating solutions that people may accept. Change agents realize that conflict may surface issues that people need to examine honestly and resolve before they can work in harmony. Conflict, thus, can lead to stronger relationships—provided change agents focus on divisive issues rather than personalities.

Intercede in Power Relationships

As mediators, change agents unite people having unequal power and status for achieving common purposes in organizations. Through collecting and analyzing data from various management systems, for instance, change agents can demonstrate how inequality has contributed to both low productivity and morale. This, in turn, affects relationships with the organization's external members, such as elected officials, oversight agencies, public interest groups, and the media. Thus, unless the inequality is addressed, the organization's ability to perform will deteriorate. Change agents bring to light interpersonal relationships that impede productive change and open channels for building trust among all classes.

Withstand the Paradox of Mediator

Change agents invariably find themselves drawn between the forward push of change and the backward pull of resistance. Frustrated, angry, and fearful people want things to be different; yet taking action involves risks they may not want to undertake. Change agents mediate people who want and yet do not want change to happen. They sometimes find that they are alone in trying to persuade others to change, but they must somehow find equilibrium between the pro- and antichange forces, one of the most challenging—and frustrating!—aspects of mediation.

SUMMARY

Change agents mediate transformation by creating shared interpretations of meanings among internal and external public agency stakeholders. In bringing purpose to public agencies and meaning to employees' work, change agents exhibit several important behaviors. To create common purpose and meaning, change agents reveal empathy for the complex and ambiguous environment of public organizations; yet they also inspire and encourage public employees to seek out answers and develop untapped skills for making desired changes. In facilitating change, agents must confront multiple sources of resistance, issues that political and career employees may not wish to open up, and conflict that has festered beneath tepid interpersonal relationships over time. Change agents open many closed channels of communications to allow healing. At the same time, they build structures that will guard against future dysfunctions.

REFERENCES

Manchester, W. (1983). *One brief shining moment*. Boston: Little, Brown and Company.

Ulanov, A. and Ulanov, B. (1991). *The healing imagination*. Muhwah, N.J.: Paulist Press.

CHAPTER 8

Fostering Perspective Change for Empowerment: A Skills-Based Approach

All change in the quality of a person's life must grow out of change in his or her vision of reality.
—John Powell (1976). *Fully Human, Fully Alive*

Before she left home one morning, Betty got a call from one of her former clients. The woman asked Betty to come to the hospital as soon as possible to help with accommodations for the woman's daughter. The girl had overdosed on an uncut type of street drug and was in intensive care. When Betty found the girl, the girl had tubes in nearly all of her limbs and lay like a rag doll in a crib. Unable to stand by, Betty stopped the head nurse and stated her frustrations. Betty explained she was a social worker and knew of a facility where the girl could receive comprehensive care. The nurse followed through with Betty's request and transferred the girl to the facility. There, the girl would get more than just her basic physical needs met and her records kept.

Change agents may feel an uncomfortable tension in the roles they play. On the one hand, they understand the rules, spoken and unspoken, about "how things are here." They may well be part of this system, yet they dislike the unfairness, the lack of concern, and the shortsightedness of those rules systems. They realize an important piece of service has been left out—the stories of their clients, whom Ferguson (1984) labels "cases."

The conflict leads to alienation. Lipsky's (1980) "street-level bureaucrats" show this in the extent to which they can express or repress their feelings about those whom they serve. Like the head nurse in the example, they may work on only segments of a process by carrying out their specialized roles. Taking responsibility for the "missing pieces" of care, the human needs clients reveal, is not covered in their standard job descriptions. This provides them with boundaries and also distances them from the problem. It relieves their tension, but it does little to solve the bigger problem of changing dysfunctional systems.

Change agents may effectively resolve this tension by operating *above* the system. Working *outside* it suggests using a defiantly aggressive frame of reference that only provokes defensiveness in the system. It also saps the change agent's own creativity. Change agents cannot envision possibilities for improving the faults in systems when they face continual opposition from the client system. When change agents can step back from the resistance and gain a broader perspective, however, they often develop sets of values that operate above the norms of the client group. Once they have tapped these values, the values give them greater stamina.

These higher values are the staging grounds for resolving conflict with street-level types of values. Change agents set up dialogues with clients to examine their operating norms and help them transform the perspectives. As Betty in the earlier example did, change agents enable others to see the shortcomings of narrowly defined values systems by pointing out the long-term effects on the lives of others.

NORMATIVE/REEDUCATIVE STRATEGIES

Etzioni (1961) pointed out that changing the values of followers involved a twofold process: Change agents need to transform the norms or standards on which people base their assumptions and beliefs; and change agents supplant those norms or standards by teaching followers new ones. This chapter describes how change agents alter the character of norms through leading people to examine ideologies that undergird actions. It explains how different ideologies can produce tensions and lead to conflict. Second, the chapter explains a process that change agents can use to reeducate followers. It describes techniques change agents may use to engage others in dialogue, which opens the way for in-depth, follow-up training in changing practices related to the values sets. The aim of changing these values sets and related behaviors is to promote shared values, meaning, and power. The basis of organization transformation is in concert with others. Developing a broad base of commonly accepted values permits clients to achieve consensus decisions. In the pluralistic context of public organizations, this base is essential to enhancing democratic aims and processes.

The use of perspective transformation skills, described in this chapter, is highly important to developing change agent competencies. Team building, involving individual- and group-level changes in mental models and related behaviors, is perhaps the most common form of intervention in organizations. By teaching people in small groups skills for perspective and behavior transformation, the change agent can use the design in several types of team intervention strategies.

IDEOLOGIES

Ideologies are unarticulated systems of beliefs and values that people develop and act upon within organizational settings. Ideologies link group members, but they also separate groups from one another. Billig (1976) maintains that ideologies categorize groups in terms of social divisions, such as race, gender, and class; organizational structure and processes, such as division of labor, work assignments, and rewards; and informal communication and negotiation. Although organizations may have several ideologies, Clegg (1975) asserts that the dominant group exerts influence on which ideology is generally followed when organizational members make decisions. To the extent that groups share the same ideology, they will act in harmony.

Changing ideologies involves an educational process in which people learn to see and reinterpret a situation from an expanded viewpoint. Ideologies that have viewed situations from a limited viewpoint have often produced erroneous thinking and incongruities between feelings, thoughts, and actions.

Figure 8.1 shows that ideologies are values systems that are removed five levels from actual events. From events people experience at level 1, the mind takes in certain sensory information; it stores the data as categories at level 2. To identify the categories and use them to "make sense of" situations, the mind fashions labels in level 3, much as people name computer data files to identify contents. Over time, the mind develops beliefs, or ideas held to be true, about the data inside the categories. The mind strings these beliefs together as wholes or systems of beliefs at level 4. When individuals use the systems of beliefs to determine how to act, they use the beliefs as judgments. The system of beliefs people use to guide action, or ideologies, appears at level 5.

For example, as children, we may have picked up a broken glass jar lying on the ground to look at the colors, shape, or size. If we cut our hand in the process, we learn that glass can cut us. If we see another broken piece of glass, from a jar or light bulb, or bottle, we remember our earlier experience. The mental model of "broken jar glass" has expanded to a more general model of anything having "broken glass." Along with the more abstract model, in addition, we have attached a belief about broken glass. We avoid picking it up with our bare hands. The belief, the ideology about broken glass in general, directs what we do when we see it.

In the same way, people form mental models of different experiences,

Figure 8.1
Levels of Ideology

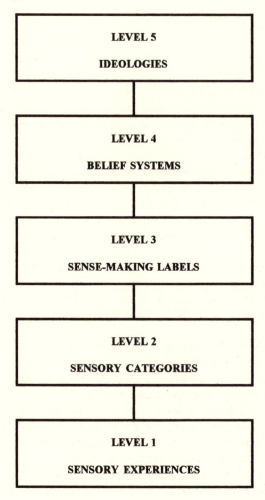

such as "drug abuser." From their experiences, people abstract greater meanings that influence their reactions. In the nurse's ideology, drug abusers were all alike. They required standardized treatment procedures and routine interactions that met basic needs. The nurse failed to understand that the "client" had special needs and a unique identity. She needed care beyond the rituals; she needed treatment that would enable her to become a fully functioning human being once again. No matter what had driven her to drugs in the first place, she needed the chance to learn new possibilities for her life. But the head nurse didn't have time to do that. To relieve her tension, she worked from the stereotype her street-level bureaucratic ideology defined (Figure 8.2).

Conflicting ideologies, as in the nurse-client case, can divide public servants and those they serve. Because people interpret situations differently, no two ideologies are identical. Yet different ideologies need not lead to divisiveness. Change agents can use skills of dialogue to turn different ideologies into resources for building a common framework for acting on particular issues.

DIALOGUE AND CHANGING IDEOLOGIES

Creating dialogue among people of diverse ideologies helps in the reeducation process. In dialogue, small groups of people discuss their interpretations of experiences they have shared with others. The discussion enables people to see how their ideologies relate to actions. Using forums for dialogue enables change agents to help others clarify their own ideological beliefs and practices with others. Dialogues can help pinpoint idiosyncracies and lead to changing the relationships between individuals and groups.

Shaping a Dialogue Session

How do change agents initiate dialogue? To begin, the change agent may wish to convene a group of 15 to 20 persons who have dissimilar ideologies regarding a particular issue. The issue selected may be of interest to a number of people but may be both controversial and complex. The change agent may lead discussion but appoint a person who is not a participant to record information on wall charts. Ideally, the dialogue should take no more than two to three hours. Participants may wish to meet away from their own organizational setting, where they may spend time in reflection.

To open, the change agent should announce the purpose of the dialogue and discuss ground rules for interacting. Because dialogue succeeds in looking at issues from multiple mental models at once, it requires participants to suspend judgment. This allows people to describe their thoughts, feelings, and beliefs about the topic at hand freely and to agree to allow others the same opportunity. Criticizing individuals or imposing one's own solution to a problem violates a spirit of inquiry.

Three important skills, illustrated in Figure 8.3, facilitate open inquiry: nonjudgmental listening, cognitive mapping, and critical thinking.

Nonjudgmental Listening

Nonjudgmental listening involves focusing on the feelings people express in statements and examining the relationship of the feelings to their beliefs and actions. Statements such as "I would like to help the girl, but I can't

Figure 8.2
Cognitive Mapping Diagram

MENTAL MODEL I			
Knowledge	**Beliefs**	**Values**	**Action**
Girl over-dosed	Needs to recover	Follow regulations; routine treatment	Monitor; give medications as directed
	Hospital gives care	Should provide only necessary care	Record treatment provided
	Girl is like other drug abusers		Follow standard procedures
MENTAL MODEL II			
Knowledge	**Beliefs**	**Values**	**Action**
Girl has special relation-ship (parent was client of social worker; sought help)	Not routine case	Should be given comprehensive care	Referral to long-term facility
	Hospital does not provide type of care she needs		

give drug abusers special treatment" suggest that the speaker feels concerned but cannot think beyond the label "drug abusers." In responding nonjudgmentally, the change agent can paraphrase the feelings in a statement that invites the speaker's elaboration. "You feel very strongly about this" encourages the speaker to verify the interpretation and invites listener empathy. It also opens the door to trusting the listener and to exploring additional options for helping. Nonjudgmental listening elicits meaning from the speaker's point of view (Rogers, 1977).

Figure 8.3
Skills in Dialogue

- Nonjudgmental listening
- Cognitive mapping
- Critical thinking

Cognitive Mapping

In addition to nonjudgmental listening, the change agent might use cognitive mapping. The change agent asks volunteers to describe their understanding of the situation as clearly and succinctly as possible. The recorder writes on a blackboard or newsprint *knowledge, beliefs, values,* and *actions* and lists under them what he or she heard. The group leader then asks the participant to draw lines that indicate how the terms are related. Figure 8.3 illustrates the head nurse ideology.

As an alternative, the change agent might have participants read a hypothetical case example and invite participants to interpret its meaning and suggest actions. The change agent can examine various ideologies that suggest themselves using Figure 8.2 as a format.

Critical Thinking

After participants have stated their beliefs, values, and thoughts concerning the topic, the change agent can invite critical reflection on meaning and implications for action. The change agent facilitates thinking critically by encouraging questions, seeking logical connections between feelings, beliefs, and actions, and aligning beliefs with actions.

Seven skills are particularly useful in fostering critical thinking (see Figure 8.4):

1. *Encourage sharing of views and feelings.* Invite all participants to speak. Moderate the amount of time people use and ask individuals who say little or nothing to share their thoughts and feelings about what is being discussed.
2. *Ask participants to cite evidence for their views.* When participants give vague or general explanations, ask them to back up their claims with specific examples or verifiable facts.
3. *Lead participants to think about how their rationales and feelings influence action.* Participants can examine the logical framework of their thoughts, beliefs, and actions through introspection and through listening to feedback from others.
4. *Ask participants to evaluate actions in light of their beliefs and note any gaps*

Figure 8.4
Critical Thinking Skills

- Share views
- Ask for evidence
- Examine rationales
- Note gaps between assumptions and actions
- Examine alternatives
- Close gaps
- Test new thinking strategies

---

between what is espoused and what is acted on. Learning takes place when people become aware of deficiencies, gaps, or flaws in the ways they think and react. The change agent or group leader can point to inconsistent logic and ask participants to suggest ways the inconsistencies can be resolved.

5. *Examine alternative solution strategies.* The change agent can facilitate discussion of options for resolving ideological dilemmas by asking participants to express alternative scenarios. The recorder should write a summary of the alternatives on a separate wall chart and post each scenario around the meeting room.

6. *Help participants agree on strategy that can reflect shared beliefs and actions.* To permit discussion from several different points of view, the facilitator might then ask the proposers to meet with five to seven participants whom the change agent assigns at random. In a 20-minute session, participants assess the assumptions and possibilities the scenario suggests and report their evaluation to the larger group. Each small group should accomplish four goals:

   - Determine the purpose of the strategy.
   - List opportunities that currently exist to allow the strategy to work.
   - List factors that work against the strategy.
   - State possible effects of choices as a whole and people with whom they are helping or working.

7. *Develop a plan to test strategy in action and establish time, place, and dates for follow-up assessment.* The change agent asks the group as a whole to select a strategy they believe will best accomplish the problem. The change agent may assist the group in selecting a particular strategy based on common purposes or design. Not every participant will agree with the strategy selected but should be willing to help support its being tested in action.

The recorder writes a summary of the strategy on which participants have agreed and also how it will be examined in practice. The plan should list who will lead the strategy, how it will be implemented, by when, and how it will be evaluated. The plan should also include a time for assessment during the implementation as well as after it has been enacted.

CHANGING GROUP DYNAMICS

Changing ideological assumptions and beliefs precedes changing actual behaviors people exhibit in groups. To align changes in perspectives with practices, change agents should follow up ideology-altering sessions with small-group training in group dynamics. By training individuals in techniques in understanding how others develop and use different points of view in interacting, change agents can enable people to put transformed ideologies into practice.

DESIGNING SMALL-GROUP LEARNING PROGRAMS

The change agent should work with the same group of individuals to provide training in group participation. Sharing power is perhaps the most critical skill in this. The change agent should explain the advantages of shared power among group participants and how the training sessions will enable participants to practice skills for sharing power in decision making.

The Importance of Power Sharing

Sharing power among group members in making decisions has several advantages. First, the ability to share power promotes identifying and achieving common aims. Second, power sharing fosters identifying multiple problem-solving strategies by encouraging and promoting the contributions of all group participants. This is important in reducing decision-making errors from limited ideological frameworks. Third, power sharing can also diminish aggression among people at different levels of organizational position and power (Maccoby, 1977). Fourth, power sharing encourages high levels of group satisfaction with problem-solving and decision-making processes and outcomes (Gardner, 1991). In summary, power sharing permits group members to obtain information from a variety of organizational stakeholders to resolve complex and controversial issues (Bryson and Crosby, 1992).

Gaining Skills for Power Sharing

Learning to share power requires the group to master several different skills. In groups having varieties of expertise, experiences, and interests in problem solving and decision making, each member has potential control of agendas, resources, and outcomes. Change agents may begin sessions by asking participants to explore the effects of organizational power and politics on group decision making. Change agents may invite participants to look at some experiences they may have had in feeling they were somehow "different" from other participants in a group setting. The change agent may use these experiences to probe feelings and examine how the feelings were linked to actions.

Commonly, participants bring up their experiences in being "bureaucrats." Often, participants feel uncomfortable when constituents, clients, the media, and politicians bash bureaucrats. This may lead to a discussion of how the bashers use power tactics to define and carry out their respective interests (Fairholm, 1993). The discussion allows participants to examine some "theories in use" that those who exercise control of information can exclude individuals and groups that do not have this advantage.

Change agents can then lead participants to see how the exclusion may become part of the formal and informal systems and structures in organizations. Participants may wish to discuss organizational policies that curtail decision-making opportunities for certain groups within the organization. They can also talk about practices that may be commonly known that also inhibit information and shared power. Change agents may ask participants to create diagrams of policies and practices that limit access to power in decision making and to describe some of the usual consequences.

Learning Skills for Sharing Power

Following discussion of the importance of power sharing and how lack of power sharing influences personal and organizational effectiveness, the change agent may lead specific skills-building activities. These expand on those developed in ideological transformation by incorporating behavioral outcomes. The activities the change agent selects to reinforce ideological transformation should combine current skill-level assessment, small-group exercises based on simulated and real-life situations, and periods of reflection and discussion. Figure 8.5 shows focal skills that change agents may wish to develop.

Finding and using common ground. Fisher and Ury's (1981) classic *Getting to Yes* spells out ways people may explore common interests in forging shared decisions. They point out that acknowledging and valuing different options are important to generating problem solutions that will produce mutual gains. In addition, the change agent may use strategies to foster creative thinking strategies to enable participants to see a "bigger picture." Such techniques as brainstorming, the nominal group technique, and synectics (Van Gundy, 1984) are especially helpful. Through producing new ideas, change agents enable participants to construct new frameworks of meaning. Words, phrases, and metaphors take on novel meanings that participants come to identify and own.

Figure 8.5
Skills for Promoting Power Sharing

Finding and Using Common Ground
- Acknowledging differences of opinions
- Valuing divergent contributions
- Willingness to envision "bigger picture"
- Demonstrating respect for thinking processes
- Searching for common meaning constructs

Opening up Communications Channels
- Creating open discussion
- Providing accurate and timely information
- Questioning

Reflecting on Group Process
- Guarding against premature closure
- Fostering critical reflection on assumptions
- Confronting and articulating "undiscussables"
- Confronting silence or overcompliance

Building Shared Commitment
- Identifying and acknowledging diverse interests
- Exploring available resources
- Finding ways for inclusive involvement

Opening Up Communications Channels. Because flow and quality of information play important roles in sharing power, the change agent should take special care to ensure that participants practice skills in openness. A particularly useful technique in doing this is the "Johari Window" (Luft, 1984). Finding blindspots, uncovering hidden agendas, and exploring unknown personal strengths are key ways in which individuals practice openness. Moreover, change agents may show participants how to obtain accurate and timely feedback from others, such as soliciting information, raising questions, and seeking assumption verification and clarification (Goyer, 1970).

Reflecting on Group Process. Change agents can give people skills for examining the quality both of the decisions they make and of interactions among themselves. Using skills for critical thinking, particularly examining "theories in use" (Argyris and Schon, 1978), helps people evaluate the validity of their thought processes. In addition, change agents should show people how to assess critically the processes by which they reach decisions.

Figure 8.6
What Influences Power Sharing?

> **Nature of Issue**
> * Perceived importance
> * Locus of responsibility
> * Population(s) affected
>
> **Individual Characteristics**
> * Expertise
> * Degree of divergence
>
> **Interpersonal Communications Relationships**
> * Styles
> * Problem-solving skills

For instance, change agents can explain the process of "groupthink" (Janis, 1972), or making unanimous and premature closure to problems. In addition, change agents should teach group members how to confront and articulate issues that have been "undiscussable." Finally, group members should be aware of the effects of nonparticipation in group settings, such as through silence or overcompliance, and explore ways to create more group member involvement.

Building Shared Commitment. In forging decisions, group members need to not only acknowledge the diversity of individual interests and contributions but also value them as means to shared commitment to decision outcomes. The recognition and valuation of diversity open up new opportunities for finding and exploiting resources to carry out decisions. Further, change agents need to reinforce the idea of continuous scanning for group member involvement, recognition, and resource use. If people do not perceive that their contributions are recognized and affirmed, they will likely end their participation in group activities (Webster and Sobieszek, 1974).

Variables in Power Sharing

To deepen understanding of how power use influences both the quality of decisions and the degree of commitment to carrying them out, the change agent may point out some characteristics that influence whether or not people share power. Three important characteristics, as shown in Figure 8.6, include the nature of the issue being discussed, levels of individual expertise, and styles of interpersonal communications.

Nature of Issue.

Perceived importance. Issues that people should seek inclusive discussion on are those that are critical, immediate, and complex (Filley, House, and Kerr, 1976). Because inclusive discussion exposes different viewpoints and a broad range of suggestions for solution, it is ideal for difficult issues.

Locus of responsibility. In taking responsibility for solving problems, group members need to assign primary, secondary, and tertiary levels of accountability. Primary responsibility should go to the person or groups who have primary "ownership" of the problem or the greatest stake in its outcome. However, groups whose interests and areas of accountability affect the outcomes need to know how they can support those having primary responsibility.

Populations affected. The goal of shared power can come about if people have a clear picture of a goal or aim and know how their interests and needs are tied to its achievement. Thus, a chief goal of the change agent is to help participants find common ground and common aims. This may require several meetings in which the change agent assists participants in creative visioning, strategic planning, and action taking.

Individual Characteristics.

Because individuals affect how reality is defined and carried out, their skills, interests, and knowledge base play important roles in bringing inclusiveness to group situations. Among the more important characteristics that affect use of power in groups are expertise and degree of divergence.

Expertise. In general, individuals having the greatest knowledge and skills in solving problems also have the greatest base of power (Bass, 1990). Those with expertise power need to make sure they invite questions, show they are open to additional information, and provide evidence for their strategies. Unless they can convince others that their expertise is being used for the good of the whole, they will lose credibility and followership (House, 1974).

Degree of divergence. Groups that have little inclusiveness tend to think and act alike. This puts them in danger of solving the wrong problem—or solving the right problem with the wrong solution (Leana, 1983).

Interpersonal Communications Relationships.

Styles. How group members share power depends a great deal on their personal preferences and styles of interaction. The change agent may provide detailed information regarding individuals' preferred communications styles by using a number of standardized instruments. Change agents should explain what results mean, how people can strengthen the positive qualities, and how they can diminish the negative results. Change agents may consult several sources of standardized tests and measurements.

Problem-solving skills. Often, group members do not receive specific training in how to solve problems. Change agents can fill this void by providing skills in identifying and diagnosing problems, using multiple sources of data collection and analysis, developing a range of possible solution strategies, building group consensus, ensuring group member involvement, and assessing solution strategy feasibility.

SUMMARY

Changing values systems and aligning mental models with actions are perhaps the most critical competencies change agents need in working with public organizations. The extent of different points of view, different systems of values, different ideologies, and different ways to act on beliefs in the public sector makes achieving shared vision and purposes difficult. Frequently, change agents must help clients understand the importance of different mental models and develop strategies for integrating the models in decision-making processes. Mastering skills for achieving shared mind-sets gives public sector clients more power in interacting with internal and external stakeholders. In sharing power, power increases.

This chapter outlined a step-by-step approach to enable clients to enlarge their values perspectives and to acquire a broader range of interpersonal and intergroup relationship competencies. Understanding the uses of dialogue and practicing them in small-group settings make up the first step. This step involves skills in listening, cognitive mapping, and critical thinking. Once clients have gained these skills, change agents may enable clients to put the skills into practice in group-based decision-making activities. Learning how to share power is one of the most important skills to acquire. Clients may use power-sharing skills in several situations calling for consensus building.

This chapter has been a prelude to building on interpersonal competencies. Part III examines how change agents may use skills in empathy, courage and compassion, and hope to encourage and empower clients. Part IV then shows how actual public sector change agents used perspective transformation and interpersonal competencies in three different contexts: a labor-management cooperative program; an intergovernmental network of clients; and a local government organization that created self-managed teams from a hierarchical organization structure.

REFERENCES

Argyris, C., and Schon, D. A. (1978). *Organizational learning*. Reading, MA: Addison-Wesley.

Bass, B. M. (1990). *Bass and Stogdill's handbook of leadership: Theory, research and managerial applications* (3rd ed.). New York: Free Press.

Billig, M. (1976). *The social psychology of intergroup relations*. New York: Academic Press.

Bryson, J. M., and Crosby, B. C. (1992). *Leadership for the common good: Tackling public problems in a shared power world.* San Francisco: Jossey-Bass.

Clegg, S. R. (1975). *Power, rule and domination.* London and Boston: Routledge & Kegan Paul.

Etzioni, A. (1961). *A comparative analysis of complex organizations.* New York: Free Press.

Fairholm, G. W. (1993). *Organizational power politics: Tactics in organizational leadership.* Westport, CT: Praeger.

Ferguson, K. E. (1984). *The feminist case against bureaucracy.* Philadelphia: Temple University Press.

Filley, A. C., House, R. J., and Kerr, S. (1976). *Managerial process and organizational behavior* (2nd ed.). Glenview, IL: Scott, Foresman.

Fisher, R., and Ury, W. (1981) *Getting to yes: Negotiating agreement without giving in.* Boston: Houghton Mifflin.

Gardner, J. (1991). *Building community.* Washington, D.C.: Independent Sector.

Goyer, K. S. (1970, March). Communication, communicative processes, and meaning: Toward a unified theory. *Journal of Communications, 20,* 1–46.

House, R. J. (1974). Path-goal theory of leadership. *Journal of Contemporary Business, 3,* 81–97.

Janis, I. L. (1972). *Victims of groupthink.* Boston: Houghton Mifflin.

Leana, C. (1983). *The effects of group cohesiveness and leader behavior on defective decision processes: A test of Janis' "Groupthink" model.* Paper presented at a meeting of the Academy of Management, Dallas, TX.

Lipsky, M. (1980). *Street-level bureaucracy.* New York: Russell Sage.

Luft, J. (1984). *Group process: An introduction to group dynamics* (3rd ed.). Palo Alto, CA: Mayfield.

Maccoby, M. (1977). *The gamesman: The new corporate leaders.* New York: Simon and Schuster.

Powell, J. (1976). *Fully human, fully alive.* Allen, TX: Argus Communications.

Rogers, C. (1977). *Carl Rogers on personal power.* New York: Delacorte Press.

Van Gundy, A. B. (1984). *Managing group creativity: A modular approach to problem solving.* New York: AMACOM.

Webster, M., and Sobieszek, B. I. (1974). *Sources of self-evaluation: A formal theory of significant others and social influence.* New York: Wiley Interscience.

PART III

When They Don't
Want to Change

CHAPTER 9

Empathy and Encouragement

Encouragement is the process of facilitating the development of a person's inner resources and courage towards positive movement. The encouraging person helps the discouraged person remove some of the self-imposed roadblocks. The goal of encouragement, then, is to aid the individual to move from a philosophy that suggests "I can't" to the more productive, "I will."

—Donald Dinkmeyer and Lewis Losonsky (1980).
The Encouragement book: Becoming a positive person.

When Gene Gavin took over as the eighth commissioner in 11 years at the Connecticut Department of Revenue Services (DRS), he found a discouraged lot. In 1993, taxpayers and the legislature were screaming for no more tax increases, yet they demanded improved services and cuts in personnel at the same time. Tax collectors were an easy target—as with death, no one likes dealing with them. To carry out the taxpayers' wishes, Gavin had to use angry, fearful, and jaded employees.

Gavin wanted to provide the efficiency and cost-effectiveness that constituents were demanding. He decided, however, to take a different approach than the slash-budgets-and-cut-people method that other state agencies had adopted. To lead DRS employees through changes, Gavin chose encouragement. Today, the agency that no one had ever dreamed of imitating has become a model not only for other state agencies but also for

Figure 9.1
Skills to Support and Encourage Change

- Positive interpersonal communications
- Enthusiasm
- Present-moment possibilities
- Celebration of successes

---

private sector organizations and many nonpartisan professional associations.

Healing public employees involves learning the skills of encouragement and support. All the bluster about doing more with less, outsourcing, and downsizing is paralyzing to employees. Encouraging stressed-out workers to develop positive attitudes, improve productivity, and serve customers more courteously is a mammoth undertaking. But through listening, finding value and opportunity in people, and communicating good tidings whenever possible, change agents can indeed lead discouraged people toward a brighter future.

RELATIONAL LEADERSHIP

Before change agents can introduce agendas for change, they have to cultivate relationships built on mutual trust, support, and concern. To do this, change agents can adapt techniques from the psychology of encouragement (Dreikurs, 1950; Dinkmeyer and Eckstein, 1996) and nondirective counseling (Rogers and Stevens, 1967). This chapter examines the relational skills of encouragement and describes techniques change agents can apply. The chapter illustrates their use in a case study of how Gene Gavin used encouragement to turn the DRS into a beacon of change.

SKILLS FOR ENCOURAGING AND SUPPORTING CHANGE

Change agents cannot force another person to think or act differently. All change has to come from the inside first. Problem solutions, motivations, and abilities to make change happen live within people. The change agent is like a catalytic converter that takes out pollutants and releases energy that was inside all the time (Combs, Avila, and Purkey, 1971).

Skills for encouraging and supporting change fall into four broad categories: communicating positively in interpersonal encounters; demonstrating enthusiasm for change; anchoring hope in present-moment possibilities; and celebrating successes (Figure 9.1). These skills are based on the Adlerian principles of psychological encouragement that Dinkmeyer and Eckstein (1996) identify in interpersonal competencies. Briefly, they include empathic listening, confidence, enthusiasm, hope, creativity, and courage.

Communicating Positively

Communicating interpersonally involves sharing meanings through speaking and listening. The exchange, however, involves understanding not only what the other says but also what words and phrases mean from the perspective of the other. Gaining this perspective requires suspending judgments and ideas. Communication involves tuning in with the whole being (Rogers and Stevens, 1967; White, 1994).

To facilitate change in others, change agents should demonstrate that they care genuinely about what others say and think. Listening in an atmosphere of mutual trust and respect offers clues to meanings. By becoming fully aware of verbal and nonverbal cues, change agents can fathom meanings as others fashion them.

To listen with encouragement, the change agent must pay attention to what is being said and also to what is left out. Listening for word choices, emotional tones, and accompanying gestures helps understanding; but topics the speaker dodges, questions or puzzles raised, or words and phrases that do not match the contextual tone indicate possible "sensitive areas" that the speaker does not wish to raise. The change agent knows that unless the speaker can voice these underlying, unspoken issues, the speaker will not accept change fully; barriers remain that will crop up whenever something rubs against them.

Communicating with empathy and yet with sensitivity to what may be bothering the speaker is not easy. It means that the change agent deliberately suspends all critical remarks, judgments, and feelings about the speaker and puts the speaker's thoughts and feelings into words (Hyde, 1994). The change agent paraphrases in such a way that he or she asks for elaboration or clarity. The change agent, for instance, may say, "You feel anger at having to do this without extra staff help?" "This makes you feel unsure of your technical ability?" "Does this mean you are having second thoughts about your decision?" By doing so, the change agent may bring into the open what the speaker may have avoided, was unaware of, or could not articulate (Gendlin, 1962).

Helping the speaker lay out hidden thoughts and feelings, moreover, enables the change agent to challenge errors. Language reveals distorted beliefs, untrue assumptions, and stereotypical thinking patterns, for example. The change agent can lead the speaker to reflect on the validity of certain assumptions. Asking for examples or evidence helps clarify and elaborate ideas.

In helping to examine logical connections and articulate feelings associ-

118 Transforming the Character of Public Organizations
118 Transforming the Character of Public Organizations

ated with meaning, the change agent maintains a respect for individual integrity. He or she assesses the logical links in relation to the background of a particular event or issue and shows understanding for the process by which the speaker drew certain inferences; in this way, the change agent separates fallacies from the person speaking. In showing respect for the importance of the individual, the change agent indicates acceptance, caring, and interest in what the person believes is significant.

The key is avoiding the temptation to control the other's thinking. As a change agent, making the other person's choices is seductive. When a change agent is invited to participate in discussing and solving a particular problem or issue, it is tempting to offer pat advice. But this denies the other the opportunity to think, exercise his or her own freedom, and explore alternatives. It even robs the participants of the learning experience that can come from trying something and failing.

To help the other gain skills for making decisions, the change agent can provide both training and support. Through education, the change agent alters the perceptual field where people create meanings. Combs, Avila, and Purkey (1971) maintain that the change agent can help change perceptual fields of meanings in three ways:

- *Build personal resources.* The change agent's goal is to help people attain self-actualization: to discover more effective and satisfying relationships between themselves and the world. This may involve attending formal skills-building courses followed by specific projects to apply in the workplace, individual coaching or mentoring, or small-group discussions.

- *Remove barriers.* The change agent not only helps clarify logical relationships through questions but also seeks to uncover attitudinal as well as physical reasons for inability to change. Providing financial, staff, and technological support is important, as is education.

- *Change goals.* Change agents help others not only to explore logical connections but also to assess the importance of goals, efforts needed to achieve them, and expected payoffs. The change agent respects the ability of the other to choose, however, and works toward building trust and mutual growth.

Enthusiasm

Change agents purposely seek out the upbeat and communicate positive linguistic imagery in order to spark actions. Change agents master the metaphor to inspire self-confidence and commitment. They show continually what Kierkegaard (1966) calls a "passion for possibilities."

Cooperrider (1990) points out that symbolic language that conveys affirmation of individuals is a self-fulfilling prophecy; if people are treated as if they are important, they will act accordingly. Cooperrider compares people's actions to the "heliotropic" tendencies of plants to bend toward sunlight and warmth to receive nourishment for growth. If people are exposed to affirmation of their own self-worth, they respond, Cooperrider says, by producing an affirmative "cognitive ecology and emotional climate" and confident action.

Change agents are people who are readily "in touch" with others. To take the pulse of what people believe, change agents take full advantage of opportunities to speak to key people who can support change. At informal gatherings, for instance, change agents may wander about from small group to small group in search of ears willing to hear. At other times, change agents are like television evangelists who thump their platforms to hundreds and even thousands at a time. They see themselves as champions, cheerleaders, and drum majors for change.

Change agents not only preach positive thinking and actions; they also model them. If change agents expect others to carry out assignments, they must do their own homework first. People will then see that not only does the change agent believe in a certain concept—he or she has actually *lived* it. Doing what they feel is important gives the change agent both credibility and authenticity.

Change agents also look for ways to celebrate. They rejoice when they hear others reach breakthroughs in their habitual patterns of thought and actions. They feel glad to see people taking critical steps toward new goals. Change agents delight to throw a party when they find there have been positive behavioral drifts.

Because they tune into positive signals, change agents are courageous riskers. They follow a vision that fills them with joy but at the same time has roots in ideas and events in the here and now. Events are like angels in stones waiting for the change agent's insights to bring them to life. Change agents convince themselves of the sureness of the visions because they have faith; they believe in a future that has shown evidence it can and has worked in others (Lawson, 1991).

Seeing the future in the present gives change agents hope. Hope has substance: real results already achieved. Hope opens up future possibilities for advancement. Thus, if a change agent sees potential in situations, believes people are capable, and provides resources for helping people achieve change, he or she can give flesh to hope.

Change agents do not expect perfection, however. They realize that setbacks and even complete failures happen in every human activity. Yet they don't look for failure either in others or in themselves. They know they find what they seek. Instead, change agents accept calamities as opportunities to try again—and next time, to do things differently. And they challenge others to try out creative alternatives.

In helping people rebound from loss and failure, change agents offer a place of warmth, openness, and mutual acceptance. Recognizing possibilities but also limitations, change agents nurture a spirit of "trying again." They help people to discover unexplored corners and create new pathways in situations that seem murky. They heal with empathy, the experience of having tried and failed perhaps again and again. They know, however, that without the cheer and coaching from those who have overcome, hope dies.

LEADING CHANGE WITH ENCOURAGEMENT: A CASE EXAMPLE

The story of the Department of Revenue Services illustrates Gene Gavin's interpersonal competencies of empathic communication, hope, and enthusiasm in healing discouraged people. The turnaround occurred through Gavin's vision of possibilities, his finding and cultivating resources within people, and his heralding success that others achieved through cooperation and involvement.

Empathy

One of the landmarks in the journey toward wholeness was Gavin's profound empathy for the people he led. He often spoke of them as "my" people. He recognized their fears of losing jobs and the meaning work had for his employees. He knew many of them personally before he was appointed commissioner. As a certified public accountant and attorney, Gavin had contact with five of the nine divisions of DRS and praised their professionalism, fairness, and courtesy. And he was well aware of the distrust that had been kindled by the frequent changes at the top and the lack of tax knowledge exhibited by many of the previous commissioners.

To connect his goals of cost-effectiveness and efficiency with his people, Gavin identified common irritants in the tax law administration. He realized that neither the public nor even the employees liked the cumbersome, vaguely written tomes; both desired simplicity and ease in administration. He remarked,

The twenty-six tax credits and the statutes that were written were so complicated that sometimes it took me, as a practitioner, [so much] more time to understand the statutes and write a memo to my clients that I had to bill them more for my time. Something was wrong with that.

Accordingly, Gavin made the simplification of tax language (in terms that laypersons could understand) a priority. He found the Small and Medium Sized Users Business Committee (SMSUBC), which the state general assembly had created that year, willing to help out. Composed of businesspeople from small- and medium-sized organizations, trade professionals, and tax professionals, the SMSUBC worked with employee volunteers to publish three handbooks the first year of Gavin's appointment: "A Guide to Connecticut Sales and Use Taxes for Building Contractors" (February 16, 1995); "A Guide to Connecticut Corporation Business Tax Credits" (February 16, 1995); and "Sales and Use Tax Guide for Manufacturers, Fabricators, and Processors" (November 3, 1995).

Since Gavin had become commissioner, the workforce had fallen by 7 percent. But Gavin insisted that no person be laid off. Instead, he did not fill jobs when employees left or retired, he transferred people to divisions with vacancies, and he retrained people whose jobs had become obsolete. He said:

I know how important a job is to people, and I don't want to cut a job. One of the things that might happen in the process is that there might be new opportunities, new retraining for people who are here. I made the commitment to them. I will give them the right training, if that's something that impacts them. I see this as an opportunity to learn something new about the agency. This will make you more valuable and keep you interested.

Stimulating a Vision of Hope

Gavin saw that the agency lacked a focus, a vision. In the wake of frequent management changes, people had no idea of what their agency was expected to do or what their particular roles were. Gavin recognized that because of this ambiguity, the nine division directors had built up "walls" around themselves and had managed each division as a business unto itself. People inside the agency did not talk with each other, and relationships with outside customers were sometimes tense.

To create a common identity among the employees, Gavin asked people to draw up their own mission statement. It gave the employees a chance to determine what they wanted in the agency and to write it down in concrete terms. After employees wrote the final version, Gavin had it printed on the backs of business cards. He pointed out that this reminded employees of their purpose and gave them a reason for serving taxpayer needs and interests. Business and professional clients as well as employees have told Gavin how that has improved their relationships. "The positive feedback," Gavin noted, "was applauded. Psychologically, that's very important. When they started getting the feedback, the sense of hard work they had put into the publications was worthwhile."

Using Symbolic Language to Encourage Change

In addition to seeing and communicating possibilities for change and stimulating others to share the vision, Gavin used many team metaphors. The Public Service Excellence (PSE) program, a variant of TQM, used cross-functional teams of managers and employees to develop and carry out incremental changes in operations. Gavin referred to the incremental changes as "base hits" and added, "When you have eight hundred and sixty people hitting a single, you have a lot of home runs by the end of the program." Sometimes, an innovation that netted large cost savings was a "grand slam."

Empowering division directors and employees to identify, carry out, and evaluate changes emerged as a result of education. Gavin coined words such as "torchbearers" and "disciples" to signify their shared interpretation and commitment to change in their own organizational units. To create an optimistic outlook for redeploying employees in the workforce reduction, Gavin proclaimed that he would "insource" work. He would develop a cadre of specially trained employees to take over the data-entry functions outside vendors used to perform during the busiest tax collection season. Through changing the frameworks of meanings of delegation and contracting work outside the agency, Gavin used words to educate employees for greater ownership of work processes and outcomes.

Celebrating Interpersonally

Gavin's approach to working with and through people was intensely personal. He often spoke of DRS in human terms, for instance, saying to employees, "The agency is listening to your ideas." He also showed that he shared their "pride in production" and used internal motivators as levers for change. In addition, he appealed for help by referring to them as equals in power: "If you help me be successful," he told them in small-group meetings, "I will help you."

Gavin used the personal approach even in all-employee messages. He relied on his broadcast mail to tell employees about their colleagues who had accomplished major results through the PSE small wins applications projects. He also announced via the broadcast line his pride in what all the employees had contributed, for example, when the Connecticut Quality Council awarded DRS its 1996 Gold Connecticut Innovation Prize. In introducing a strategic planning process and inviting volunteers to participate, Gavin held ten face-to-face meetings with all 860 employees. And each Friday, at the informal "Breakfast with the Commish," he listened to whatever employees wanted to tell him.

And the Applause Keeps on Coming

Gavin's personal, direct, and participatory approach to leading organizational change inspired others to bring about changes. In developing team-based "small wins" of the PSE, employees had to question why they had been doing work as they had always done it. In developing an understanding of problems and issues, employees opened up for critical inspection many of their unquestioned assumptions that framed the organization's culture. In addition, because they had training in problem solving, the commitment of their directors and the commissioner, and delegated authority to make changes within two to four weeks in how they did work, employees developed their own ideas for future changes. In fact, in their employee newsletter, employees recognized colleagues who had begun incremental changes on their own.

The favorable responses had a "snowball" effect, Gavin commented. Employees began to experience rapid success with new ideas they had introduced; in fact, one private sector official said that employees accomplished in six months a particular reform that would have taken anywhere from two to three years. External customers have been so pleased with the changes that they have built internal bases of support for DRS. One contractor newsletter, for example, praised "Gavin's Posse" of employees who prosecute home improvement contractors refusing to pay taxes. The contractor newsletter asked members to contact the DRS "Discovery Unit" if they knew of tax violations.

Gavin commented, "We're getting a lot of business and industry people and taxpayers saying 'We want to talk to DRS because they seem to be getting things done quickly and fairly.' "

The federal government has also taken note. In 1995, the U.S. Congressional Ways and Means Committee, hearing of the DRS's successes, cited Connecticut as one of three state models of innovation. The committee asked the DRS to share its revenue-finding tactics with the Internal Revenue Service. The commitment to the commissioner's goals of cost-effectiveness and efficiency, moreover, influenced legislative appropriations. When the legislature became aware of how the 860 DRS employees recovered over $900,000 in lost revenue, they granted Gavin's request for funds for the 1977 vintage computer system.

SUMMARY

The DRS case study shows the possibilities for transforming discouragement into hope through what Covey (1991) calls an "abundance mentality." Change agents recognize that resources not only abound but also multiply when they work with people to create change. Teaching others activates new meanings and new possibilities and gives individuals power to make changes where one is. Others see it, learn from it, and make their own changes. Change with an "abundance mentality" is like passing the light of one candle from one person to another until a whole room is lit.

The process begins with a vision of possibilities. Hope is the future embedded in the present; it waits for encouragement to unfold it. It comes to life when people begin to question taken-for-granted assumptions, realize problems or pain, and search for ways that will bring wholeness. Inevitably, they find what they seek. It may mean removing some psychological, emotional, or situational barriers, and it may involve costly mistakes as well. But when people find they have achieved what was before only a vision, they celebrate. They invite others to parties and share what they have done.

In leading change from the inside out in public agencies, change agents can help discouraged people recover meaning. Adler (in Dreikurs, 1950) points out that suffering results from difficulties that come between the three roles individuals play in life: work, or contributing to the welfare of others; friendship, pertaining to social relationships; and love, the emotional bond between humans. Leading change involves helping people discover and celebrate personal significance through empathy, hope, and encouragement.

REFERENCES

Combs, A. W., Avila, D. L., and Purkey, W. W. (1971). *Helping relationships: Basic concepts for the helping professions.* Boston: Allyn and Bacon.

Cooperrider, D. (1990). Positive image, positive action: The affirmative basis of organizing. In S. Srivastva and D. L. Cooperrider (Eds.), *Appreciative management and leadership: The power of positive thought and action in organizations* (91–125). San Francisco: Jossey-Bass.

Covey, S. R. (1991). *Principle-centered leadership.* New York: Simon and Schuster.

Dinkmeyer, D., and Eckstein, D. (1996). *Leadership by encouragement.* Delray Beach, FL: St. Lucie Press.

Dinkmeyer, D. and Losoncy, L. (1980). The encouragement book: Becoming a positive person. New York: Prentice-Hall.

Dreikurs, R. (1950). *Fundamentals of Adlerian psychology.* New York: Greenberg.

Gendlin, E. T. (1962). *Experiencing the creation of meaning.* New York: Free Press.

Hyde, R. B. (1994). Listening authentically: A Heideggerian perspective on interpersonal communication. In K. C. Carter and M. Presnell (Eds.), *Interpretive approaches to interpersonal communication* (179–195). Albany: State University of New York Press.

Kierkegaard, S. (1966). *Works of love.* New York: Harper.

Lawson, D. M. (1991, December). Language for change. *Individual Psychology, 47* (4), 456–463.

Rogers, C., and Stevens, B. (1967). *Person to person: The problem of being human.* Walnut Creek, CA: Real People Press.

White, K. W. (1994). Hans-Georg Gadamer's philosophy of language: A constitutive-dialogic approach to interpersonal understanding. In K. C. Carter and M. Presnell (Eds.), *Interpretive approaches to interpersonal communications* (83–114). Albany: State University of New York Press.

CHAPTER 10

Confronting Change with Courage and Compassion

Most ailing organizations have developed a functional blindness to their own defects. They are not suffering because they can't solve their problems but because they won't see their problems. They can look straight at their faults and rationalize them as virtues or necessities.
—John W. Gardner (1968). *No Easy Victories*

Jim didn't want to fire Alice; he really didn't. But he had to. Alice usually came to work a half hour late. Each time, she made excuses. Sometimes it was the usual story about her broken-down eight-year-old car, Washington traffic on rainy mornings, or a power outage during the night that messed up her alarm clock. Other times, she invented more creative tales: She had sudden attacks of colitis. Her bathtub had overflowed. She had run out of the diet colas she drank for breakfast.

Nonetheless, Jim liked Alice. She was still the bubbly, outgoing, funny young woman he had hired just a year before. But he knew something serious was wrong. Alice had just gone through a divorce. She was taking medications and seeing a counselor. He had to start documenting her attendance, reporting her frequent absences, and discussing suspension with labor relations. He couldn't do it; but in the meantime, his office productivity was sliding downhill fast.

Change is like a cloudburst that shuts down a ball game in the eighth inning with the score tied. Like most of us, Jim doesn't embrace change. His feelings blocked doing what he knew had to be done to restore peace in the office. Eventually, Jim overcame his feelings, and after giving Alice a 14-day suspension, she resigned.

Jim ultimately acted with compassion. According to Matthew Fox (1979), compassion is an act of justice. It relieves pain and allows people to experience wholeness. Compassion is letting go of ego in order to free oneself from it and to deliver others from oppression.

Is firing someone compassionate? Yes, if the compassion frees other people from injustice. Alice's lateness, lying, and continual abuse of "the system" created inequalities that oppressed her coworkers. She continued to receive pay as others, but she worked less and received no punishment when she violated rules applicable to all employees. Understandably, the coworkers rebelled. To restore peace and justice, Jim had to act justly.

Confronting organizational problems requires compassion. In playing roles as mediators, change agents have to let go of their own feelings and allow the self to experience the pain of unjust practices that corrupt organizations. From taking on the perspective of those experiencing the problems, change agents can derive an accurate picture of "what is" and what people desire. Identifying the gaps is the first step to closing them.

This chapter provides skills for closing the gaps and bringing peace and justice to organizational realities. It does this by describing some common sources of resistance to change in government organizations from three sources: individual, organizational, and political. The chapter maintains that the three sources interact but that the political ideology that originated organizational structures and programs influenced the organizational culture strongly. Hence, to change government organizations, change agents must focus on transforming the pervasive political ideology.

Raising sensitive issues in government organizations is particularly tricky because of the underlying political ideology. Individuals may attempt to deal with the ideology through a variety of cover-ups and games. Addressing political ideology through people requires the change agent to use both an indirect and a direct approach, depending on circumstances. By developing a relationship of mutual trust, by gathering and presenting data from a variety of sources, and by cultivating a climate of inquiry, change agents can change the predominant political ideology that contributes to many organizational problems.

Expanding the theme of trust building, we'll explore how change agents may use skills of empathy and encouragement to help people overcome resistance to change. We'll look at how a change agent incorporated empathy and encouragement in leading a state agency from despair to hope. Subsequent chapters describe ways that change agents can foster interpersonal relationships that pave the way to organizational change. The last chapter outlines a strategy for undertaking change through systemic diagnosis and intervention.

Figure 10.1
Sources of Resisting Change

- Fear
- Possible retaliation
- Perceived powerlessness
- Dislike of being disliked
- Clinging to the status quo
- Feeling overwrought

CONSIDER THE SOURCE

Where resistance originates in the organization also makes a difference in how people respond. It can come from any one of four organizational levels: from within individuals, from individuals as they interact, between units in agencies, or between agencies and various interdependent stakeholders. The four levels are not neatly separated, however. Resistance at one level ultimately affects all levels because individual beliefs, values, and actions define and influence "reality."

Individual Sources of Resistance

People confront change using several general tactics. Briefly, they may not recognize change and thus take no action; they may recognize change but deny it is important to them; or they may recognize change but take inappropriate actions to resolve it. In the last category, people may fabricate any number of games to avoid dealing directly with problems they know they must confront.

The change agent helps people identify and define opportunities for change. For people who do not comprehend that their thinking and behavior patterns interfere with their performance effectiveness, change agents provide information that helps them see the need to change. For people who do not see the relevance of change (for themselves), change agents can use a systems approach to point out how various problems and issues relate to their own interests. However, even after people have become aware of the need to change, they still often refuse to make adjustments. Hence, change agents need to understand that people confronting possibilities for change will show resistance. Some common sources of resistance are fear; possible retaliation; perceived lack of power, status, and influence; dislike of being disliked; preference for the status quo; and feeling overwrought (Figure 10.1).

Fear. People do not change because they fear consequences. Change often suggests that something within their area of self-responsibility is inadequate. They feel something must be wrong with them. This also exposes a sense of vulnerability. Weaknesses leave people prone to disparagement and open to attack from the outside, presenting challenges that require an extra effort of strength and confidence to surmount.

Fear becomes a self-fulfilling prophecy. What people fear often comes about. A story was told of a perspicuous old man who washed his hands five or six times a day to avoid getting a cold. He bragged that the technique had kept him from getting a cold for over two decades. In the process of continual hand washing, however, he developed a bad case of dermatitis, and the rough, red skin spread from his hands to the rest of his body.

Lack of Power, Status, or Influence. In bureaucratic organizations in particular, people at the "street level" may feel they have little ability to change "the system." In organizations in which red tape clogs operations, people have little discretion in making even minor changes in enforcing rules. They may see suggesting improvements to standard operating procedures as a waste of time.

Possible Retaliation. When people confront conditions within organizations that require change, they may struggle with telling their superiors. Bosses usually have the authority for making changes, but they also have accountability to their superiors for managing problems. Because they may look bad to their superiors, bosses may fear exposure themselves. They may blame people who brought the problem to their attention and even punish them for pointing out flaws. People who bring up issues put their careers at risk. The stories of managers who harassed and ultimately fired "whistleblowers" exemplifies this.

Dislike of Being Disliked. Change may pit friends and associates against each other. In an organization that values harmony, especially among management and top officials, raising issues of change may lead to expulsion. People who go against the prevailing cultural norms and practices are not seen as team players.

Clinging to the Status Quo. People may feel comfortable with the way things are for several reasons. They may not have personally experienced problems that others have voiced. Further, they may have grown used to a particular condition and accommodated their thinking and behavior to it. They may have even been rewarded for not making waves.

A secretary to a lawyer in a government agency once declared she used five different "in-baskets" for getting material to her never-on-schedule boss. For less important matters, she used the in-basket by the window; "pretty important" issues landed in the one on his desk; "extremely urgent" ones fell into his chair. That way, he couldn't possibly avoid overlooking hot ones. Rather than changing the multiple in-box organizing system to

Figure 10.2
Organizational Barriers to Change

- Fragmented political systems
- Lack of central accountability
- Political ideologies
- "Lookin' good" syndrome
- Loyalty
- Low empowerment and risk taking

---

one that would take less time, however, the secretary continued the extra work year after year. It made her feel needed, she remarked.

Feeling Overwrought. Making changes involves mustering not only courage but energy. It requires people to see ideas through, to encourage change in others, and perhaps more important, to make changes in their own ways of doing things. Mounting a change campaign may turn up burned-out team members.

Change involves frustration. Even when people plan and implement change programs carefully, they can experience setbacks. Budgets may be sliced; key people may leave; others may continually criticize both the idea and the method. Stress accumulates and leaves people even more vulnerable to mistakes.

Organizational Barriers to Change

In addition to individual reasons for resistance, organizations can obstruct change (Figure 10.2). In public organizations, barriers often arise from the fragmented political systems that undergird agencies. The fragmentation produces lack of central accountability, diffused responsibility for results, and reduced empowerment and motivation for taking risks.

Fragmented Political Systems. Public organizations contend with multiple and often contradictory sources of power. The elaborate system of checks and balances of power in the U.S. government allows for limited jurisdiction in making and carrying out laws. This produces overlapping boundaries of responsibilities and duplicated programs and sets up "turf wars" at every organizational level that has a degree of jurisdiction for a particular program. It makes government slow, inefficient, and legally focused.

Lack of Central Accountability. The multiple and limited jurisdictional controls lead to narrow focuses and limited accountability for results. Finding an individual who can make a final decision is sometimes nearly impossible. Decisions are often referred upward and typically to an office having highly specialized or technical expertise. Legal and engineering professionals often receive the questions and advise administrative managers. But because other branches of government or departments within an agency require consent, administrative advice is circumscribed. The accountability issue goes beyond the argument of "too many cooks in the kitchen." It is more like which cook has the authority to stir which pot on whose stove.

Political Ideologies. Perhaps the most contentious sources of resistance to change in government organizations are political ideologies. Political ideologies define the mission and structures of agencies, the fragmented systems of checks and balances of power, and the lack of central accountability.

Unlike private sector organizations, public agencies come into being primarily through compromised political ideologies. Representative elected officials enact legislation that reflects a hodgepodge of political beliefs, values, and interests. Usually vague, the legislation grants administrative authority to an agency, bureau, or committee. Legislation thus establishes mission and proscribes program operations.

The prevailing ideology within the legislation sets the tone for how the agency reports to a legislative oversight committee. In the case of the U.S. Department of Education, for instance, the legislation that created the agency was enacted through the efforts of educators concerned with the low status of education in the federal system, various civil rights interest groups, and elected officials concerned with the school achievements of American students in comparison to those of the Soviet Union. The mission of the Department of Education reflected a concern for both quality of instruction and improving equal access to education. The agency obtained support from "liberals" and consequently evolved programs and a management culture that reflect egalitarianism.

In relation to organizational change, many of the efforts to improve government productivity emanate from political ideologies. That these ideologies drive the purpose, scope, and outcome from outside in and top down makes organizational change an imposition. Career employees have little input into the decisions made by political appointees—and no stake in outcomes. This lack of authentic participation intensifies individual, interpersonal, and interorganizational unit resistance.

Political ideologies produce three key outcomes that block organizational change. The first two, the "lookin' good syndrome" and the "loyalty" factor, arise because of a need to influence voters' perceptions of results. If apparent good results come from a particular program or service, it reflects well on the elected official who introduced it. This helps the possibility for reelection and also enhances the careers of administrators who work with the elected officials. The third factor, low risk taking, is especially apparent when the organization undergoes imposed, top-down change.

"Lookin' Good" Syndrome. Because of limited and overlapping controls, frequent leadership changes, and truncated loyalties, elected officials preoccupy themselves with developing a favorable public image. If outcomes of legislation produce positive attributes, politicians hold them up as proof that their policies work. Negative results, on the other hand, are the other party's fault. Although program outcomes are often unpredictable, politicians monitor them scrupulously. Even if results cast shadows on political authors, politicians strive to "look good" for their constituents. They mine angles, obscure effects, and human interest stories in search of cosmetic gold.

Loyalty. Career managers learn that to get raises, promotions, and tenure they must become spokespersons for their political superiors. Their jobs depend on how laudably they perform. Consequently, they tuck away and ignore issues that may create "bad breath" in public events. Bureaucrats who raise issues innocently—obstacles that prevent them from doing their jobs effectively and efficiently—find they need courage. Often, ideas that would save taxpayer money, services that could shorten signature approvals, or innovative techniques from a training seminar go undeveloped. Ideas that interfere with the implicit loyalty/job rewards exchange process not only risk failure but may damage the initiator.

Low Empowerment and Risk Taking. Some organizations, in addition, have a history of failed change attempts. Old-timers invariably bring them up when they hear about a new idea. They may argue: "If it ain't broke, don't fix it." "We tried that last year, and it didn't work." Or, "Been there, done that." People often wish to separate themselves from change programs they perceive as risky.

In multilevel bureaucracies, professional turf signifies status. Professionals pride themselves on work "their department does." Because they have the skills that are important in accomplishing the work, in addition, professional elites accumulate a certain status. Further, to differentiate themselves, professionals will distinguish their work from others carefully and guard it jealously. Patent attorneys in one agency, for instance, may distinguish themselves from labor-management attorneys and may state they have greater status because their practice is more specialized than those who handle a variety of employee/management disputes.

Because of professional specialization that separates employees into discrete job classes, "buck-passing" is quite common in bureaucracies. A customer who needs the required signatures to submit a claim often finds the process nettlesome. Even worse is trying to pinpoint exactly who is accountable for resolving a particular problem. The responsible agent may be in another department in another state.

CONFRONTING SENSITIVE ISSUES

Working with people to confront resistance to change involves seven chief actions. In brief, the actions must establish a climate of trust; examine organizational formal and informal relationships; pay attention to voices from the organizational boundaries; select where and when to confront carefully; gather, analyze, and discuss data on organizational problems from several sources; note what people do not address; and state your own questions, puzzles, feelings, and frustrations. The keys to working through resistance are honesty, openness, and participation.

Create a Climate of Trust

The public sector change agent can begin to address individual, organizational, and ideological areas of resistance by developing a reciprocal positive and trusting relationship with people whom change affects. The change agent can accomplish this by promising to adhere to ethical standards of confidentiality and anonymity. In addition, the change agent can demonstrate knowledge of a particular situation or the historical and cultural context of an issue as a basis for determining the type of change strategy to use. This provides credibility as well as competence and assures people that the change agent has their best interests in mind. Moreover, the change agent can provide copies of interview, survey, and document analyses to people to solicit their verification, which enables the change agent to maintain visibility—a factor that greatly enhances trust.

Examine Organizational Relationships

In identifying and defining organizational problems and issues, change agents study the relationships of people, the work they do, the connections between the work to the overall performance of the agency, and the relationships of the agency and its multiple constituency. Analyzing the formal structures and processes as reflected in various types of legislative and agency documents can provide some clues; however, charting the informal structures and processes, particularly the ways in which political ideologies influence how and why people do—or do not do—work, reveals much.

Cultivate Marginal Voices

Because of the diffused character of power and influence in government bureaucracies, people who work in units closest to the public and in field operations often have different viewpoints than those who manage the agencies. In addition, people who have not had access to shaping policies and practices, such as women and minority employees, have stories that shed much light on why organizations fail to perform optimally. Listening to the perspectives of marginal people can also provide the change agent with ideas that may affect change.

Choose Timing and Place to Confront

Change agents need to select when and where they present information that may provoke resistance. People may be more receptive to information if the change agent has cultivated their trust. Therefore, the change agent can present sensitive or difficult information best after he or she has established a relationship of candor. Prematurely sharing the information will likely evoke protection, denial, or withdrawal from the change process. If the change agent establishes trust and follows up sensitive information with support and specific suggestions for change, the change agent will minimize resistance.

In addition, because the change agent establishes confidentiality, he or she should meet with people privately. Further, the change agent must present information only to those who have the power to change conditions. Leaking information to people who expect change but who cannot control it breaches trust.

Use Multiple Data Sources

The change agent should collect, analyze, and discuss information regarding change from several different sources. In addition to people at the organization's margins, the change agent needs to assess perspectives from individuals associated with the change issue. The different perspectives will likely generate questions that the change agent may wish to raise. Sharing stories from diverse perspectives and inviting those with the power to implement change to comment will reduce resistance. This technique enables people to gain an objective picture of what is going on. It allows them to suspend their own mental models and seek more comprehensive meaning. The change agent can facilitate dialogue that culminates in shared meaning by helping people to focus on issues continually, articulate their concerns and questions, and probe suggestions for alternative explanations.

Look at What Is Not Said

Often, such individual sources of resistance as fear, lack of influence, or the feeling of being overwhelmed will prevent people from revealing the most important aspects of problems. The change agent suspects this in situations such as meetings that end in agreement, people who work overtime without complaint, and organizations that have "open door" policies.

Primary indicators that people are coerced appear in body language suggesting compliance and silence.

Articulate Fears, Concerns, Puzzles, and Frustrations

Change agents use their selves as instruments of change in two ways: indirectly and directly. Indirectly, change agents act as mirrors that reflect the pain people are feeling in organizational settings (Rogers, 1961). Through data collected and analyzed from surveys, interviews, observations, and organization performance documents, change agents can present a composite view of experientially defined reality. Often, the picture change agents present begins to question the prevailing political ideology and its effects on how and why people work.

Change agents can also confront change directly through expressing their own feelings, fears, and questions to people whom change affects. Articulating uneasiness, questions regarding assumptions, and concerns about possible outcomes of a decision, for instance, may allow the change agent to unmask resistance. Once the change agent brings unexamined issues to light, he or she may present them for discussion and resolution.

A change agent once sat in a meeting between a supervisor and his staff of three professional and three clerical employees. The staff members requested the meeting to discuss problems they were having regarding the supervisor's short temper. Al believed he communicated authoritatively and provided sufficient information and lead time for staff to accomplish their assignments. However, the staff considered Al overbearing, often holding back important information, and leaving the office for long periods of time without telling anyone where he was.

During the meeting, Al took charge. When his secretary reminded him about his persistent absence, Al became defensive. The change agent interrupted Al, however, by telling him that she felt he was "stepping all over" his secretary's feelings. Al began to berate the change agent. But when the change agent asked why she should be the target of Al's anger, he stopped yelling. After a period of silence, Al agreed he had been too forceful. When the change agent asked him to think about what his staff was saying (and interrupted whenever he started taking over), Al started to listen.

A CASE EXAMPLE: RAISING SENSITIVE ISSUES

Change agents can confront change in government at any one of four levels: individual, interpersonal, interorganizational, or intraorganizational. Further, issues that trigger confronting a particular change can arise from within an individual, from interpersonal relationships, from day-to-day work experience, or from legislative mandates that produce top-down change from the outside. Change agents may encounter resistance from any of these levels or combinations of levels.

In the following example, a change agent in a mid-sized federal organization described how she intervened at the individual and interpersonal levels. The case reflects a strong political ideology of top-down control and its detrimental effects on subordinates. The change agent confronted the adverse effects using monitoring and coaching to change the manager's mental models and mitigate the political ideology.

Sharon Garrett was a mid-level manager who had come into government after working as a crisis counselor in a privately owned enterprise. As a volunteer, she gave telephone counseling to people facing crises. Not only did she confront the emotional and often irrational situations people described, but she also probed people's intellectual understanding of the situations so that they could develop a broader perspective of reality.

When Sharon started, she found working in a large bureaucracy chaotic. She quickly learned that her coworkers never confronted their superiors.

Sharon managed to survive, however. Her first supervisor, a female, spotted Sharon's ability to facilitate discussions among different interest groups with which the agency interacted. Sharon was particularly adept at bringing potential conflict situations under control, always working toward consensus decisions. All this changed, though, when Sharon's supervisor left and Dr. Overby took over. It didn't take long for the more open style of the woman manager to disappear. Sharon recalled:

The level of accountability he required was incredible. In meetings, for instance, he would have tasks to be carried out, dates, and who was responsible. That was a very good system, mechanically. It was clear who was responsible for what. But it was also a threatening way of doing business. Minutes were distributed to divisions and posted out in the hallways. So if someone were having problems, if things weren't going well, it was public information for everybody. Sometimes the reason the task didn't get completed was not under the control of the employee.

Because Dr. Overby was new and didn't know the agency's external stakeholders, however, he relied on Sharon to fill him in. Sharon gave him tips on how to handle disagreements among clients and volunteered to help with the more difficult interactions. But she was more concerned about how he handled his own staff.

Sharon had seen how morale had plummeted after Dr. Overby arrived. She recognized the anger in herself and in the staff. But should she step in? If so, how and when? She stated her dilemma:

It was risky, obviously, and I think probably the only reason why I did it was because it was so serious. If that behavior continued, it was going to have a serious impact on a lot more than just the person the behavior was directed at.

Sharon's answer came when she realized Dr. Overby trusted her. She noted that Dr. Overby "respected my judgment and my opinions, and I sensed that he would try to change." She decided to intervene.

She planned her strategy carefully. She decided to meet with Dr. Overby when he was not busily engaged in a project. Before she met with him, moreover, she planned what she was going to say, anticipated some of Dr. Overby's responses, and thought about what she wanted him to do afterward.

She decided an initial discussion to describe the staff situation as she saw it, her concerns, and her skills as an intervener would prepare Dr. Overby for seeing the situation from the staff's point of view. She also offered to help him interact with a more open demeanor. She gave him specific techniques for asking questions, inviting reactions, and becoming less controlling in his relationships with staff.

Sharon pointed out that Dr. Overby did act "a little bit defensively" after she met with him. But after the second meeting, Sharon saw "a small change in the total behavior." She believed that this small change suggested that he had tried. He "did hear something I said," she commented, "and I feel like it did have some merit. I tried something and I really reinforced it every time he did." She added:

I was willing to take the risk—I was so upset. It was so unfair to those people. But I felt I developed a relationship with that person, and it was okay to do that. I think that is the part where you use your judgment in that way depending on what your relationship is like.

SUMMARY

Confronting change with compassion enables the change agent to understand deeply how injustice and inequality cost people's well-being and the organization's productivity. The high price, however, may make people unwilling or unable to examine and correct abuses. Their resistance stems from a discontent that they cannot confront directly and leaves them with an anger that erupts in work relationships. Organizational structures and processes bear the load of anger and also reinforce the unjust and unfair practices.

Change agents need courage to root out deceit and harm in political ideologies and taken-for-granted organization practices. To match courage with the conviction that such beliefs and practices should change, the change agent can practice skills of building trust, carefully collecting and diagnosing organizational data from different and diverse viewpoints, presenting information in confidence, and articulating questions, puzzles, and uneasiness, especially with what people are *not* voicing.

Hannah Arendt (1964) described conditions within people, bureaucratic structures, and political ideologies that engender feelings of powerlessness to change. Bureaucratic organizations leave people feeling that they are replaceable parts; to keep their job security, they must remain loyal to superiors.

Breaking the cycle of fear, distrust, and insecurity requires the change agent not only to practice compassion and courage but to teach those skills to others. When people take responsibility for their own needs to change, they free themselves from injustice and inequality. Mary Douglas (1986) suggests that a solution to such injustice is fostering the belief in "extrarational principles": beliefs, values, and practices that go beyond the everyday paradigms of organizational reality. To encourage such thinking and responding, change agents need to practice skills of empathy and encouragement consistently.

REFERENCES

Arendt, H. (1964). *Eichmann in Jerusalem* (Rev. ed.). New York: Viking Press.
Douglas, M. (1986). *How institutions think*. Syracuse, NY: Syracuse University Press.
Fox, M. (1979). *A spirituality named compassion*. San Francisco: HarperCollins.
Gardner, J. W. (1968). *No easy victories*. New York: Harper & Row, Publishers.
Rogers, C. R. (1961). *On becoming a person*. Boston: Houghton Mifflin.

CHAPTER 11

Hope as the Imperative for Transformation

The revolutionary act of hope is . . . the opening up of situations which want to stay closed, and the contradiction of systems. . . . It is power in action, never satisfied and never incarnated.
— Jacques Ellul (1973). *Hope in Time of Abandonment*

In the movie *Gandhi*, a Hindu soldier visits the place where Gandhi is fasting. The soldier confesses that he has killed a Moslem child and feels a great deal of guilt. He asks the Mahatma how he can free himself of the pain he feels. "I know a way out of Hell," Gandhi whispers. "You must find a Moslem boy and raise him as your son."

Hope in a difficult situation is a path out of apparent hell. It recognizes the anguish of present circumstances, but yet it uses the circumstances as a means of change. Hope enables people not to escape difficulties but, rather, to transcend them. And it looks to the difficulties themselves, finds an innovative way out, and calls for taking action.

Change agents encounter people searching for ways out of over-whelmingly bad situations. They may be managers confronted with deep budget cuts that entail staff reductions, employees working under a supervisor who makes Rasputin seem angelic, and task forces that have to make a politically driven, yet unpopular, program work. Change agents help people who face what for them are entrapments and find keys from inside that will set them free. Change agents are hope finders in what many people see as hopeless situations.

WHAT IS HOPE?

Change is the possibility of hope. Change raises expectations that a desirable future will begin from the brokenness of people and relationships within present organizational environments. But change also raises fears, uncertainties, doubts, and backward glances toward a time when things seemed better. In the process of change, people move along an emotional continuum between exhilaration and despair. Change agents recognize the tensions people feel and try to create an equilibrium—an acceptance and reassurance that ultimate good will yet succeed.

Hope as a Push-Pull

A roller-coaster ride describes how people often respond to the possibilities of change. On roller coasters, people begin the ride with a desire to break a monotony of sameness, lack of stimulation, or inability to find challenge and thrill in their lives. The risks they take in beginning the ride are fairly safe; there is a predictable beginning and end, and fortunately, accidents happen rarely. Many have ridden roller coasters before and use their previous experience to reduce fears of running into something unexpected. They also share their adventures with others who have goals similar to theirs, and there is a high probability that those goals will not be met.

In getting into a roller-coaster car, people also act on the belief that what they do in the present will bring about the ultimate goal they seek in the future; present and future are connected in that moment they climb aboard. People appear to be the same when the ride ends, but in reality, their perspectives have changed them based on what happened during the ride and, with that, their views of themselves and others.

Antecedents of Hope

Change agents often wonder why clients wait so long before asking for help. Usually, by the time clients seek assistance, problems and issues have become unmanageable. There are several possible reasons for why clients do not begin to hope for change. Figure 11.1 describes some of the more common reasons.

Discouragement. People have become used to lack of response to their contributions in organizations. Supervisors may have denigrated and even chastised them for taking risks, thinking differently about an issue and suggesting an innovative approach to dealing with it, or succeeding at a complex and unique assignment. Coworkers, too, may have scorned employees who do not conform to norms of mediocrity—people who call attention to issues that need resolution.

Apparent fulfillment. People may come to accept situations that they

Figure 11.1
Antecedents of Hope

- Discouragement
- Apparent fulfillment
- Privilege and position
- Resignation
- Rule binding

---

believe pose no immediate threat to them. To those who believe they are safe, there is little need for hope.

Privilege and position. In hierarchical organizations, people at or near the top may insulate themselves from day-to-day problems. Information they receive from lower echelons comes prepackaged. To prevent alarm and possible retaliation, lower-level managers and employees bear positive information that will enable top officials to "look good." Those who filter information engage in elaborate cover-ups, deceptions, and oppressive, silencing tactics. Consequently, top-level officials are unaware that people at the shop levels contend with difficulties and are frequently shocked and puzzled when they do find out.

Resignation. People become inured to silence, disparagement, and the futility of change. They may have tried many times in the past to change but each time encountered obstacles they couldn't overcome. They have learned not to challenge wrongdoing. They may know of improprieties, but they feel powerless in voicing their concerns. Nobody, they feel, listens.

Rule Binding. Bureaucratic organizations limit hope by killing innovations. Conformity to rules boxes people in and offers them little autonomy to "think outside the box." Rules prevent uncertainty and problems that come from exercising discretionary authority, but they also overshadow possibilities for changing the status quo.

Change Agents and Shamans

When change agents enter client systems, it is often the worst of times for those whom the problems have affected for a long time. Because clients often see little realistic hope for changing conditions and solving problems, they may see the change agent as a shaman. Shamans change the seemingly unchangeable by invoking magical powers. Shamans are agents of change, but they manipulate powers without necessarily touching people on the sidelines. Ellul (1973, 39–40) points out that organizations with their formidable technical systems and relentless structures lull people into taking "refuge in ancestral activities of magic and occult, of nighttime and

Figure 11.2
The Cycle of Hope

- Phase 1: Recognition of Desire to Change
- Phase 2: The Inevitable Jerk
- Phase 3: Breaking the Fall and Revisioning
- Phase 4: Search and Renewal
- Phase 5: The Big One
- Phase 6: Dealing with Aftershocks: The Crisis of Meaning
- Phase 7: Resurrection

---

dreams." Clients become spectators who, by going through rituals change agents introduce, feel change happening. Like shamans, these change agents fix systems but leave the people running them unchanged.

Real hope comes when people go through struggles. They experience derision, roadblocks, threats to their own self-confidence, and silence. Going through change in search of hope involves losing one's way at times, feeling alone, and continual questioning of motives and tactics. It is a recognition that change agents cannot turn what is water into wine. That is an act of faith, of trusting in one's own powers and in the pull of a compelling vision of possibilities.

THE CYCLE OF HOPE

Figure 11.2 outlines a cycle of events that the possibility of change produces. Like a roller-coaster ride, the cycle begins with the desire for change—something different, new, better, or less burdensome. As people encounter events in organizational change, they learn. Their perspectives change, and with that, they confront additional choices for responding. Change agents help people explore meanings of these events and also choices and possible consequences. As cocreators of possible futures, change agents and clients build pathways as they move through unfolding events.

Phase 1: Recognition of Desire to Change

Hope begins with emptiness. It is a recognition that things are not going well, people feel unhappy and frustrated, and that what was expected failed to deliver. If there were no possibilities for change, however, the recognition would turn into despair. Yet with *this* particular feeling of emptiness, there is that chance. Hope sparks the possibility that something will change: A problem will be solved, people will be more satisfied with their work, and the old regime will capitulate. Hope as the possibility of change enlarges perspectives and stirs up exhilaration.

In addition to the recognition, hope dawns as the possibility that people can do something about their circumstances. Hope gives people the idea they are not powerless. They have the capacity for making differences; they create resources. They are confident, strong, and autonomous.

Phase 2: The Inevitable Jerk

The thrill of starting change lasts about as long as when a roller coaster reaches its first crest. The bottom falls out of enthusiasm when people contend with negative feelings and emotions. They often come to them as screaming accusations: "What did I get into? I didn't expect other people to back out once they made the commitment to help." "What if this fails?" "This is more than I want to take on right now." "The pilot project isn't going well." To deal with the tensions, people begin to put up defenses. They make excuses, deny what is happening to them, try to bail out, and blame others—especially the change agent for drawing them into this mess in the first place.

Phase 3: Breaking the Fall and Revisioning

Change agents intervene before doubts, fears, and anxieties produce the first signs of decay. The timing and context of "jerks" are critical. They usually come at critical phases of the change process and call into question motives and methods. Change agents watch for the convergence of circumstances and the birth of a vision as a guide. Embedded within threats are also opportunities for improving the change strategy, such as refocusing the aims, including people who may have been overlooked in the original needs analysis and intervention design, or aligning goals to achieve more realistic ends. Change agents can scan the patterns of circumstances to detect a new vision—one that will lead the way more accurately and with greater promise. Seeking opportunities to learn meanings of jerks and their uses in the evolving change process is the means for moving out of troughs.

Phase 4: Search and Renewal

Obstacles seen as opportunities intensify searching for ways out. New areas of knowledge open up, new resources suggest themselves, and new energy pulses through those who have resolved the first crisis of hope. Innovative ideas multiply, and clients giddily let them run. The change process accelerates, and what people now hope for renews their strength.

The renewal produces results. Conditions believed unchangeable produce unimaginable results. Those involved in the change realize their contributions have paid off. People celebrate in the realization that hope has dawned.

Phase 5: The Big One

When people undergoing change with renewed energy and vision hit minor dips and turns, they slip them into the enlarging perspective. Plans seem to be paying off, and worries and fears experienced earlier appear to have vanished. Clients may revel in the institutionalization of change and believe the worst is over. It is even tempting to sit back and enjoy the roller-coaster ride until it's over.

Never underestimate the power of the dark side, as Luke Skywalker in *Star Wars* found out.

As every hope blossoms, it also carries within itself seeds of destruction. Change successes have a way of unleashing evil elsewhere in the organization. People who feel threatened may react—and not so subtly. Earlier in the book, a training program for women managers was described. The program had been developed to boost women's competitiveness for managerial jobs in a federal agency. The program exceeded the designers' expectations. Its popularity among participants came from its effective design and implementation. One thing that designers were not permitted to change, however, was the management culture. Top agency officials agreed to the affirmative action officer's demands for opening paths for more women to enter managerial positions, but they also foresaw possible backlash in the "old boy" network. Fearing revolt and wanting to reassert their controls, the top administrators forbade program designers from training participants' managers to support the program. After two years of successful implementation, the top officials abruptly canceled the program.

Phase 6: Dealing with Aftershocks: The Crisis of Meaning

When clients experience the fall of a successful program, they often retreat into states of being that are sometimes worse than those before the change program came into being. In fact, in some cases, it is a near-death experience. Figure 11.3 shows some of the various degrees of hopelessness that may follow change that died.

Emptiness. People who spent their time, resources, and energy may feel exhausted. Worse, the end of an important dream left them little base on which to recover their losses.

Disappointment. People often feel let down emotionally following the collapse of an idea. The idea represented their aspirations for something better. It also represented people's own best thoughts and motives. In dealing with loss, people become disappointed in themselves and others. Disappointment, in turn, can lead to dissolving bonds of trust that people had so tenuously built (Desroche, 1979).

Figure 11.3
Degrees of Hopelessness

- Emptiness
- Disappointment
- Sadness
- Frustration
- Despair
- Loss of meaning and purpose

Sadness. Failure of change can often trigger depressed emotions. Sadness drains energy for taking on new ventures and keeps people from climbing out of troughs. Moltmann (1983) describes a "tristesse" that fills all living things with decay.

Frustration. Stopped change may arouse anxiety, an ambiguous feeling that things are out of phase. Frustration affects reactions of individuals in the office and at home in sudden fits of anger and outbursts of rage. Frustration can also inhibit the willingness to take on a future change project.

Despair. If people experience repeated frustration and have little encouragement to try to change again, they eventually lose their will to change. Moreover, they may come to expect that *any* change will inevitably result in unfulfilled hopes.

Loss of Meaning and Purpose. People who lose hope entirely often sink to a point of anomie. They lose track of who they are, where they are going, and cease searching for purpose. When the opportunity comes for them to change, they are impotent.

In *The Iceman Cometh*, Eugene O'Neill describes the aftermath of people's lives that have lost meaning through losing hope. Appropriately at a place called Harry Hope's Hotel, characters in the three-act drama portray the paradox of hope. Each character at the gin mill has had a dream of what life could be like through following a cause, a movement, or a crusade. Each one has clung to a pipe dream that has left them only shreds of self-respect. Hickey, the "Iceman" of death, comes in the guise of salvation; he tries to rouse those who are hanging on by promising them salvation from their illusions. Each character rallies, but only briefly. Coming to terms with the absurdity of their struggles to change and the inevitability of destruction of all hopes in death, each character realizes the potency of defeat.

Phase 7: Resurrection

O'Neill is far too nihilistic; in reality, few people succumb to death in life. Opportunities for change exist even when people experience low points in the change cycle. In our Western culture, however, lack of success or a project gone wrong is a failure; and failure brings condemnation (Brueggemann, 1973). The frame of failure keeps people from developing hope and the will to try again. When people succeed at getting through the stigma nonsuccess in this culture has handed them, they do break through the illusion of failure. But breaking free is something they need help with—and from an agent of change who can lead them through a reframing process.

Real hope comes from the other side of "reality" (Brueggemann, 1979; Muyskens, 1979). Change agents help clients reframe nonsuccesses by envisioning what the processes look like from a future state. Moreover, change agents help people realize they are not, in fact, powerless. Through their own choices, people can create the possibilities they desire.

A good example of this is the popular *A Christmas Carol*, by Charles Dickens. In the last visit from a spirit just before Christmas Day, Scrooge sees his own funeral being held. He is amazed at how people dislike him, even in death. He comes to realize that the fortune he had gained by cheating employees didn't matter in perspective. At the same time, however, Scrooge realizes it is not too late to change his stinginess. Scrooge discovers his autonomy and, in so doing, realizes he does not have to accept the pronouncement others may give him after he dies. For Scrooge, freedom to choose breaks the spell of hopelessness and puts him on a new path toward a more desirable future. Brueggemann (1973, 45) explains that freedom for change and newness comes from those who have been "exiled, emptied, and made alterable."

The cycle of hope is neither smooth nor straightforward. Hope reflects the forces that enter into all human experiences themselves; yet hope transcends them. From the fits and starts of life events and the seeming lack of meaning they often present to us, somehow we see a vision that takes us to a different vantage point. We see things in another light, and our meaning perspective begins to clear up. Without the disruptions and discontinuities in life experiences, we would not become mature people. Abrasions and surprises, Brueggemann (1973, 47) notes, are gifts we don't want to receive. After a roller-coaster ride, we may stagger a bit. The ride, however, has changed us: We'll go again.

THIRTEEN WAYS OF SEEING A SEED

Change agents help people find hope through examining possible futures from different viewpoints. The process is similar to going to a doctor for an eye examination and having an image become sharper and clearer through adding one lens over another. Hope finding involves changing both the ways we think about change and the ways we act on it. To activate the possibilities of hope, we have to find new ways to describe potential futures; our lenses of language and culture simply aren't adequate.

The discussion of the discontinuous cycle of hope points to hope's paradoxical nature. We may carefully envision the possible as it lies unformed within a tangled-up situation. We may even set up conditions that will allow the possible to take shape and flourish in the way we expect. But to allow hope to take life, we have to give it up to other hands. We have to allow forces to carve hope. We cannot control how hope evolves.

Hope goes into a black box, and what comes out may have little resemblance to what our intentions and interventions desired. As a created thing, hope is neither positive nor negative; it simply "is." We may manufacture meaning, however, in the labels we attach to what emerges. And in naming it, we also set up how we react to it (Averill, Catlin, and Chon, 1990).

To avoid limiting the meaning of hope, however, we may use metaphors to describe its paradoxical character. Metaphors leave room for us to find multiple meanings in the "gifts and surprises" we may not have expected or wanted. Through metaphors, we may find different paths to getting out of hell.

METAPHORS OF HOPE

From a discussion of the cycle of hope, we see at least seven possible metaphors that depict dimensions of hope. We can compare hope to (1) good/bad seeds, (2) embracing pain, (3) deconditioning us from rigid expectations, (4) valuing uncertainty, (5) a countersystem community, (6) a guiding vision, and (7) a transcendent value.

Hope as Good Seed/Bad Seed

When plans for change produce what we expected or even more than expected, we celebrate. What we have planted comes to fruition and produces delightful results. When the results disappoint our expectations, however, we confront a puzzle. We may question our methodologies, the feasibility of our plans, people with whom we have worked, or even our own competencies. When hope disappoints us, we often resort to ex post facto reason finding and convenient ways to explain what happened. In our efforts to solve the mystery, we assume that what occurred failed.

If we were to look at disappointments, however, we might find an opportunity for further growth and future productiveness. "Failed" changes are untapped answers.

In a military organization, a woman manager had tried to gain recognition of her competence among the all-male staff by putting in twice as much work as needed in completing a project or task. She believed that by overpreparing and scrupulously editing reports, for instance, her male colleagues would see how bright she was. When the intended result did not happen, but in fact caused even more resentment among the men, the woman was bewildered.

Instead of blaming herself or her colleagues, however, the woman began searching for ways she might show her competencies differently. As she searched, she discovered a key to the male system of success: In meetings, the men would put out only as much effort as necessary to complete a task. The norm became binding, and anyone who overproduced was ostracized. In subsequent reports, the woman followed the "rule" and subsequently won respect for her contributions.

Hope as Embracing Pain

In a similar manner, "bad news" often carries possibilities for change. But instead of denying negative feedback, we need to welcome it. Sometimes, we have to go through hell before we reach heaven. Moltmann said that hope doesn't take us from the pain of time but takes the pain of the temporal on itself. It is the basis for new thinking and planning. Pain and deprivation, like failed change, can become the means we use to escape.

Jim Wray spent several years as a prisoner of war in a North Vietnamese dungeon. A pilot, he was separated from his surviving crew members and other American soldiers for many months. During the solitude, however, Jim and the other prisoners developed an elaborate scheme of communicating with taps on walls. The code system enabled the men not only to exchange ideas and information but also to keep their emotional states of being healthy.

Hope as Deconditioning

Ellul (1973, 229) observed that hope is the work of "deconditioning"—the opposite of propaganda. Hope challenges concrete situations we hold to be true, obvious, and unimpeachable (Muyskens, 1979, 130). Hope calls into question our cause maps, mental models, and ideologies. Pat explanations for why things happened as they did do not satisfy our hunger. Until we can examine our assumptions uncritically, we cannot find shreds of hope amid disasters.

A famous example is the Hawthorne Experiments in the late 1920s and early 1930s (Stillman, 1988). Elton Mayo and Fritz Roethlisberger were studying the effects of varying rewards on workers at Western Electric's Hawthorne, Illinois, plant. The experiments were based on the prevailing assumption that people would work harder if they received more pay. To the researchers' surprise, however, results showed workers put financial rewards below recognition. The discovery led to the use of nonfinancial rewards and incentives to motivate people and to the beginning of the human relations approach to management.

Hope as Valuing Uncertainty

Predictability is hardly a watchword for bureaucracies. Ideally, bureaucratic organizations produce order, routine, and depersonalization of decisions to bring about efficiency and effectiveness of services. In reality, and particularly in the public sector, bureaucracies are battlegrounds for hosts of diverse interests. Overlay the chaos with a climate of general public apathy and mistrust toward government, politicians who replace bureaucratic organizations with loosely connected, contracted-out structures, and career staff who can't find any more to do less with. Change in public organizations becomes a challenge in dealing with multiple forms of uncertainty.

Hope in uncertainty leads to creative coping methods, however. Hope begs change agents to keep the present open and provisional—to evaluate the meaning of events in light of what occurs. Developing understanding also sharpens tools for dealing with obstacles.

In one federal agency in which numerous budget and staffing cutbacks had leveled hierarchical status, managers and employees were forced to operate as coequals. Instead of a manager in authority making all the decisions, the responsibility was shared. In fact, managers and staff often rotated positions; who was once the supervisor became the supervised. The arrangement created several positive by-products in addition to enabling the organization to solve the leadership problem. People became aware of each other as potential resources, conflict diminished as people developed and followed a common goal, and people developed greater sensitivity to the roles of managers and to employees. During the period, people showed more willingness to share risks, commitment, and loyalty.

Hope as a Countersystem Community

When people encounter "the big one" obstacle in the cycle of hope, they face a major dilemma. Choices open to them include turning back, quitting altogether, or forming a countersystem. Each choice entails its own risks. But creating a system that challenges opposing forces requires extraordinary courage. It is also the option that produces a counterargument.

Forces that work against hope are also the ones that inhibit change: satisfaction with the way things are, fear of taking risks, acceptance of defeat, and insulation. Discovery of the blocks to change creates the first encounter with the dominant system of norms and practices. Those who continue on in their fight to correct the system realize their need to form a coalition. The "countersystem," as Brueggemann (1973, 14) refers to it, creates a reality that assails "muteness, fulfillment, and technique." The countersystem calls bold attention to deficiencies in the prevailing system but also exhibits norms and behaviors that embarrass the status quo.

Many reformist movements came about because they believed in the possibilities change could bring. Reform groups often had beginnings in violence but continued on the force of resolve. The U.S. Civil Service Act of 1883, for instance, established a merit-based system for hiring and promoting bureaucrats. It followed as an outcry to the assassination of President James Garfield in 1881 by a disgruntled contender for a political position (Stillman, 1991).

Hope as Guiding Vision

Breaking free from constraining systems, in addition to courageous action, comes about through choosing an encompassing vision. The vision that guides hope often comes from the outside and takes on authenticity because it galvanizes common beliefs and values within people. The vision that leads people on journeys of hope is one that unites, creates new symbols for meaning, and energizes.

The guiding vision is often a common spiritual experience that people share, tell about, and pattern their lives by. For Paõlo Freire (1990), the guiding vision was one of human liberation from unjust, oppressive orders. The vision centered on "true generosity" as the wellspring of transformation:

True generosity consists precisely in fighting to destroy the causes which nourish false charity. False charity constrains the fearful and subdued, the "rejects of life" to extend their trembling hands. True generosity lies in striving so that these hands—whether of individuals or entire peoples—need to be extended less and less in supplication, so that more and more they become human hands which work and, working, transform the world. (29)

Hope as Transcendent Value

Hope is not utopia—in the sense that it dulls people to pain in present circumstances; but neither is it content with what exists. Hope provides a balance between what is real and what is ideal by anchoring a guiding vision in present possibilities.

The present possibilities, as Frost and Egri (1990) show, are positive attributes of conditions. To a great extent, these attributes are connecting points of change. Frost and Egri describe criteria for selecting the attributes, including using values that transcend the material conditions of the world, finding constructive intent that will produce enduring change for the betterment of self and others, integrating traditional polarities creatively, and selecting practices aimed toward the collective good (289–322).

To transcend means to operate "as if" the desired changes were already in place. People who are about to undergo a team-building intervention in an organization, for instance, are seen as people who are worthy individuals, who have the capacity and the willingness to change, and who have potentials within them to find and work from a common base. Treating people "as if" will also lead them to live up to the label; they will become that which they are called.

SUMMARY

In leading people through difficult situations in organizations, change agents require hope. Hope allows people to realize the complexity of the pain they confront. It entwines their spirits and inspires them to change. Hope presents a guiding vision that illumines paths that people would not necessarily choose for themselves as escapes. When hope comes, it gives oppressed people choices and the realization that in choices there is freedom. Hope transcends past, present, and future. It brings together hurting people and gives them the courage to speak out against injustice with a common voice. Hope replaces fear, pain, and aloneness.

How does hope build and nurture a common voice? Part IV presents several ways in which change agents have brought hope to people facing difficult choices for change. It describes how labor and management cooperated in improving worker quality of work life, how diverse constituents solved major public problems, and how people used individual and organizational learning strategies to empower themselves.

REFERENCES

Averill, J. R., Catlin, G., and Chon, K. K. (1990). *Rules of hope.* New York: Springer-Verlag.

Brueggemann, W. (1973). *Hope within history.* Atlanta: John Knox Press.

Desroche, H. (1979). *The sociology of hope.* London: Routledge & Kegan Paul.

Ellul, J. (1973). *Hope in time of abandonment.* New York: Seabury Press.

Freire, P. (1990). *Pedagogy of the oppressed.* New York: Continuum Press.

Frost, P., and Egri, C. (1990). Appreciating executive action. In S. Srivastva and D. L. Cooperrider (Eds.), *Appreciative management and leadership: The power of positive thought and action in organizations* (289–322). San Francisco: Jossey-Bass.

Moltmann, J. (1983). *Theology of hope.* Minneapolis: Fortress Press.

Muyskens, J. L. (1979). *The sufficiency of hope.* Philadelphia: Temple University Press.

Stillman, R. J., II. (1988). *Public administration: Concepts and cases* (4th ed.). Boston: Houghton Mifflin.

Stillman, R. J., II. (1991). *Preface to public administration: A search for themes and direction.* New York: St. Martin's Press.

PART IV

Change through Creative Involvement

CHAPTER 12

The Art of Cooperation: A Case of Management-Union Joint Problem Solving

With is a pretty good preposition, not because it connotes democracy, but because it connotes functional unity, a much more profound conception than that of democracy as usually held.
—Mary Parker Follett (1926). *The Giving of Orders*

Although cooperative planning and carrying out change in public organizations are essential to success, they are even more important when clientele have high numbers of union members. If management does not include union members from the beginning and throughout the intervention, it is not likely to gain union support. Having the support and cooperation of union members enables management to develop creative strategies, higher degrees of employee participation and commitment, and enhanced productivity. Nearly 40 percent of all public employees belong to unions, compared to only 11.2 percent in the private sector; and the numbers are increasing (Baird, 1994; Myers and Killeen, 1994).

Implementing organizational change, in addition, requires understanding cooperative labor-management agreements, often for several different types of unions. Union membership may range from blue-collar workers to clerical personnel; professionals also may belong to various unions. In some government organizations, even managers are unionized. Explaining the intent of an intervention, discussing some possible ways the intervention will affect union members, inviting suggestions on implementation, and working with officials to assess outcomes help management gain insight as well as support.

The support is also vital in that unions often regard interventions skeptically. In interventions calling for employees and management cooperation, unions may perceive their bargaining power eroding (Cutcher-Gershenfeld, 1984). Moreover, some unions have observed management using cooperative programs to downsize or lay off workers where productivity is at stake (Gold, 1986). Management may also demand or impose wage cuts and benefit concessions during cooperative ventures. Finally, some unions have found that if their locals or chapters are weak or that members easily fall prey to management's attempts to weaken the union, the project can have a negative effect on the bargaining power of the union (Reisman and Compa, 1985). In sum, unions fear losing power in preventing unilateral management decisions (Mangum and Mangum, 1993).

This chapter describes how management and union officials were able to implement successfully a quality-of-work-life program in a northeastern state government. Through analysis of case examples of several health care facilities in the state, the chapter identifies elements that can help management and unions develop programs that benefit not only management interests in productivity enhancement but also union interests in enhancing worker morale and job satisfaction. It concludes with some tips that will help change agents introduce interventions in unionized environments.

QUALITY OF WORK LIFE

Quality-of-work-life (QWL) programs are examples of cooperative programs often found in public organizations. Stimulating motivation, commitment, and performance since the 1970s, QWL programs foster worker participation in such issues as pay, job security, workplace decisions, and self-development.

QWL programs have several common features: There is a specific allocation of funds set aside specifically for cooperative projects. Funds are negotiated between the parties in the collective-bargaining agreement. Further, the approach to QWL is "bottom-up" (Eaton and Voos, 1992).

QWL programs have introduced several innovative work processes in the public sector. For instance, QWL programs have reduced job-related ambiguity and conflict (Israel, House, Schurman, Heany, and Mero, 1989; Kochan, Katz, and Mower, 1985). At the same time, they have improved worker attitudes (Norsworthy and Zabala, 1985); lowered grievance rates (Ichniowski, 1984); and decreased price-cost margins (Cohen-Rosenthal, 1985; Karier, 1985). Among the other benefits QWL programs have brought are (1) increased communications between employees, coworkers, and supervisors through promoting more accurate performance expectations and organizational policies and procedures; (2) additional social support; (3) improved psychological health and well-being; (4) improved job satisfaction; and (5) reduced absenteeism and turnover (Jackson, 1983).

In implementing QWL programs, both management and union must cooperate from a position of equal strength. Management and union can do this if they both see productivity improvement as a common goal. Management may agree to form QWL programs, in part, to become more competitive and reduce labor costs (Hecker and Hallock, 1991). Jennings, Smith, and Traynhem (1986) point out that management must provide assurance of continued cooperation, even when organizational changes occur. Union officials, moreover, need to remove collective-bargaining issues from the participative process and agree to communicate joint activities. Both union and management officials must communicate trust in their decisions and support.

Qualities for Success

Reviewing conditions that facilitated labor-management cooperation in the survival of joint programs, Eaton (1994) identified five key variables: good labor relations, concessions, fragmentation of representation, integration of bargaining and participation, and strict limits on the overlap of bargaining and participation.

Difficulties in Government

Quality-of-work-life programs in the public sector face several constraints, however. Chiefly, public sector organizations do not have the ability to raise funds but rely on legislative appropriations for their livelihoods. The dependency relationship limits the type of influence tactics that public sector unions may use. For instance, public sector unions, unlike private sector counterparts, do not have the right to strike or to engage in work slowdowns to demonstrate their dissatisfaction and inhibit management activities (Sulzner, 1982).

Because of the different economic and political configurations of public sector organizations, union commitment to cooperative problem-solving projects appears to differ from that of private sector organizations. In the public sector, unions have different organizational objectives, processes, and outcomes. For example, public sector unions have fewer options to negotiate work assignments than in the private sector. Levine (1991) maintains that private sector unions may bargain about virtually any topic, use strikes and lockouts as economic weapons, and negotiate security through fee structures. In the public sector, on the other hand, the Taft-Hartley Amendments to the National Labor Relations Act limit the scope of bargaining, and mandate that labor disputes must be resolved through third-party intervention, and that strikes are illegal.

Second, the morass of laws, rules, and regulations governing personnel management discourages government managers from trying innovative approaches. Levine (1991, 105) notes: "Labor and management have developed a rigid attitude against cooperation as a result of the level of mistrust that has developed; some fear that increased productivity due to cooperation may be used to justify job loss."

Third, motivational incentives in the public sector differ from those in the private. Public employees experience higher needs for achievement (Guyot, 1962) but lower levels of job satisfaction than their private sector counterparts (Porter and Mitchell, 1967); fewer intrinsic rewards (Rainey, 1987); and more inconsistent managerial support (Keehley, 1992). Erez and Arad (1986) point out that the gap between achievement and satisfaction often leads to lower productivity.

A SUCCESSFUL CASE EXAMPLE

The case is based on an internal program evaluation of a QWL project negotiated by a state and a 1,300-member public sector health care union in 1983. The public union, which had a traditional collective-bargaining relationship, was the first state bargaining agent to embark on a cooperative program through negotiations. In 1983, the state health care agencies along with health care employees established a QWL program. The QWL program was designed to improve the work environment and skills and morale of health care employees in an atmosphere of mutual trust and cooperation.

The program established eight specific goals:

1. To create an environment in which employees could work constructively for the betterment of their clients.
2. To assist in making the delivery of quality health care a rewarding career.
3. To create an environment where individuals' contributions would positively affect clients.
4. To develop a safety and accident reduction program.
5. To develop ways to address the effects of excessive absenteeism on client care.
6. To develop skills for dealing with the changing nature of health care delivery.
7. To establish child care programs.
8. To develop training programs in awareness of quality-of-work-life issues.

From 1983 to 1987, volunteer labor and management representatives worked collaboratively while continuing in their other work responsibilities. In 1987, the state steering committee established a QWL office and hired a staff director; the committee hired an assistant and a part-time secretary in 1989. The permanent staff conducted training in local health care facilities, reducing the cost of hiring outside consultants. The steering committee also established facilities steering committees in each agency to oversee management and union problem-solving teams. In addition, the committee hired two consultants to conduct feasibility studies and to provide training in team problem solving.

The consultants trained the cross-functional problem-solving teams in problem definition, idea generation, alternative selection, project identification, and funding proposal techniques. The teams prepared proposals and sent them to the facility steering committees for consideration. Professional staff members continue to attend regular training to stay abreast of the latest developments in labor-management cooperation. The office also contains a clearinghouse for labor-management training materials, videotapes, and research.

Types of Projects

Pilot Project: Child Care. Believing that an increasing need for employee child care was an important first project, the steering committee of state agency and deputy commissioners, top union leaders, and a third-party neutral met to discuss alternative ways to meet the need. Steering committee leaders agreed during negotiations to set aside funds not only for child care but also for other initiatives that could improve the quality of life in the workplace.

Subsequent Projects. After establishing child care centers, the QWL program added 13 other projects: safety training, nursing preceptorship, building an employees' lounge, wellness program, physical fitness, work scheduling, attendance incentives, literacy, smoking cessation, employee recognition, team-building training, space consolidation, and staffing. Many of the projects were determined by local worksite joint labor-management cooperative committees, and a few originated at the statewide level through the top-level union leaders and agency heads. By 1993, 1,300 workers and managers were collaborating on 31 projects.

SOME KEY PROJECT RESULTS

The QWL projects produced several important outcomes in terms of long-term monetary savings, work innovations, and improved union-management working relationships. Some of the more notable benefits included improved management-employee communications, cost reductions, and future project funding.

Communications Relationships

An analysis of interviews of three management and three union officials revealed that improving the quality of labor-management relationships was by far the most important outcome of the cooperative problem solving. The improved communications relationships produced 11 major by-products:

1. Increased toleration
2. Deepened commitment to the process among both management and union
3. Increased creativity in problem-solving ability
4. Willingness to cooperate in future projects
5. Enhanced trust and respect
6. Greater goal clarity
7. Higher tolerance for risk taking
8. Empowerment of all employees
9. Moving beyond stereotypic categories to seeing uniqueness of people
10. Heading off major problems in the future
11. Improved capability to fulfil mission

Cooperation strengthened relationships with management, such that grievance management has been less confrontational. A union interviewee observed that management is more willing to listen to and respect workers' feelings in decisions. When a downsizing was announced, she noted, the cooperative relationship enabled the people to discuss the issue without feeling angry: "Everyone felt good about the outcomes." Another pointed out that management recognized that "employees really liked their jobs and valued collegial support and encouragement."

The improved relationships have not diminished the ability of the unions to raise and negotiate work-related issues, however. In particularly troublesome areas, an ombudsman or mediator has been appointed. A management official cited a project that involved employee scheduling:

Before cooperations, scheduling had been worked out through negotiations. When management and labor couldn't work it out that way, however, they agreed to call in an outside mediator. Through the mediator, they were able to resolve the scheduling problem without filing a formal grievance. After that [the agency] saw the value in cooperative problem solving and began to take on other cooperative projects.

A union leader noted that "management has lessened its view of controls, while unions have less feeling that they are being coopted."

The observation is contrary to the conclusion of Perline and Sexton (1994) that management that perceived union relationships as cooperative was less willing to open decisions to union input. Apparently, union respondents in the present study perceived greater opportunities for such input, feelings of mutual trust and respect, and satisfaction and commitment to their jobs. Management, in observing changes in employee motivation and productivity through joint problem solving, was more receptive to future possibilities for cooperation.

Cost Reductions

The QWL program reduced by 30 percent workers' compensation costs and cut mandatory overtime. A survey of health claims, in addition, showed a savings of $10 million in compensation safety. In interviews with the consultants, eight union members pointed out that injuries, compensation claims, and safety violations had decreased since the cooperative problem-solving projects had been initiated. One noted, "It helped put safety language in the contract. For years, this had been fought for. It is odd that this is something management should have done as a principle."

Spinoff Funding

The initial success of the child care project led not only to its continuation but also to several other interventions in the workplace. The cumulative cost savings that the QWL projects netted became a strong argument for the continued funding of the entire QWL project. From an initial investment of $60,000 in 1983, funds steadily increased over each of the successive collective-bargaining agreements to a high of $450,000 in the early 1990s.

Local labor-management cooperative teams were successful in using their existing QWL committees as "laboratories" for other types of funding. For instance, QWL-inspired smoking cessation projects were initially funded through QWL and subsequently funded through health care cost containment funds. Many of the safety project teams were able to access loss control grants in the agencies with the greatest need, especially mental retardation and mental health. QWL funds were used to launch projects, and once they were established, agencies assumed more of the projects' costs.

A Downturn

A severe recession and the need to cut back government services, however, strained the QWL program. Beginning in 1989 and lasting until 1993, the state eliminated 140,000 jobs. To save additional money, various state and local government services were contracted to private sector organizations at lower operating costs. When the job cuts were at their peak in 1993, the state threatened to cut funding for the public QWL program.

In 1994, although the state did eliminate many of the funds, it did establish a public sector award for excellence in quality similar to the private sector Malcolm Baldridge award. The award recognized the importance of quality improvements, such as those the QWL program had introduced earlier. In addition to the state verbal support, however, the sites having existing QWL programs received technical assistance from several private sector organizations with similar QWL programs. On a voluntary basis, the private organizations donated training materials and invited QWL members to participate in training events and participated in planning and designing joint ventures.

Areas of Concern

Interview data from both management and union respondents suggested that the QWL program produced several important innovations in the workplace but left some problems little changed. Although management and employees communicated a great deal more effectively because of the QWL programs, many respondents described a continuing tension between those who have the authority to make decisions and those carrying them out. One respondent in a focus group pointed out that management gives only continuing "lip service" to genuine power sharing. The respondent added that this is particularly notable among top-level officials. Another respondent maintained that in spite of the training in making joint decisions about workplace problems, many managers have failed to let go of over-controlling interpersonal communications styles.

Other respondents described their satisfaction with the differences QWL had made in their own work areas but added that the cooperative problem-solving process had not completely changed the corporate culture. Many management and union leaders were reluctant to discuss linking the co-operation to other forms of organization change. One central outcome was the tendency to revert to a top-down decision-making style and a resulting mistrust among labor and management.

Several respondents, in addition, mentioned they faced many types of external pressures throughout the QWL program. Participating in a quality-of-work-life team took much of their time. Planning, discussing, and working out the details of implementing changes took place in addition to their normal workloads. This created tension in their own lives but also raised management's objections. An additional deterrent was having to demonstrate accountability for use of taxpayer funds. At a time when the state slid into a deep recession, taxpayers scoured budgets looking for items to chop. Many taxpayers saw the QWL funds as frills and the training for labor-management cooperation of little direct payoff to the state.

The perception of low rate of returns, and the backdrop of reduced state funding for the QWL program, was in part the reason for decreased amounts of training in cooperative problem solving. For example, several interviewees believed training should have been more extensive. One management official remarked, "More credence has been given to management development in terms of valuing human relationships and being proactive instead of reactive. This should have been so without training."

A union representative, moreover, noted that training should be for all union members, not just leaders. Group facilitators, in particular, should receive continual training as well as process feedback to improve their skills. Training is crucial for those who enter projects in midstream; these are people who lack understanding of initial project objectives and who may have difficulty breaking into already established group relationships.

A Summary of the QWL Program

The case study of the QWL program indicated that public sector union support for QWL enhanced the well-being of employees through such projects as wellness, day care provisions, and additional educational opportunities. It also enabled the state to save tax money by reducing employee compensation claims, compensatory overtime, and grievance management. Further, it fostered improved interpersonal communications relationships through continuous training, publishing results of programs, and mutual labor-management trust. In a time when diminished funding brought widespread layoffs in both the public and private sectors, the QWL project created opportunities to expand allocated funding and produce highly productive results.

In summary, the study suggests that QWL programs have succeeded in the public sector because of four key conditions:

- Mutual trust permits opportunities for direct participation in achieving specific, measurable, and agreed-on goals.
- Participation enhances motivation to achieve goals even in the absence of monetary rewards. As research suggests, the desire to achieve is of greater value to public sector employees than to private sector employees.
- Evaluation interview results demonstrate improved work processes and relationships, cost-saving innovations, and operating cost reductions. These benefit union-management relations, enhance worker morale and productivity, and produce tax-dollar savings.
- Union and management develop bonds of trust that encourage future participation in problem solving.

IMPLICATIONS FOR CHANGE AGENTS

The case study clearly shows that management-union cooperation in planning and implementing organizational change can take place successfully, provided certain conditions exist. First, unions have to demonstrate a high commitment to cooperative relationships. Strong union commitment to QWL resulted in reductions in grievances, consensus regarding employee well-being, and lowered operating costs.

Management must also provide adequate and continuous resources to employees working on improvement projects. These resources include funds not only for project start-ups and ongoing development but also for training in using new work techniques. Perhaps of most importance, however, is management's willingness to change the prevalent style of interpersonal communications from control to openness. Notably, the basis for such participation is mutual trust. Through trust-based commitment, employees and management can introduce innovative programs and work processes jointly, produce a highly satisfying climate, and create opportunities for improved communications.

The success of the QWL program indicated that many fears unions often express in engaging in cooperative programs need not become realities. First, downsizing need not follow gains in productivity. The state continued to fund QWL projects in spite of other state and local government reductions in funds, programming, and staff. Second, union participation reduced the costs of operating programs and services. Finally, management officials do not always seek to co-opt workers or to weaken union influence.

TAI CHI AND CHANGE AGENTRY

Engaging public organization change through cooperative labor-management programs is like leading a pair of martial arts players. The objective of success in a Tai Chi match is not to show competitive advantage over the other; the greater aim is to achieve gains through a triple-stage process of respect, discipline, and commitment as a way of life. Cooperative programs are less like wrestling matches in which the stronger opponent wins but, rather, more like a dance in which partners coordinate moves to create a harmonious whole.

Respect

Respect for the other is a foundation of cooperation. Respect comes from a positive estimation of the other's resources and strengths and the notion that the other could use them with discretion. The fact that the other might engage the resources is always a possibility; but when the other reciprocates and decides to withhold using the resources, respect is a powerful deterrent to war.

Management has the right to terminate, but unions have the right to participate. If neither recognizes the advantages of the other, war can break out. Employees under fear of layoffs go through the mechanics of implementing change. Change agents help deter war, however, by helping management and unions realize the relative strengths the other has. Instead of fights, the change agent shows them how to dance.

Discipline

Learning the rudiments of dancing, however, does not require much commitment. After mastering fundamental steps, dancers can become more proficient. The logic behind the steps—the meanings of moves and their possible effects on the moves of other dancers—requires extensive practice. Change agents can teach the rationale of cooperation to management and union officials and reinforce the strategies of change through guided practice sessions, coaching, and modeling. When players slip backwards, change agents can help them regain balance.

The goal of the change agent, like the Tai Chi master, is to instill self-discipline. The principles for achieving balance of strengths and the advancement of a common goal can work if players internalize them. Internalization involves prolonged periods of introspection and action in which people practice self-discipline, reflection, and dialogue. Through introspection and discussion, people see interpersonal situations from different angles. They also make values, beliefs, and actions congruent with respect to setting and attaining mutual goals.

Commitment

Discipline, however, has its limits. Temptations to return to control, withhold information from employees, and forego delegating responsibilities can reestablish mistrust between management and employees. In times of crises, such as budget and staffing cuts, the temptation to take charge is especially strong, and managers may not rely on self-discipline to see them through.

What they need is commitment—an act of will. Commitment as will is a conscious choice of letting go. Through commitment, people cut out attitudes and actions that inhibit creative ideas, tear down positive self-regard, and destroy empowerment. Commitment is also a rebuilding. It involves selecting attitudes and actions that will accomplish a greater or common good. Choice is not an act of will to meet one's own ends but is done with reference to others' needs and interests. Commitment springs from the realization that the greater good comes from people identifying and sharing the many untapped resources within them.

Times of crises test commitment. Crises call for abandoning what no longer works and searching for what can. Crises force finding common ground and the cooperation of many different people. In difficult times, such as those public organizations now find themselves in, joint management and union investment in developing employee needs and talents is critical. By pointing out this common interest and the importance of improving the overall quality of organizational life, change agents can help management and union officials strengthen their commitment to productivity and personal empowerment.

The following chapter examines ways change agents used diversity among people to build common ground and commitment to solving major socioeconomic problems in an urban area. Through the leadership of change agents in clusters of interest groups, transformation occurred. Instead of coaching dancing partners, change agents in this chapter coordinated waltzes on a ballroom scale.

REFERENCES

Baird, C. W. (1994, Fall). The Dunlop Commission report: Friends of unions. *Government Union Review, 6,* 1–42.

Cohen-Rosenthal, E. (1985, Autumn). Orienting labor-management cooperation toward revenue and growth: Employee involvement programs stressing revenue generation have greater potential than those emphasizing cost containment. *National Productivity Review, 4,* 385–396.

Cutcher-Gershenfeld, J. (1984, May). Labor-management cooperation in American communities: What's in it for the unions? *Annals of the American Academy of Political and Social Science, 473,* 76–87.

Eaton, A. E. (1994, April). The survival of employee participation programs in unionized settings. *Industrial and Labor Relations Review, 47*(3), 371–389.

Eaton, A. E., and Voos, P. B. (1992). The ability of unions to adapt to innovative workplace arrangements. *American Economic Review, 79*(2), 72–76.

Erez, M., and Arad, R. (1986, November). Participative goal setting: Social-motivational and cognitive factors. *Journal of Applied Psychology, 71,* 591–597.

Follett, M. P. (1926). The giving of orders. In H. C. Metcalf, (Ed.), *Scientific Foundations of Business Administration.* Baltimore, MD: Williams and Wilkins Co.

Gold, C. (1986). *Labor-management committees: Confrontation, cooptation, or cooperation.* Ithaca, NY: Cornell University Press.

Guyot, J. F. (1962). Government bureaucrats are different. *Public Administration Review, 22,* 195–202.

Hecker, S., and Hallock, M. (Eds.). (1991). *Labor in a global economy: Perspectives from the U.S. and Canada.* Eugene, OR: University of Oregon Books.

Ichniowski, C. (1984, June). *Ruling out productivity? Labor contract pages and plant economic performance.* Cambridge, MA: (Working Paper No. 1967). National Bureau of Economic Research.

Israel, B. A., House, J. A., Schurman, S. J., Heany, C. A., and Mero, R. P. (1989). The relation of personal resources, participation, influence, interpersonal relationships, and coping strategies to occupational stress, job strains and health: A multivariate analysis. *Work and Stress, 23*(2), 163–194.

Jackson, S. E. (1983). Participation in decision making as a strategy for reducing job-related strain. *Journal of Applied Psychology, 68*(1), 3–19.

Jennings, K. M., Smith, J. A., and Traynhem, E. C. (1986). *Labor-management cooperation in a public service industry.* New York: Praeger.

Karier, T. (1985, February). Unions and monopoly profits. *Review of Economics and Statistics, 62*(1), 34–42.

Keehley, P. (1992, August). TQM for local governments: The principles and prospects. *Public Management, 74,* 10–16.

Kochan, T. A., Katz, H. C., and Mower, N. R. (1985). *Worker participation and American unions: Threat or opportunity?* Kalamazoo, MI: Upjohn Institute for Employment Research.

Levine, M. J. (1991, February). Legal obstacles to union-management cooperation in the federal service. *Labor Law Journal, 42,* 103–110.

Mangum, G. L., and Mangum, S. L. (1993, July–August). Assessing alternative employment relations systems. *Challenge, 36:* 29–37.

Myers, K., and Killeen, B. (1994, April). Building union-management partnerships. *Quality Progress,* 95–97.

Norsworthy, J. R., and Zabala, C. A. (1985, July). Worker attitudes, worker behavior, and productivity in the U.S. automobile industry. *Industrial and Labor Relations Review, 38,* 544–557.

Perline, M. M., and Sexton, E. A. (1994, July). Managerial perceptions of labor-management cooperation. *Industrial Relations, 33*(1), 377–385.

Porter, L. W., and Mitchell, V. F. (1967). Comparative study of need satisfaction in military and business hierarchies. *Journal of Applied Psychology, 51,* 139–144.

Rainey, H. G. (1987). Reward expectancies, role perceptions, and job satisfaction among government and business managers: Indications of commonalities and differences. *Proceedings of the Academy of Management* (Atlanta, GA), 357–361.

Reisman, B., and Compa, L. (1985, May–June). The case for adversarial unions: A traditional labor-management relationship, rather than one based on concessions and cooperation is best for both sides. *Harvard Business Review, 63,* 22–24.

Sulzner, G. T. (1982). The impact of labor-management cooperation committees on personnel policies and practices at twenty federal bargaining units. *Journal of Collective Negotiations, 11*(4), 37–45.

CHAPTER 13

Creating Community in Government

Community does not solve the problem of pluralism by obliterating diversity. Instead, it seeks out diversity, welcomes other points of view, embraces opposites, desires to see the other side of every issue. It is "wholistic." It integrates us humans into a functioning mystical body.
    —M. Scott Peck (1987). *The Different Drum*

Providing solutions to difficult problems that affect all of society is one of government's primary purposes. Problems such as homelessness, AIDS, hunger, and environmental pollution threaten the quality of life not only for just a handful of unfortunate individuals but for all people. Yet the widespread and deep cuts in funds, staff, and technology have drained governments' ability to respond.

Cuts affect poor children perhaps worst of all. The Children's Defense Fund (1995) paints a shocking picture. Nearly one in four homeless persons is a child under 18. Over 1 million families are waiting for public housing. When poor children do have homes, more than half their family's income is spent on rent. Available housing, moreover, tends to be substandard, infested with rats and mice, overcrowded, and cold.

Ruth Crone, like other Washington, D.C. area residents, sees it every day. On her carpool commute for work from suburban Maryland, the executive director of the Metropolitan Washington Council of Governments (COG) experiences the diversity of a large metropolitan area. Its overall wealth has not prevented urban or suburban blight nor insulated its residents from social or infrastructural problems; yet the Washington metropolitan area, with all its complex, interjurisdictional problems, also contains wealth: wealth of skills, commitment, and resources.

Ruth realizes the challenges both to the children's futures and to those of the 4 million other people in the D.C. area. She is not discouraged, however. In fact, since she took over the COG in 1991, she has led 18 neighboring jurisdictions in making many innovative changes. Working with businesses, nonprofit organizations, and civic interest groups, COG collaborated with policy makers to increase public housing availability, expand foster care services, augment drug treatment and prevention education, and reduce water and air pollution. By forming partnerships, COG created resource bases for tackling some of the most insurmountable obstacles to community well-being.

Developing partnerships, however, requires skills for changing the ways that governments have traditionally interacted with both external and internal clientele. Coordinating information flow among different interests for reaching consensus, for instance, requires flexibility and responsiveness. However, in bureaucratically structured organizations such as COG, authority levels tend to filter information, making it easy to lose sight of a larger purpose. As a result, narrow political or mercenary interests often supplant decisions that would benefit a wider population. Preoccupation with the details of programs, in addition, can lead to decreased enthusiasm and creativity.

This chapter addresses these concerns in showing how Ruth Crone as a change agent used the right mix of intervention skills to create "community." The chapter contends that effective partnerships with different government interest groups depends in large part on the ability of the change agent to transform bureaucratic norms into a shared commitment to reaching common goals. Change agents facilitate such transformation through influencing diverse interest groups, making them realize how social problems affect the well-being of the greater society.

WHAT IS COMMUNITY?

Communities are social groups that meet together periodically to talk, share resources, and strive for mutually defined goals. Groups by themselves are not communities, however. Communities have interpersonal relationships that bind people together and enable them to interact closely. Working together on mutual interests, improving the common welfare, and making conditions better for future members are the hallmarks of community. There is typically a great deal of cordial intimacy among the participants. Communities share tacit knowledge and implicit trust.

Communities form when people face common crises successfully over time. They learn to use shared resources to accomplish goals that sustain,

Figure 13.1
Skills of Community Building

- Trust
- Inclusiveness
- Dialogue
- Identifying larger meaning
- Cultivating mutual respect
- Developing commitment to caring
- Fostering creativity

---

protect, and ensure the continuity of the group. Developing a particular set of symbols, such as language and customs, provides unique identities for community members and also serves as vehicles for communicating solidarity.

To meet common needs and purposes, communities solve problems through active participation. Historically, governments began as communities and became more bureaucratic as problems increased in complexity. Still, the need to have a face-to-face relationship to share problems and concerns has not diminished. Community relationships permit people to share the problems they have in common—and encourage each person to contribute solutions. Therefore, for government programs and services to truly benefit society, government needs to cultivate community support vigorously.

SKILLS OF COMMUNITY BUILDING

To encourage diverse social, economic, and political interest groups to develop innovative solutions to complex common problems, change agents can practice these skills: trust, inclusiveness, dialogue, identifying larger meaning, cultivating mutual respect, developing commitment to caring, and fostering creativity (Figure 13.1).

Trust

Trust is the foundation of community. Trust is the knowledge that you are respected for who you are, the assurance that others treat you as they do themselves, and the confidence that people's actions match their intentions. Without trust, there can be no honesty, commitment to the best interests of the group as a whole, and lasting change.

A lack of trust produces fear, which brings with it a multitude of problems. When organizations wrestle with the possibility of layoffs, for example, high-ranking officials may keep information secret. Not surprisingly, employees often interpret this as lying and play several defensive games as a result.

In one state agency, rumors of downsizing and mergers circulated for months after the conservative governor had appointed an associate as commissioner. The commissioner, who had been a career official before her appointment, gave out mixed signals. She approved a training program that enabled staff to form problem-solving teams but rarely endorsed the program. When staff members asked her for guidance, she postponed meetings. Over several months, confused and worried staffers fought with each other and with other departments. One day, only through reading the employee newsletter, two staff members discovered that their supervisor had been given a "pink slip." The atmosphere of secrecy was destroying the community of the agency.

Inclusiveness

Inclusiveness requires an unambiguous recognition of each individual's inherent worth as a human being, with a special focus on the contributions that each person can make to enhance both individual and group potential. Inclusiveness not only values diversity, but it goes a step further and actually uses it as a means to develop bonds of strength and unity. Inclusiveness creates sensitivities to issues that may otherwise go unnoticed—but could make the difference in succeeding with change.

Words and the meanings they connote reflect the extent of inclusiveness in small groups. A female human resources director in municipal government had initiated several programs to enhance the self-esteem and feeling of empowerment among women and minority employees. In the municipality, men held most managerial jobs and had developed a culture of "machoism." They used the term *boss* freely until the human resources director pointed out the demeaning effects it had, particularly on African Americans. Raising the concern helped stem the use of *boss* in meetings and other cross-jurisdictional functions.

Dialogue

Because people construct reality according to frames of reference that have meaning to them and describe their beliefs, thoughts, and attitudes in dialogue, dialogue produces insight. To assess the meaning of reality, change agents need to suspend their own critical judgments and listen to understand how others relate thoughts and feelings. Dialogue, especially from different points of view, widens the pool of information needed to solve particularly complex problems. Dialogue also encourages organizational members to share their commitment to resolve commonly faced issues.

Several conditions are necessary in order for real dialogue to take place. Individuals must set aside their status-based positions of power and listen to others as equals. Doing this requires training people to identify assumptions and analyze them critically. This may produce conflict, but the conflict should focus on issues and *not* on the people offering information. Moreover, dialogue facilitators need to recognize and affirm contributions and connect them to the larger purposes the group hopes to accomplish. Dialogue provides channels for information, personal acceptance, and solutions.

Identifying Larger Meaning

Dialogue often creates and transmits symbols that point toward commonly understood meaning. Symbols capture common threads of meaning and weave them into tapestries that people understand as a complete picture. Change agents use metaphors and rituals as types of symbolic forms to describe or characterize "reality" as people experience it.

In a federal agency that was downsizing, a change agent met with a small group of workers in a particular division and asked them to draw pictures of how they saw people and events. Several employees drew managers as snakes, dragons, and spiders. Their feelings of fear and pain stood out vividly in pictures of animals, people, or things being impaled, eaten, or burned alive. When the change agent asked for verbal descriptions from the employees, however, people did not speak up. The experience of sharing feelings and thoughts united the group around a common crisis; talking about it on a verbal level, however, not only increased the distance from their tacit understanding but also created the possibility that an outsider—the change agent or even some of the managers involved in the downsizing—would destroy their sense of unity.

Cultivating Mutual Respect

Community is characterized by deep and interdependent ties. It is strongest when people realize that to meet their own needs they have to consider the interests, needs, and welfare of others. Changes in one part of a work unit, division, or organization affect the lives of others through a steady ripple effect. Because people in a community want a better workplace for themselves and those who follow them, they examine the decisions they make today critically, because they will impact the organization as a whole both today and in the future.

In one government labor-management relations office, for instance, the manager worked closely with an employee representative to solve problems before they escalated. The manager and the union spokesperson jointly published helpful pamphlets that described frequent problems that managers encountered with employees and ways they could take action. The manager and the union representative also cotrained other managers in workshops, which enabled the managers to practice proactive, employee-centered supervisory techniques.

Developing Commitment to Caring

Change agents encourage people to take responsibility for the welfare of others. By highlighting the interdependency of people—what affects one person affects everyone—change agents can influence mutual concern and action taking.

In one state agency, managers rarely thanked employees for their contributions. Employees received cost-of-living pay increases but not verbal compliments or plaques. Managers seldom held meetings with employees, and when they did, they showed little commendation of individual or team effort. Employees, having few incentives for finding excitement in where they worked or joy in what they did, quickly lost the motivation to contribute their best efforts.

When a new agency head took over, he decided to intervene. One of his first acts was to compel managers to write "thank you" notes to employees. At first, managers laughed at the idea; but when the agency head followed up by checking with people who received the notes, managers began taking it seriously. The agency head, working with an outside consultant, held a management retreat to examine morale issues and identify some strategies that would resolve them. In addition, he began holding a series of informal but private discussions with small groups of employees and encouraged them to provide him with honest feedback. In turn, he shared his vision of how he hoped people in the agency would begin feeling that they were valued.

To supplement the discussions, the agency head created cross-functional teams that worked on specific problems of trust, communications, and valuing diversity. Over time, the managers came to realize the importance of participation in problem solving, openness in sharing feelings, and recognition of people for making the agency a more enjoyable place in which to work.

Fostering Creativity

Governments have tough problems to solve, limited financial resources, and massive barriers of red tape with which to contend. Yet creative thinking offers a too-often-untapped plethora of solutions. First, however, organizations need to foster a climate that accepts different ways of working, encourages innovative strategies, and is committed to continuous learning. The key to creativity is an attitude of openness.

In a federal agency, a human resources manager had to train all employees in a performance appraisal system that was based on setting and achieving measurable work objectives. As with most government organizations, operating objectives were imprecise; there was little direct correspondence between what the agency, the work unit, and the individual employee did. Further, the manager received no funds for implementing the system but was told the money would have to come from "overhead."

To cope with the constraints, the manager formed a cross-agency task force of managers, professional and technical employees, and clerical staff. The task force, composed of a highly skilled and experienced representation of the 5,000-member agency, developed a plan to train internal trainers, use in-house personnel staff to write policies and work plans, and provide technical assistance to help managers and employees write performance objectives and plans. The task force met periodically for six months to assess how well their plans were being implemented and adjusted their strategies when the policies or the training programs ran into problems. Within a year, the agency had accomplished its goal and had spent under $5,000.

USING COMMUNITY-BUILDING SKILLS

In creating community from among 18 county governments in the Washington area and scores of businesses, philanthropic and nonprofit organizations, and citizens groups, Ruth Crone used many of the skills we've already examined. These skills are evident in the seven strategies Ruth used to develop consensus, coordinate shared resources, and achieve common goals (*People and Partnerships*, 1995). They included collecting, analyzing, and disseminating data; sponsoring conferences and workshops; initiating committees, task forces, and forums to debate policy options; sponsoring research and demonstration projects; cosponsoring programs; administering grants; and recognizing and rewarding individuals and groups meeting larger social goals.

Collecting, Analyzing, and Disseminating Data

Change agents use data to bring about changes in people's thoughts and actions. COG creates a variety of data-based reports and shares them with the regional community. For instance, COG recently conducted a rent survey that challenged the figures the Housing and Urban Development (HUD) agency had issued, which underestimated the cost of affordable housing in the area. As a result of the study, 11,500 rental units that would have been excluded by HUD's new guidelines remained eligible for subsidies. The report also resulted in approximately $290,000 in additional federal subsidies for local administrative support.

Sponsoring Conferences and Workshops

In addition to printed data, change agents can use information through educational events to alter mental models and produce committed action. One example was COG's "Fostering Together" program for 250 foster parents and child welfare professionals in the area. To share information regarding the need for adequate foster care providers and for adoptive homes within the larger community, COG teamed with a local television station and a private sector foundation to produce the *Wednesday's Child* program. Each week, the *Wednesday's Child* program features foster children available for adoption and referral information for interested viewers. In 1995, COG set up a Foster Care Hope Line that in one year handled nearly 1,100 calls from area residents. In addition to the *Wednesday's Child* program, COG has recently worked with a local radio station to collect and distribute toys for foster children during the Christmas holidays.

Initiating Committees, Task Forces, and Forums to Debate Policy Options

Through dialogue, clientele can examine issues from multiple viewpoints and use the different insights to weld commitment to action. COG's Transportation Planning Board facilitated discussions and strategic planning among citizens, elected officials, and interested public and private organizations. The discussion, which COG named "Getting There," developed a consensus of vision for the Washington area's transportation system in the next century. To widen the discussion and planning process, COG dispatched a "vision van" to solicit input from people at such places as subway stations, schools, shopping malls, and community centers. As a result of the information, the Transportation Planning Board completed a final vision that became a blueprint for future planning.

Sponsoring Research and Demonstration Projects

Conducting applied research, and sharing results and implications, is another way to influence thinking and acting. Using a Gallup poll of 1,700 residents and nearly 500 businesses to determine the top environmental concerns of the area, COG joined with other Maryland, Virginia, and District of Columbia governments to sponsor an air quality research and action program. The program, "ENDZONE—Partners to End Ground-Level Ozone," also enlisted the help of government agencies, businesses, civic groups, and health and environmental organizations. The combined groups provided area residents with information about, and solutions to, the ground-level ozone problem.

The cornerstone of the campaign was the ozone forecasting program through which a team of meteorologists and technical staff from the University of Maryland, the Maryland Department of the Environment, the Virginia Department of Environmental Quality, and COG prepared the forecasts on predicted ozone levels for the next day. The team wrote a booklet, *Air Quality Forecast and Action Guide*, based on the research. It used a simple, four-color chart to designate ozone levels, weather conditions associated with those levels, and corresponding health and air pollution reduction actions, such as "Code Orange" for approaching unhealthful air quality and "Code Red" for unhealthful ground-level ozone levels.

Cosponsoring Programs

Working with other interests can not only result in shared commitment to particular objectives but also strengthens bonds among the interests themselves; the rewards of participation are often quite tangible. One of the ways COG encourages continued involvement is through providing members cost savings. The Cooperative Purchasing Program that COG administers has saved COG members more than $1.25 million in gasoline, diesel fuel, and heating oil purchases. The savings resulted from combining the requirements for a commodity or service from one or more jurisdictions and using the volume to obtain better unit pricing. By lowering administrative costs, moreover, additional savings resulted.

Administering Grants

In addition to gathering, assessing, disseminating, and discussing data, change agents can support collective action through providing project funding. One example is COG's use of a Federal Highway Administration Grant to launch a "red light running" enforcement program. Working with local police chiefs and the U.S. Department of Transportation, COG helped to reduce the number of traffic accidents caused by drivers running red lights.

Recognizing and Rewarding Individuals and Groups Meeting Larger Social Goals

To encourage community-wide acceptance of policies and programs, change agents reward people who have used innovations to achieve particular objectives. One example is COG's goal to encourage environmental stewardship through recycling. To promote the idea that recycling is valuable, COG usually gives local employers awards for outstanding achievements in recycling, waste reduction, recycled product purchases, and environmental education. COG supplements the awards program by describing the awardees' programs and practices in a regional markets directory that also lists processors and what materials they accept.

SUMMARY

In their historical roles as solvers of society-wide problems, governments are primary community-building agencies. In fulfilling their vital roles, however, governments face several obstacles. Citizens, legislatures, and the media clamor for greater accountability for public funding and quality of services but have not provided sufficient moral or material support for governments to perform their roles fairly and equitably. When governments fail, or are perceived to fail, trust declines and community cohesiveness deteriorates. The perceptions become reality, forcing a vicious downward spiral of decreasing productivity, increased distrust, and additional failures.

Change agents can help break this cycle. By forming a variety of mutually beneficial ties with civic, business, professional, and academic organizations, they can allow other community affiliations to more clearly see the common needs people face. The partnerships galvanize concern, commitment, and resource contributions.

Building community bonds rests on practicing seven core relationship skills: trust, inclusiveness, dialogue, identifying larger meaning, mutual respect, caring, and creativity. Without developing interpersonal relationships, people cannot adequately solve problems affecting both themselves and their communities. But when mutual problems are solved, they not only address current conditions but also prepare for a healthier environment for future generations. Thus, to the extent that communities improve their well-being, the greater the likelihood they will survive.

Teaching people skills for community building, however, is never easy. Change agents frequently confront barriers such as distrust, fear, outdated and erroneous cause maps, turf protection, stereotypes, and a lack of the basic technological skills necessary for change. The aim is to reduce the misinformation and interpersonal bias before introducing innovations. The next chapter describes ways in which the change agent can introduce innovations through integrating both individual skills building and organizational learning.

REFERENCES

Children's Defense Fund. (1995). *The state of America's children yearbook 1995.* Washington, D.C.

Peck, M. S. (1987). *The different drum: Community making and peace.* New York: Simon and Schuster.

People and partnerships: Metropolitan Washington Council of Governments 1995 Annual Report. (1995). Washington, D.C.: Metropolitan Washington Council of Governments.

CHAPTER 14

Holistic Learning: Integrating Individual and Organizational Change

No man can reveal to you aught but that which already lies half asleep in the dawning of your knowledge. The teacher who walks in the shadow of the temple, among his followers, gives not of his wisdom but rather of his faith and his lovingness. If he is indeed wise he does not bid you enter the house of his wisdom, but rather leads you to the threshold of your own mind.

—Kahlil Gibran (1966). *The Prophet*

A key outcome of organizational change is teaching people how to take responsibility for directing their own learning. Change agents can teach skills for diagnosing problems, suggesting interventions, and helping people restructure work processes and outcomes to achieve particular organization goals. But unless people learn new ways of thinking and doing (and adapt change agent suggestions to their own conditions), organizational change does not occur. People have to do the hard work of making changes.

This chapter enables change agents to understand their roles in facilitating change, as equippers, brokers, influencers, and exhorters. It also describes the processes that individuals use in learning organizational settings. Individual responsibility for learning depends on motivations, opportunities, rewards, and satisfaction. Moreover, organizations share responsibilities for helping members learn through improving such processes as communications, rewards, and management functions. The chapter illustrates how change agents can fulfill their roles of connecting individual and organization learning processes and systems through a case study of self-managed project teams in Windsor, Connecticut.

WHAT IS HOLISTIC LEARNING?

Holistic learning assumes that people learn with their whole beings. Human learning processes integrate cognitive functions, such as recall and memory, with affective functions, such as valuing and believing, and result in some form of change. The change can be observable, as when individuals perform a skill or task they were not able to perform before learning. The change can also be nonobservable: Individuals learn when they experience a flash of insight, when they become aware of a gap in information, when cognitive maps no longer "make sense," or when they see situations differently than they did before. Learning affects all areas of an individual's mental, emotional, motivational, and physical realms of being (Vaill, 1996).

Holistic learning also depends on the richness of the context in which people live. Environmental cues trigger ideas, feelings, and questions, for instance, that individuals interpret and act on. Change agents can facilitate an enriched learning context through presenting cues as factual material, arranging small-group discussions, and providing testing and assessment activities.

Holistic learning also assumes that people learn from each other (Merriam and Caffarella, 1991). Because people construct meaning from environmental cues, holistic learning depends on the depth of interaction that takes place between people. In many organizations, bureaucratic structures prevent people from sharing vital information, giving honest opinions about particular topics, or talking about matters that touch on feelings, spirituality, or home and family life. Holistic learning opens channels that permit integrating personal and professional realms.

THE ROLES OF THE CHANGE AGENT IN LEARNING

In bringing about holistic learning, the change agent plays both direct and indirect roles. Direct roles involve teaching skills in a structured or deliberate format to achieve specific outcomes. Classroom instruction is the most common form. Indirect roles are catalytic. In playing these roles, change agents influence learning by modeling certain behaviors, providing coaching or counseling, or changing information flow systems in organizations.

In performing either direct or indirect roles, change agents accomplish four primary objectives: to equip people with skills, attitudes, and abilities; to connect people with resources for putting new ideas, information, and strategies into action; to influence motivation to learn; and to encourage people to take responsibility for making specific changes in their work environments.

Equippers

Change agents provide skills, attitudes, and abilities to help people to either improve their performance of particular tasks, learn new tasks, or prepare for future responsibilities. Most often, this comes about through training programs. Change agents identify key "end states" and direct people toward them. Change agents often develop performance measures that indicate whether learners have adequately reached the goals and whether the behaviors will transfer successfully to workplace settings to solve particular problems.

Change agents reinforce formal skills by using their own behaviors, values, and attitudes. This may occur as training program participants observe how the change agent views problems, frames solutions, involves others, and solicits feedback for support, guidance, and assessment. Ideally, the change agent who teaches skills formally is available following training sessions as mentor and coach. For optimal transfer of learning to the workplace, the change agent coaches and models skills for the managers of individuals who have undergone formal training. Because managers provide opportunities, skills reinforcement, and rewards, they are pivotal in augmenting formal learning (Broad and Newstrom, 1992; Goldstein, 1993).

Resource Brokers

Change agents help individuals locate or create resources for adapting new skills, abilities, and knowledge for the workplace. Location may involve connecting people with additional knowledge or experience in particular areas through networks. Professional associations, for instance, have many sources for facilitating continuing education.

In addition, change agents help organization members identify and develop resources that may previously have been unknown or underutilized. This involves removing obstacles, such as inadequate information flow, a lack of knowledge regarding policies and procedures for performing particular tasks, and limited access to technical resources and funds. Many obstacles lie in organizational culture norms and practices. The "glass ceiling," for instance, has prevented many talented women and minority employees from contributing fully and adequately to organizational programs (Morrison, 1987).

Because brokering resources and removing obstacles often require advocating specific changes in organizational policies and practices, change agents work directly with top management. In public organizations, the dual elected/careerist organizational structure makes this difficult. Change

Figure 14.1
Disincentives to Individual and Organizational Learning

- Inadequate prior learning
- Insufficient time
- Little perceived job relevance
- No organization support

---

agents may not know which manager in which department has the authority to make decisions about policy, personnel, or budget issues. Accordingly, the change agent must use influence tactics with a widely different set of clients and create a basis for broad consensus in decision making. To complicate matters further, the change agent's recommendations often end up as committee decision items; this could mean the committee holds lengthy discussions and reaches compromises before they make a final decision.

Motivators

Change agents influence not only the "how" of performance but also the "why." They help people value learning as a means of improving both their personal and their professional competencies. Motivation is a product of change agent influence and learner valuation. To motivate people to learn, change agents connect purposes and outcomes of learning with various levels of human needs within learners. Maslow (1987), for instance, identified the needs for basic survival, security, belonging, self-integrity, and self-actualization as influencing actions. By connecting human needs with reasons for trying out change strategies, change agents can influence motivation.

People themselves must attach value to the change strategies, however. Not only must they see the relevance of these strategies to personal and professional needs, but they must also recognize the relationship of the strategies to their immediate work situations. To make this connection requires people to identify both the obstacles and the catalysts of adaptation (Lewin, 1951).

Some main reasons why individuals do not feel motivated to make changes are the following (Figure 14.1).

Inadequate Prior Learning. People may lack fundamental skills for understanding and applying the change strategies. Change agents may have to reteach such skills as basic reading and listening comprehension, writing, and computation before individuals are ready to begin learning more complex skills sets. In addition, change agents may enable people with little or no experience opportunities to learn from performing similar tasks and skills in a simulated or laboratory learning context. Change agents may use such skills as assessment, feedback, and coaching to ensure participants can perform the skills outside the training environment and in the actual workplace (Broad and Newstrom, 1992).

Insufficient Time. Widespread organizational restructuring has required people to fill two or more jobs. Working 12-hour days leaves little time and energy to attend conferences, workshops, or professional meetings. Moreover, cramped schedules in which people perform administrative, professional, and managerial tasks leave little time to reflect on processes or learn from doing (Mezirow and Associates, 1990; Schon, 1987). Few people have the skills necessary to (on their own) analyze their work process relationships, make adequate and correct diagnoses of problems, and devise innovative strategies to correct dysfunctions. Change agents can work with managers and employees to restructure work to allow for on-the-job learning.

Little Perceived Job Relevance. Unless people can see direct relationships between what change agents teach and on-the-job situations in which they can apply ideas and strategies, they have little incentive to apply skills. Moreover, because many organizations devote less than 5 percent of their overhead budgets to human resource development, they do not sponsor training that lacks a measurable return on investment (Killian, 1976). Programs developing human relations, stress management, and interpersonal communications, the "soft skills," are essential to job performance and productivity but may take several months or years before they bear fruit. Change agents should address this by developing a draft learning contract with training participants to use following training. Participants identify specific tasks they perform and want to improve, or tasks they may perform in the future. With their managers, participants negotiate how they will use the training. Furthermore, change agents may work with participant managers prior to training to plan costs, expected and measurable outcomes, and net dollar returns.

No Organization Support. Organizational cultures may inhibit learning not only because people do not see the relevance of learning but also because such learning may threaten the status quo assumptions and managerial power structures. These organizations may sanction what Argyris and Schon (1978) call "defensive routines," such as filtering and distorting information sent to internal and external constituents, uncritically accepting assumptions as valid, and creating and disseminating cause maps that uphold and substantiate status quo practices. Organizations may erect boundaries around certain functions and isolate certain tasks as sacrosanct. Learning that inquires into the issue of functions often triggers turf wars in which learners become casualties.

To improve the likelihood that organizations will value training, change agents can make training programs integral components of an overall change effort. They can train managers and employees as a natural work team by encouraging a new approach to work.

In addition, change agents can use training to prepare people for organizational changes. One example occurred as a change agent worked with a public organization that was redesigning its automated information systems. The change agent facilitated a team of cross-agency subject-matter experts from across the organization to identify both obstacles and opportunities for systems improvement. To prevent the team from reverting to the existing system that had contributed to the current dysfunction, the change agent spent a day training the team in creative thinking techniques. This enabled team members to envision a state that could be achieved realistically, allowed critical thinking and feedback, and also produced a novel system.

Encourager of Responsibility Taking

Ironically, even as change agents strive to open up organizations, some members may still refuse to accept significant change. By creating conditions that empower people, in large part by improving management structures and systems, change agents enable people to overcome this reluctance. Preparing people through education is a critical first step. This involves providing job-related knowledge, teaching people how to analyze, diagnose, and intervene in the problems that affect them. The change agent must clearly demonstrate how theoretical information can be applied to existing organizational processes and systems, including redesigning work relationships to facilitate on-the-job learning and satisfaction. In brief, the more individuals involved in the change can make changes they feel necessary to make their jobs easier and more productive, the more commitment they will have to "owning" the change.

STRATEGIES FOR INTEGRATING INDIVIDUAL AND ORGANIZATIONAL LEARNING

Because all areas of individual existence participate in learning processes and because individuals construct organizational realities, learning that affects people also affects organizations. The task of the change agent is not only to strengthen the likelihood that individuals will want to learn but also to create opportunities and rewards for people to *apply* learning. The change agent can facilitate this by integrating individual and organizational change strategies (Figure 14.2).

Figure 14.2
Integrating Individual and Organizational Learning

- Use incremental approaches
- Train others in consulting skills
- Use project consultant teams
- Align policy and practice synthesis
- Redesign work flow

Use Incremental Approaches

In public bureaucracies, short-term operating goals, fragmented account-ability and resource structures, and multiple, overlapping, and often con-flicting political and administrative interests make large-scale change difficult to achieve. An incremental approach works best. Incremental change improves conditions within specific operating units. These condi-tions, however, often extend beyond the units into other areas of an or-ganization. Accordingly, change agents need to involve individuals whose functions in some way contribute to a focal problem affecting many units.

Incremental changes to organizational systems enable people dealing di-rectly with focal problems to solve them. Making small-scale changes en-ables people to take responsibility to act. People closest to the focal problem are in perhaps the best position to solve it (Elden and Levin, 1991). Their familiarity should be used as a blueprint for tracing relationships of the focal problem to other parts of the organization. These people can also identify additional resources that can be brought to bear in solving the problem. And they also have the basic knowledge and skills necessary to create novel solutions.

In addition, incremental changes benefit organizations in that they do not require large budget expenditures and layers of hierarchical approval. Typically, they become part of individuals' day-to-day job responsibilities and thus do not cut into other units' domains. Incremental changes, more-over, produce tangible, quick-turnaround results that signal "lookin' good success" to election-wary politicians.

Train Others in Consultant Skills

Change agents may integrate the incremental approach with team train-ing to enhance both individual and organizational learning. People dealing with small-scale, focal problems on a recurring basis are candidates for training in consultant skills. Change agents may teach such people skills in

developing contracts or agreements for making changes, diagnosing problems, collecting and analyzing data, presenting data and recommendations
for solution strategies, recognizing and confronting resistance to change,
collaborating in solution generation and implementation, and assessing and
evaluating implementation strategies (Lippitt and Lippitt, 1986).

Use Project Consultant Teams

Following training, the change agent can increase the chances that participants will attain key outcomes and will adapt skills, knowledge, and
concepts if people work in teams. Teams of three or four participants may
select a project that addresses a particular focal problem or issue shared by
a number of people across organizational boundaries. Working with managers and others having an interest in solving particular work-related problems, participants can form a consultant team (Hirschorn, 1991).

They develop a contract with people with whom they will work. This
contract addresses such requirements as (1) problem description; (2) data
collection and analysis strategies; (3) data presentation and solution generations; (4) implementation strategies; (5) estimate of time, staff, technical,
and financial support; (6) expected outcomes; and (7) assessment and evaluation strategies (Broad and Newstrom, 1992; Margulies and Wallace,
1973).

Project teams strengthen learning in several ways. First, they examine
multiple viewpoints, exploring different solution options and inventing
strategies. This is accomplished by permitting an interpersonal exchange of
information that typically leads to synergistic thinking and commitment to
unified action. Second, teams reinforce what individuals have learned and
extend concepts and skills to broader contexts. Third, they use multiple
forms of power and influence to accomplish their tasks. Not only do teams
expand expertise as a form of power, but they also have "connection
power" with top managers. This gives teams both legitimacy and status.
Fourth, they bring turf issues to light. Teams find solutions that meet common needs rather than narrowly defined organizational interests.

Align Policy and Practice Synthesis

Change agents also work to help organizations align policies and practices that have contributed to focal problems. Change agents can act both
as spokespersons for the teams and as advocates for changing how people
perceive and enact job roles. Working with midlevel, executive, and non-
career managers, change agents can help those in positions of power examine the relationships between cognitive frameworks and follower
interpretation. Through data collected, analyzed, and presented to people

whom change affects, change agents can encourage people to align frameworks with interpreted reality.

Redesign Work Flow

To examine the relationships between practices and policies, change agents can conduct training and follow-up coaching to help managers and employees in project teams redesign work. Redesigning work allows people to experience greater motivation from more intrinsically satisfying work and opportunities for learning on the job. In analyzing how they perform tasks, managers and employees can diagnose problems (Weisbord, 1991). With the technical guidance of change agents, managers and employees can target specific goals and design solution implementation plans.

CASE EXAMPLE: SELF-MANAGED PROJECT TEAMS

In Windsor, Connecticut, town manager Albert G. Ilg successfully integrated individual and organizational learning in introducing the novel concept of self-managed teams. Begun as a pilot project in 1990, self-managed teams provide employees with decentralized decision-making authority, opportunities to create innovative solutions to problems, and intrinsic rewards from controlling the management of work processes. Self-managed teams not only have increased efficiency through the use of total quality management techniques but also have sparked employee enthusiasm and creativity.

Self-Managed Teams

Self-managed teams are cohesive groups of employees who design, develop, and carry out services to internal and external customers. Such teams may consist of lead employees or team leaders who work on a specific process or major subprocess. Wellins, Byham, and Wilson (1991) and Carr and Littman (1990) list several common leadership responsibilities self-managed teams share:

1. Planning, controlling, and changing their own work conditions
2. Setting goals, developing performance indicators, and tracking project goal progress
3. Preparing budgets
4. Coordinating with other units
5. Administering contracts
6. Determining training needs
7. Participating in cross-organizational training programs

8. Hiring and disciplining members

9. Taking primary responsibility for quality of services and products.

Self-Managed Teams in Windsor Town Government

Begun as one of two pilot projects in 1990, the Family Services Unit is responsible for providing individuals and families with day care, individual and group counseling, case management, leisure activities, and emergency financial support. The unit does not have a manager, but it does have a service unit leader. This person oversees budget and cost accounting of services and coordinates information with the town council and other agencies and with citizens. The 23-member service unit meets weekly in small, function-specific groups with the service unit leader to plan services, make operating decisions, and discuss needs and opportunities for training. An organization chart appears in Figure 14.3.

The four-person youth and family services therapy counselors team uses problem-solving processes typical of a service unit. Before the pilot team was formed, the town's counseling program had a lengthy waiting list. One of the team's first goals was to devise an intake system that would schedule people for appointments soon after they asked for assistance. To meet the goal, the team decided to assign appointments by degree of problem severity. People who were experiencing a crisis saw a counselor immediately. People with less serious problems made counseling appointments, but their assigned counselor gave them helpful information to read before they met. The solution erased the waiting list. Each of the four team members oversaw the team's five functions: personnel, budget, quality and statistics management, program administration, and community liaison.

Training

Since the pilot, the town's 187 full-time employees were reorganized into eight service units. Each service unit receives continuous training in such areas as principles of TQM, customer service, teamwork, problem solving, and management and leadership skills. Participating in training programs allowed employees to learn of common needs and implementation problems; it also helped them develop a broader perspective of the organization by learning from each other.

Although the self-managed teams do not have "bosses," they do use a strategy team to coordinate and manage cross-cutting issues and work flow design. Volunteers from each of the eight service units serve on the strategy team. Commonly, they discuss internal and external customer needs, analyze customer service delivery processes, align individual service unit missions with customer needs and organizational service strategies, discuss

Figure 14.3
An Organization Chart of the Town of Windsor, Connecticut

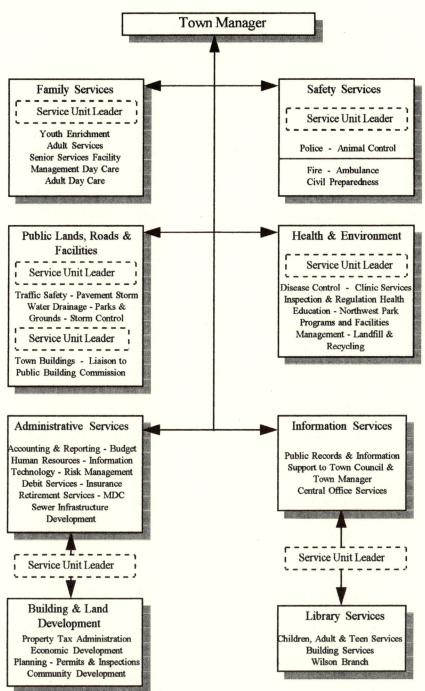

options for redeploying service unit team members to resolve cross-cutting organizational problems, and develop statistical performance measurements and tracking systems.

Obstacles and Strategies

Town Manager Ilg encountered several forms of resistance when he introduced the self-managed team concept to the nine-member town council. He discussed the concept for five years both with the council and with top career managers and union officials, arguing that the town could provide public services more efficiently through a dual approach of serving customer needs and using participatory management.

Ilg noted that midlevel managers resisted the most. "Getting midlevel managers to stop giving orders and begin coaching," he said, was the most difficult barrier. The conversion took several years to complete.

The management processes, according to Ilg, inhibited productive changes in several ways. By using command and control decision-making techniques, managers shut off knowledge of what needs others had. Consequently, managers set goals that lacked clarity and focused on narrow interests. Because decisions required several levels of signatures, service provision dragged and lost gusto. Conflict between organizational levels and among the town's departments raged. Employees experienced high levels of mistrust.

"There were too many internal customer service roadblocks to timely service," Ilg pointed out. "Employees who were used to unsuccessful change attempts in the past refused to believe the service unit approach would work."

Some employees, moreover, have had difficulty accepting the team-based approach. Unfamiliar with making their own decisions, these employees experienced anxiety in performing their new participatory roles. Midlevel managers in the organization, in fact, decreased, from 11 to 7—an event that saved the town more than $100,000 in operating costs. The *Hartford Courant* (Swift, 1991), in an interview with various team members, quoted a town garage mechanic, who noted, "The building is us now. You're not just coming to work to do what somebody else says." But the employee admitted that the work team took time away from hands-on mechanic work. He added that people did not like empowerment and would rather "just do the job."

Although the town provides training, some employees, such as the garage mechanic, do not feel it is adequate. In particular, people believe training should increase communications competencies, budgeting skills, and quality measurements.

Ilg also noted that employee union representatives expressed fears of layoffs. But he steadfastly maintained that the team structure was an honest effort toward changing a culture that had for years been unsuccessful—and it would *not* result in loss of employment. The team concept, moreover, would be introduced gradually. Ilg added that no one's responsibilities would be dropped until everyone was trained and confident of their abilities to manage whole job responsibilities. He stressed that the implementation of the teams would conform to existing union contract language.

Ilg persuaded the town council to accept the program based, in large part, on his extensive record of public sector innovations, having served for nearly 25 years as town manager, introducing numerous economic and community development projects. In the early 1970s, Ilg set up a child development center that parents paid for themselves from tuition fees. He also attracted commercial development to Windsor. Corporations such as Cigna Insurance settled in the community and generated half of the town's tax revenues. This kept citizen tax bases low. Ilg also brought in a landfill operation that today saves the town tipping fees. He also introduced the concept of a health maintenance organization (HMO) through obtaining a $1 million federal grant.

Even before coming to Windsor, Ilg had scored an impressive record of innovations. As assistant town manager of Oak Ridge, Tennessee, he had worked with the town manager to convert the city from a federal reservation and site of the Manhattan Project to a municipal government. This involved hiring nearly 250 employees and starting police and fire departments from scratch.

"In a number of ways," Ilg remarked, "Windsor has been a laboratory. The council here has always created an environment that permits experimentation. They've not been afraid to let me try things."

SUMMARY AND OBSERVATIONS

Ilg's record of accomplishments as a change agent resulted from his vision of empowered teams and his leadership in enhancing organizational improvement. In particular, he shared creative ideas, built consensus with several organizational stakeholders, used small-scale team experimentation, and devoted a great deal of time and financial resources to educating employees continuously in participatory leadership techniques.

In performing his role as change agent, Ilg removed many of the hierarchical structures, such as decision-making levels and processes that prevented direct customer contact. This provided employees with opportunities to redesign their jobs and enrich their roles. With training in skills to help them perform their new roles, moreover, and team-based experiences to apply the skills to common problems, these workers developed abilities that had lain fallow.

The possible inadequacy of training, however, and the apparent absence of any significant coaching somewhat limit the development. Accordingly, those who feel ill-equipped to fulfill their newly empowered roles experience feelings of irrelevance to their jobs and a desire to return to the old, familiar hierarchical relationships in which managers made all the decisions. Training and coaching in large doses seem essential to the informal learning that people encounter from team experiences.

Change agents typically experience dilemmas in guiding people with different learning needs through various changes. One of Ilg's dilemmas was similar to Fromm's (1941) question, "Can people really handle freedom?" If not, what can—or should—the change agent do to turn things around? A bigger question, however, is, Should the change agent help at all?

The next chapter tackles this vitally important question. It explores the values dilemmas that change agents so often encounter when leading change in government bureaucracies.

REFERENCES

Argyris, C., and Schon, D. A. (1978). *Organizational learning*. Reading, MA: Addison-Wesley.

Broad, M. L., and Newstrom, J. W. (1992). *Transfer of training*. Reading, MA: Addison-Wesley.

Carr, D. K. and Littman, J. D. (1990). *Excellence in government*. Arlington, VA: Coopers & Lybrand.

Elden, M., and Levin, M. (1991). Cogenerative learning: Bringing participation into action research. In W. F. Whyte (Ed.), *Participatory action research* (127–142). Newbury Park, CA: Sage.

Fromm, E. (1941). *Escape from freedom*. New York: Farrar and Rinehart.

Gibran, K. (1966). *The prophet*. New York: Alfred A. Knopf.

Goldstein, I. L. (1993). *Training in organizations* (3rd ed.). Pacific Grove, CA: Brooks/Cole.

Hirschorn, L. (1991). *Managing in the new team environment: Skills, tools, and methods*. Reading, MA: Addison-Wesley.

Killian, R. A. (1976). *Managing human resources: An ROI approach*. New York: AMACOM.

Lewin, K. (1951). *Field theory in social science*. New York: Harper and Row.

Lippitt, G., and Lippitt, R. (1986). *The consulting process in action* (2nd ed.). San Diego, CA: University Associates.

Margulies, N., and Wallace, J. (1973). *Organizational change: Techniques and applications*. Glenview, IL: Scott, Foresman.

Maslow, A. H. (1987). *Motivation and personality* (3rd ed.). New York: Harper and Row.

Merriam, S. B., and Caffarella, R. S. (1991). *Learning in adulthood: A comprehensive guide*. San Francisco: Jossey-Bass.

Mezirow, J., and Associates. (1990). *Fostering critical reflection in adulthood*. San Francisco: Jossey-Bass.

Morrison, A. (1987). *Breaking the glass ceiling: Can women reach the top of America's largest corporations?* Reading, MA: Addison-Wesley.

Schon, D. A. (1987). *Educating the reflective practitioner*. San Francisco: Jossey-Bass.

Swift, M. (1991, November 17). A quarter century of Ilg. *Hartford Courant*.

Vaill, P. B. (1996). *Learning as a way of being*. San Francisco: Jossey-Bass.

Wellins, R. S., Byham, R. C. and Wilson, J. M. (1991). *Empowered teams*. San Francisco: Jossey-Bass.

Weisbord, M. R. (1991). *Organizational diagnosis: A workbook of theory and practice*. Reading, MA: Addison-Wesley.

PART V

Wholeness in Organizational Transformation

CHAPTER 15

Change as the Ethics of Concern

What does it mean to be concerned about something? It means that we are involved in it, that a part of ourselves is in it, that we participate with our hearts. And it means even more than that. It points to the way in which we are involved, namely, *anxiously*.
—Paul Tillich (1955). *The New Being*

Changing organizations from the inside out involves making and carrying out a series of ethical choices. The change process, by definition, requires inquiring into problems and issues that have blocked effectiveness and efficiency. It entails turning up and sorting through past records of choices and their effects on present functioning. The records come from interviews with people who have experienced problem situations or have heard about them in organizational stories. Records also include organizational policies and practices. Inquiry looks at current relationships between organizational structures, power, and people. Inquiry seeks to understand how values and actions began and how they perpetuated themselves. In the process of asking, the change agent encounters ethical dilemmas on many fronts. An example occurred recently in a state agency that began to examine issues of mistrust on personal and departmental levels. The acting agency head had appointed a cross-functional task force to pinpoint concerns and to make recommendations for addressing them. The highest priority went to the segregated parking system.

Senior staff and managers had parking spaces reserved for them that were close to the main entrance of the headquarters building. Clerical, lower-graded, and junior professionals, however, had to park behind the lot and walk several hundred yards to the building. In winter months, it was particularly troublesome because the agency seldom plowed the lower-graded employee lot completely. When less-senior employees parked in the reserved spots, they received tickets, but senior staff parking in the employee lot did not. The issues the task force raised were not about convenience but rather of injustice. Dismantling the segregated parking lot policy symbolized a storming of the agency bastille.

For over 20 years, employees had lived with a two-tiered status system. For various reasons, however, bringing it up for discussion was off limits. The previous agency director had not only sealed the issue from dialogue but had added injustices on top of it. One particularly irksome practice was hiring external consultants and friends to carry out projects, particularly those internal staff could have done themselves. Unqualified people filled top agency positions, and their seductive mannerisms chafed both insiders and people outside the agency. The actions reinforced the perception that status makes its own rules.

Initiating inquiry opened many old wounds, but the acting director was willing to take the risk. Unless the task force could pull out the deeply rooted injustices, beginning with the parking lot, healing would not occur. The dilemma of healing, however, raised even greater problems. How much more would surface? How would the new issues affect the already damaged workforce? Would doing so ultimately solve the injustice problem, or would it create further divisions between the more privileged and the less so? Moreover, whose values should pave the way for a more egalitarian workforce? And what guarantee would there be that new policies would not get at the root problem? Would the old injustice crop up again in spite of reform efforts?

Change induces anxiety because change agents face ethical dilemmas with each choice they make. Ethics are principles that people interpret from a framework of moral values and apply to specific situations. Dilemmas result when the moral values collide and produce ambiguous consequences. In the case example, a key ethical dilemma involved the clash of status quo, elitist values versus egalitarian ones over rights to parking. The acting director was hemmed in the middle. If he acted on the basis of his prerogatives as one of the elites, he would have protected his own interests and endeared the support of colleagues. But this would have alienated the lower-status employees even more. Instead, he chose to forego his own status-based values set and adopt values that would enhance the greater good. It was still questionable, however, in that the lower-status people could have rejected the move on the belief that he was "buying them off."

This chapter examines ethical dilemmas involved in changing organizations, particularly in the public sector. It describes five major contexts

Figure 15.1
Contexts of Ethical Dilemmas

- Individual values
- Organizational culture
- National culture
- Universal values
- Situational values

---

where moral values in ethical dilemmas may arise and describes eight factors that contribute to problematic roles and responsibilities. From this, the
chapter proposes a values assessment change agents may use to resolve key
dilemmas.

CONTEXTS OF ETHICAL DILEMMAS IN ORGANIZATIONAL CHANGE

The frameworks by which people interpret moral values and apply them
to given situations may come from one or more contexts. Briefly, these
include frameworks from individuals' socialized values, organizational culture, social or national culture, "universal" values, and situational values
(Figure 15.1).

Socialized Values

People acquire values from participating in numerous social institutions
over a lifetime. From family environments, people learn such norms as
caring for others, taking responsibility for one's own actions, and contributing resources to the common good. From schools, people learn to integrate cognitive skills with values associated with application of knowledge;
learning to value knowledge as a means for achieving a goal, winning peer
recognition, and improving financial status, for instance, carry through
from childhood to adulthood. Religious institutions, such as churches, syn-
agogues, and mosques, provide additional values by which people evaluate
"rightness" of particular attitudes and actions. Socialized values continue
to evolve as individuals mature.

Change agents may experience dilemmas that come from people's previous social role experiences. Some employees may resist training that does
not have an explicit payoff, such as for promotion or pay increase. Other
employees may believe that certain moral issues affect relationships at
work. For instance, a supervisor refused to grant medical leave above the
agency-established limits to an employee with AIDS. The supervisor be-

lieved the employee "deserved" the disease because of the homosexual life-style that the employee had selected.

Organizational Culture

Organizations have their own particular values that they hold as true and good. Values, according to Schein (1985), form an important foundation to organizational culture. Values provide the stage from which organizational members define, assess, and act, as they did in the parking lot case.

Organizational cultures have an overarching character, or unique identity. Organizations also contain variations, however. Subcultures may have dissimilar values because of differences in geography, clients served, and organizational structure.

Headquarters and field offices of single agencies exemplify this. Headquarters offices, because they often serve a broader clientele, have many specialized functions. To coordinate services effectively and efficiently, headquarters offices have multiple layers of authority. In contrast, field offices tend to be smaller, serve diverse needs of specific clientele, and have fewer levels of authority. In field offices, flexibility through decentralized authority structures is essential.

The differences, moreover, influence the types of values and behaviors people in headquarters and field offices have. Because people in field offices have more face-to-face interactions with clients, relationships are more personal and less concerned with following rules rigidly. Headquarters staff, on the other hand, may use formal rules more often.

Changing values and practices, particularly when they counter those the organization upholds, takes much time and may occur only in certain parts of an organization. Introducing change in a large, bureaucratic office frequently requires selecting conditions that will most likely bring success. Good candidates include offices that have an innovative manager, low degrees of interpersonal conflict, sufficient implementation resources, and records of previous successful changes. In introducing change, the change agent must assess the degree of readiness of organizations to adapt.

National Culture

Geert Hofstede (1991) points out that each nation has cultural values that mentally program people to think and act in common ways. Studying over 117,000 people in a multinational corporation in 51 countries, Hofstede identified four central values systems that characterize different nations. In brief, these include power distance, uncertainty avoidance, individualism-collectivism, and masculinity-femininity.

Power distance is the extent to which a society accepts the fact that power in organizations is unequally distributed. In high power distance countries, such as India, people rarely speak out against injustice for fear of losing their jobs. In the United States, which has a moderate degree of power distance, people tolerate higher levels of dissent.

Uncertainty avoidance is the extent to which a society feels ambiguous situations pose threats. Through using many formal-legal codes, for instance, some countries provide specified ways for dealing with uncertainty. Rules-following provides security. In Germany, for instance, offices close promptly at 4:30 P.M. even if people wait in line for service. If U.S. officeworkers did this, the angry customers would complain to management of rudeness.

Individualism-collectivism is the extent to which individuals are expected to care for their own needs in relation to a larger group or clan. In the highly individualized United States, for instance, people are expected to provide for their own medical health coverage. In Sweden, however, the state assumes the responsibility.

Masculinity-femininity is the extent to which a nation emphasizes traditional "male" and "female" social roles. In highly "masculine" countries, such as Austria, men are expected to be assertive, and women, nurturing. Workers in masculine countries achieve measurable goals and value performance, but in feminine ones, harmonious interpersonal relationships supersede goal achievement.

In general, organizations mirror the cultural values of the larger, national values systems. Thus, in the United States, organizations tend to have overarching values of high individualism, moderate masculinity-femininity and uncertainty avoidance, and low power distance. As noted, however, organizations vary according to formal structure, geographical centrality, and clientele. Government organizations have different cultural values. They tend to show high degrees of individualism, masculinity, uncertainty avoidance, and power distance.

The differences in government versus nongovernment U.S organizations pose change dilemmas. For instance, government employees may resist working in cooperative, team-based projects. Teams require high levels of interpersonal skills to succeed in carrying out tasks. Further, decentralized authority relationships may create situations in which standard operating systems do not apply. People may experience high levels of anxiety and frustration. In addition, rewards frequently do not go to individual contributors but to the team as a whole. Over time, motivation and productivity may both lag.

Universal Values

Denhardt (1988) points out that philosophers have continually debated whether there are certain "universal" values that give standards for conduct. "Deontological" or universal values are standards that people use to evaluate actions. Mackie (1990) acknowledges that judgments may involve subjectively evaluating "goodness" or "rightness," for instance, but they do so on premises widely accepted as true. Brink (1989, 7) notes that the universal values are "independent of our beliefs about what is right and wrong."

Many professional associations as well as public and private organizations define the meaning and application of universal or deontological values in codes of ethics. In particularly murky situations or in crises, codes of ethics spell out what behaviors organizations sanction and which they punish.

Codes of ethics tend to reflect organizational culture values and norms. Based largely on an organization's mission, history, and values that have produced "success," the ethics become accepted ways of doing things. Violations bring trouble. One military organization, for instance, had a strict report-for-duty norm. Each employee was expected to be on post at 8:00 A.M. sharp—a tradition that stemmed from the Revolutionary War era. When a new supervisor who had begun working in the organization during one particularly snowy winter excused a 15-minute tardiness because of weather, the unwitting supervisor received a verbal reprimand.

Situational Values

Other scholars maintain that there are no universal values, but, rather, people decide the goodness or rightness of actions on whether such actions achieved a desirable goal. "Teleological" or "end-state" values derive their justification from situational conditions. Frederickson (1997) maintains that most of the values in public organizations stem from situations. This is true especially when situations, such as budget appropriations, lie beyond people's control. For instance, a manager may defend spending large, unused funds for expensive computer software in the third quarter of an annual budget cycle to keep the money from going back to Congress. Keeping technologically current, a valiant end state, sanctioned the spending.

In organizational situations, people may understand the universal values tacitly but may differ in how they apply to particular situations. For instance, a manager who took a plane trip to Dallas "on business" also extended the trip to visit an old friend in a nearby city. He defended taking the trip and said he did not charge the government for the extra travel. He interpreted the trip as falling within his legal duties as a manager, but his staff saw it as a way to have a vacation that would not have occurred otherwise.

Change agents who confront use of situational values in public organizations find them difficult to reverse for several reasons. Some managers and employees may believe that the paper-intensive, rules-bound public agencies force them to find shortcuts. Moreover, people who find loopholes in legislation look for means to give them flexibility and discretion. Such mavericks often become enshrined as heroes in agency folklore and their tactics copied. Third, situational values embed themselves in informal organizational culture over time (Schein, 1985). Spending third-quarter budget funds, for instance, is widely accepted as a means for exerting power over resources external bodies control.

The tension between universal and situational values not only creates ethical dilemmas but also complicates organizational change. Agency managers and employees may not realize the discrepancy between what they believe as true, honest, and fair and what their practices reveal. The organizational culture may further screen understanding by winking at ways managers get around paperwork roadblocks. Gathering, analyzing, and presenting data that indicate gaps between espoused ethics and practice may generate widespread resistance.

THREE-PRONGED ETHICAL DILEMMAS

Change agents often find that dilemmas converge from multiple sources at once. Not only do they face values dilemmas within themselves and within the people with whom they work; change agents may find that dilemmas also have roots in organizational structures, processes, and cultural practices. Dilemmas may stem from values within individuals, from the work environment, and from relationships between people and their contexts.

Perspectives play a key role in defining the dilemmas. In the parking lot case, for instance, the acting agency head faced a dilemma on a personal level: He wanted to make a change in the elitist management parking spot allocation, but he was one of the elites himself. He not only risked losing a benefit that had come to mean a reward for status and longevity; he also risked angering his colleagues who may not have wanted to forego their privileges. Formal speeches, newsletters, and public meetings would have given him an opportunity to reinforce his commitment. Over time, employees and managers would perceive a consistent message, and the possible differences in perspectives would diminish. To do nothing, however, would be to leave the suspicious doors ajar and invite sabotage.

ETHICAL DILEMMAS OF ROLES AND RELATIONSHIPS

White and Wooten (1986) suggest that many ethical dilemmas, in fact, originate in how the change agent and client define their roles and negotiate relationships as the change process unfolds. They identify eight key issues

Figure 15.2
Sources of Ethical Dilemmas

- Client trust
- Client dependency
- Termination
- Contract
- Client identification
- Appropriateness of means
- Depth and scope of interventions
- Degree of flexibility

(see Figure 15.2) that affect how the change agent and client define their roles and relationships.

Client Trust

Change agents and clients must believe that they can rely on an honest account of the problem situation, appropriate diagnostic and intervention techniques, accurate and anonymous data feedback, and open sharing of feelings and concerns. During the phase in which the client describes a problem or issue, for example, withholding information can destroy trust. The client may mislead the change agent, such as describing a situation that the client believes warrants a particular change intervention. Often, change agents accept the problem as the client presents it as a "given" and fail to see a hidden agenda. The client, moreover, may ask the change agent to conduct a team-building session in order to find evidence for firing a "thorn in the flesh" employee. If the change agent provides data and cites the source of disparaging remarks, the change agent breaches confidentiality.

Client Dependency

Change agents risk creating a dependent and even codependent relationship with clients. By definition, change agents enter situations where things are not going well. The client wants relief and expects immediate answers. Quite often, people experiencing problems expect change agents to work miracles and endow them with near divinity. Clients follow change agent advice uncritically.

Moreover, change agents develop a codependency relationship with clients. If change agents want a particular situation to change to meet the client's demands or expectations, they may collude or make the data fit.

For external change agents, the reward might be continuation of the contract; for internal change agents, it might be to not make a powerful person "look bad."

Termination

In addition to the dependency that may build up between a change agent and client, the inability to provide tools for transferring the change may interfere in the relationship. Often, change interventions disappear with the change agent or a client who is particularly charismatic. People who must make the change happen on a day-to-day basis lack the technical skills; financial, technical, and staff resources; and the motivation for doing so.

Contract

Change agents have both a formal as well as a psychological contract to help clients. When the two contracts are out of line, tension erupts. Commonly, change agents function as "an extra pair of hands" (Block, 1981). A client may have change agents implement a particular solution based on the change agent's particular expertise. If the change agent does not have the latitude or the discretion to make changes, however, their skills—and commitment—deteriorate. Working to help a client, but not having a formal or written contract, moreover, is extremely dangerous. The arrangement may lead to possible abuse, frequent conflict, and scarred future relationships.

Client Identification

In public organizations in particular, the plurality of interests prevents exact identification of who "owns" the problem. In one instance, a client in a field office of a large federal organization had issued a contract to train the trainers. Because the contract ultimately involved headquarters human resources professionals who were being reorganized into service teams, however, the contract scope was changed to providing training and organizational development. Finally, to ensure that each human resource professional in the agency would be getting the same competency training, the contract became the property of a career development psychologist. For nearly six months, the three officials discussed who should receive what training and for how long.

Appropriateness of Means

Change agents, as indicated, may have little discretion in deciding how to resolve a particular problem. However, even when they do have the leeway, they may fail to integrate technological with human concerns. For instance, productivity improvement programs may achieve targets but, in the process, result in fewer numbers of people needed. If managers fail to communicate the intent of the program and to provide employees options for career development, the intervention is unethical. In addition, clients who use team-building sessions as "quick fixes" to complex problems in organizational structures, processes, and cultures jeopardize the intervention.

Depth and Scope of Interventions

Often, the change agent faces the dilemma of how much to change over what period of time and with what level of resources. Optimally, the intervention will occur when the organization has prepared users to adopt the changes, has set up a network of internal and external supporters, and has allocated sufficient financial, technological, and staff resources for carrying out the process. Yet because public organizations cannot generate their own operating budgets and secure the support of diverse interests before undertaking change, change agents must spend a great deal of time and energy on preparing the organizational infrastructure. It entails proactively soliciting inside commitment, helping multiple levels of clients adopt a common and overarching purpose for change, and making small, yet highly visible changes in the work flow, staffing pattern, and budget allocations.

Degree of Flexibility

Change agents face a dilemma in applying certain interventions in particular situations. In spite of careful problem diagnosis, sufficient data collection and analysis, and client commitment and collaboration in solution finding, things can still go wrong. Agencies may have an unexpected change of leadership, key supporters may leave the organization, or budget cuts could force reorganizations. Change strategies need built-in flexibility. This means having a backup plan with alternative strategies and resources.

Because of the uncontrollable political changes at the top of organizations and unpredictable year-to-year budgets, an incremental "small wins" strategy may work best. This allows people most closely associated with the intervention to change functions affecting their work. It also provides control over processes and enhances their confidence and organizational commitment. Small wins also give quick turnarounds with high, tangible payoffs.

CREATING AN ETHICAL CONTRACT

Ethical dilemmas entail choices that have both predictable and unpredictable consequences. To gain some control over potentially uncontrollable circumstances, however, change agents can set up their own codes of universal ethics with clients. Usually called the "contracting" phase of the consulting process (Lippitt and Lippitt, 1986), this phase sets out not only agreements regarding roles and responsibilities but also work relationships. To foster ethical processes throughout the whole program, the contract should define core values and expected outcomes of both client and change agent and should build in formal and informal reviews.

What might the "code of ethical concern" cover? Some questions to spark reflection, discussion, and recommitment to universal values should arise at key turning points in the change process. From Lippitt and Lippitt's descriptions of phases of consultancy, we can ask some key questions (see Figure 15.3).

Precontracting Phase

Universal Values.

- What universal values are involved? For instance, justice, equality, honesty, peace?
- What is my personal goal in helping?
- Are the universal values in the project compatible with my own beliefs?
- What would I like to see happen as a result of this project?

Expertise.

- What specific skills do I have that I can use on this project?
- What skills will I need? Are there resources inside the organization I can use? Are they willing to contribute? Where else might I obtain additional help?
- What specific role do I want to play in the helping process? For instance, expert, advocate, collaborator, extra pair of hands?

Support.

- What financial, technological, and staff resources does the organization have to help me?
- Are there people in positions of power who are willing to advocate or

Figure 15.3
Asking Ethical Questions

Precontracting phase
- Universal values
- Expertise
- Support

Contracting phase
- Client identification
- Values espoused versus praticed

Data collection, analysis, and feedback phase
- Accuracy
- Confidentiality
- Openness
- Creativity

Implementation phase
- Flexibility
- Independent critique
- Client resource level

Assessment and evaluation phase
- Multiple measurements
- Short- and long-range implications

Termination
- Follow-up training
- What was learned

---

sponsor changes? If so, what are their interests? Are they compatible with the universal values?

Contracting Phase

Client Identification.

- Who are the principal stakeholders in the project? Which stakeholder has ultimate responsibility for implementing change? Does this person have the authority, power, influences, and resources necessary? If not, what needs to be built into the agreement that will ensure the change can be carried out as agreed upon?

- What are the interests of the stakeholders? Are the interests compatible?

How do these interests mesh with universal values? With my own interests in the change?

Values Espoused versus Practiced.

- What values does the initial client describe in the problem situation? Is this in accord with what the other stakeholders describe?
- What are the nondiscussable issues? How have they been handled? For instance, ignoring, punishing, slighting?
- What concerns do the stakeholders express about exposing the problem? What values underlie their concerns? What fears are suggested?

Data Collection, Analysis, and Feedback Phase

Accuracy.

- How will feedback be gathered?
- What assessment tools will be used in analyzing the feedback? What measures of reliability and validity do the tools have?
- Are inadequate cause maps in use? How can these be corrected?

Confidentiality.

- Is it possible to identify contributors from the data?
- Will information help solve the problem? What information is critical? Unnecessary? What information is missing? How will that be obtained?
- What steps will be taken to ensure anonymity and confidentiality?

Openness.

- What types of resistance manifest themselves? What assumptions do these forms of resistance suggest? Have the assumptions been made public in an atmosphere of trust?
- Have some data sources been overlooked? Are they important to understanding and resolving the problem at hand?

Creativity.

- Is there evidence of locked-in thinking regarding possible solutions to the problem? What can be done to loosen this?
- Who are the opinion leaders in the organization? Can they be used to adapt innovative solutions to their work areas?

Implementation

Flexibility.

- What obstacles to achieving the desired outcomes are present in the organizational structures? Work processes? Culture? What mechanisms may be used to convert the obstacles into assets?
- What contingencies in staffing or budgeting in particular might occur during the change process? How is the organization able to communicate changes without "losing face?"
- Is the organization change mandated? What degree of input from staff is available and rewarded? Can this be expanded?

Independent Critique.

- How will issues raised that are beyond the scope of the project be resolved?
- Is there sufficient diversity of thinking styles and experiences to examine the implementation strategy and its possible effects on employee interests? Other organizational structures and processes?

Client Resource Level.

- Does the client/organization have the necessary staff, budget, and technological resources to carry out the strategy?
- What additional training will need to occur to support the change strategy?

Assessment and Evaluation Phase

Multiple Measurements.

- What multiple measures of effectiveness and efficiency are used? How are they determined? How are they communicated?

Short- and Long-Range Implications.

- Are there any unintentional consequences? How have they been managed?
- What "midcourse corrections" in the assessment need to be made?
- What long-range use of evaluation data will be made? How will this affect the future of the organization?

Termination

Follow-up Training.

- Have users of innovations received adequate training?
- Have the original problem areas been resolved to the client's satisfaction?
- What follow-up sessions will be necessary? What will be the change agent–consultant role?

What Was Learned.

- How have my own interests been met? What have I learned?

THE IMPORTANCE OF ASKING QUESTIONS

Changing organizations is a thoroughly human, nonlinear process. Because there are no hard and fast recipes for changing organizations, the change agent's best tool is asking questions. Suspending judgment amid the eddies of organizational change enables the change agent to examine how people involved define and carry out their roles and relationships. Assuming people negotiate meanings open-endedly prepares the consultant to observe, record, reflect, and question accurately.

The "rightness" and "goodness" of how people define and enact roles and relationships involve a similar process. By helping people look at some gaps between universal and situational values and their effects on actions, change agents can use the inquiry process to promote ethical conduct. Particularly important are decisions stakeholders must make that will affect not only effectiveness and efficiency but also others in the organization, external clientele, and long-term operations. Inquiry that examines change from a broader frame of reference creates a more ethical basis for resolving dilemmas.

TOWARD PERSONAL INTEGRITY

Perhaps the greatest challenge facing change agents is developing organizational commitment to sharing responsibility for change. Frequently, units that people have pinpointed as "problem areas" become targets of change. "They" receive improvement, but "we" don't need any. Organizations, however, operate holistically. "Problem units" invariably affect other units. Unless organization members collectively—acting as a community—can come to see their roles in creating and maintaining the problem areas, change will produce isolated and ineffective results.

Ethical climates foster shared responsibility. Sharing resources to resolve common problems benefits the entire organization. In creating shared responsibility, change agents help organizational units practice universal community values, such as shared responsibility, caring, and commitment.

How does the change agent bring organizational members to this state? The human nature of organizations and the use of self as an instrument of change provide the key. Change agents teach skills, but they also model important attitudes, values, and behaviors. Being a person of integrity oneself plays a leading role in the modeling process. The last chapter shows how change agents can develop skills to enhance personal integrity and foster shared responsibility for change.

REFERENCES

Block, P. (1981). *Flawless consulting: A guide to getting your expertise used*. San Diego, CA: University Associates.

Brink, D. O. (1989). *Moral realism and the foundations of ethics*. New York: Cambridge University Press.

Denhardt, K. G. (1988). *The ethics of public service*. Westport, CT: Greenwood Press.

Frederickson, H. G. (1997). *The spirit of public administration*. San Francisco: Jossey-Bass.

Hofstede, G. (1991). *Cultures and organizations: Software of the mind*. London: McGraw-Hill.

Lippitt, G., and Lippitt, R. (1986). *The consulting process in action* (2nd ed.). San Diego, CA: University Associates.

Mackie, J. L. (1990). *Ethics: Inventing right and wrong*. London: Penguin Books.

Schein, E. H. (1985). *Organizational culture and leadership*. San Francisco: Jossey-Bass.

Tillich, P. (1955). *The new being*. New York: Scribner.

White, L. P., and Wooten, K. C. (1986). *Professional ethics and practice in organizational development*. New York: Praeger.

CHAPTER 16

Cultivating Integrity in Change

Responsible servants . . . cultivate, as a conscious discipline, a lifestyle
that favors their optimal performance as an antibureacratic influence,
over a lifespan of mature living. They bring their own unique amelior-
ative influence to bear on the pervasive bureaucracy.
      —Robert K. Greenleaf (1966). *Servant Responsibility in a*
                                       Bureaucratic Society

In the days when computers took up whole rooms, the Internal Revenue
Service processed tax information on magnetic tapes. They would then
truck them to little towns in the West Virginia mountains and tuck them
away in nearby caves. Back and forth they would run, year after year. In
the late 1980s a task force met to figure out what to do about the woefully
outdated data-processing system. Like other task forces before it, however,
this one had to give it up. They were promised a new system—three years
before—and decided the old one would have to make do, even if it was on
a respirator.

Big government left with the collapse of the Great Society over 30 years
ago, but many government agencies still live in the ice age by default. Widespread constituent dissatisfaction with public sector performance resulted
in seizing more control. Politicians helped scale back, downsize, rightsize,
and reorganize until agencies lost both stature and status. With fewer resources, however, agencies are expected to accomplish near-heroic objectives.

Unless government employees regain constituents' respect as public servants, however, doing more with less will drain their integrity to the bone. *Integrity* is often used to mean "strict adherence to a moral standard when making judgements." Another meaning, however, is the one that reflects the outcome of organizational change: "wholeness." Integrity as wholeness is based on May's (1996, 20) three principles: Persons of integrity have (1) a coherent set of values, (2) mature development of a critical point of view, and (3) a disposition to act in a principled way. Instead of obeying a set of rules strictly, public servants who act with integrity use disciplined judgment and behavior that achieve optimal results for the general public good.

Integrity is the core of public service. As Cooper (1991, 64) points out, the public employee is a "citizen for the rest of us." He or she is a person who exercises authority on behalf of others and also becomes a "witness for the common good." Public servants use integrity to inspire community vision and action.

Frederickson (1997) adds that integrity in service produces benevolence. He points out:

It should be the purpose of public administration to have a concept of public that is based on benevolence. Embodied in the notion of benevolence is the sense of service, which has long been associated with public administration. Similar, too, is the belief in a commitment to a greater good and the dedication of one's professional life to that end. It is no wonder that there has been a loss of public regard toward public service; such regard can be reclaimed only by a public administration that esteems the public through benevolence. (47)

Benevolent service seems to have drowned in organizations that have quenched employees' spirits. Organizations that have put political gains above common welfare, that have enforced codes of silence in the wake of injustice, and that have pressed for more but have given less have produced the dysfunctional employee Merton (1940) described over 50 years ago. Merton notes that in such bureaucratic organizations there is a tendency for employees to displace goals for processes; employees become so obsessed with doing a particular job that they forget the larger purpose they are achieving.

Merton's "goal displacement" produces employee disconnection. People detached from their mission exhibit such behaviors as poor job performance, dissatisfaction, willingness to leave, and poor interpersonal relationships. Mission disconnection also affects their lives off the job, especially in home, family, and community relationships. It influences personal health as well. Disconnected employees create problems for themselves and those around them.

Change agents can play a revitalization role, however, in their quest to provide meaning, commitment, and value to public employment. The key is changing the negative connotation of *service* from servitude to servant-hood.

Servitude is demeaning. It appears in the statement taxpayers frequently make to public employees about "paying their salaries." It implies taxpayers have rights to direct government employees' work, but it is based on a market concept that has no relationship to work done in the public interest. If anything, public employees are "representatives" of that interest. They do the public's work because they believe it is in both their own and the constituents' best interests. Stivers (1993, 77) points out that the role is "strikingly performative." She adds, "In carrying out their responsibilities, public administrators display the content of their individual characters to all observers and spur some, at least, to nobler aims—virtue 'by contagion,' Hume called it."

In each case example in this book, change agents spent much of their time and energies helping employees realize the bigger picture. Instead of having a narrowly defined specialty area of responsibility, public employees played enriched roles. By combining their expertise with knowledge, financial and technical resources, and influence from business, professional, and community groups, public employees redefined their purposes in relation to the organization's mission.

Change agents can help public employees realize integrity by helping them improve the difficult conditions and outmoded organizational systems under which they must work. To help public employees develop integrity, change agents begin the process from the inside first. The agents have a vision of the possible and communicate an expectation that others can achieve it as well. Change agents also model the values, attitudes, and behaviors that will lead to the desired future state. To convert visions and values into shared commitment and tangible outcomes, change agents work with a diverse clientele to form a community of public servants. In playing catalytic roles, change agents orchestrate integrity, the basis of servanthood.

This chapter describes seven vital processes that facilitate integrity. It illustrates the seven processes with examples of how change agents in previous chapters led the transformation of people and organizations. The chapter sums up the change agent's roles and competencies in leading public organizational change from the inside out by encouraging individuals to take action.

THE SEVEN "RE's" OF BUILDING INTEGRITY INTO CHANGE

The prefix *re* plus a verb means "to do again." It implies looking at an occurrence with the idea of changing it. It incorporates thinking about an action and how people have defined it, identifying areas for improvement, making changes, and assessing outcomes. To "re" is to facilitate integrity.

Figure 16.1
The Seven "Re's" of Building Organization Integrity

- Recover wholeness
- Redefine mission
- Remove obstacles
- Recommit people
- Reengineer structures
- Reskill continuously
- Reenergize self-awareness

In the case examples of change, "re" described seven key ways change agents fostered integrity: (1) recovering wholeness through healing; (2) redefining central mission and purpose; (3) removing obstacles; (4) recommitting people to purposes through participative actions; (5) reengineering bureaucratic structures; (6) reskilling to foster continuous learning and development; and (7) reenergizing through self-awareness and action (Figure 16.1).

Recovering Wholeness through Healing

Change agents bring about wholeness within organizations through healing individuals, interpersonal relationships, and work systems problems. By the time change agents intervene, however, problems affecting wholeness have produced widespread pain. They are like splinters one doesn't know have gone through the skin until red, swollen, and blistery scabs appear. People define and react to pain differently, however. Some people yowl, whereas others barely wince.

Change agents help people to understand not only differences in the meanings of issues as they have interpreted them but how collective interpretations have affected problems over time. Patterns of inaccurate cause maps, outmoded beliefs, and allness appear in tracing common interpretations of meaning. Change agents bring the inaccuracies to light through critical and reflective dialogue.

As organizations function holistically, each system, function, or process as humanly envisioned, defined, and enacted is interdependent. What occurs in one area, or what fails to occur, ultimately affects other areas. Once individuals and groups begin to understand the interrelationships of problems, define their own thinking inaccuracies, construct a larger map of the impacts of problems, and share in solving them, healing begins. Scott and Mitchell (1988) note:

This recognition, and the renunciation it demands, may be the first step toward wisdom for most of us in management. It may help us to reduce the venom in organizations that comes from evil, whether systemic, individual, or normative. It may help us cultivate in organizations, like the woman in the garden, a certain tenderness and compassion toward others without which we cannot flourish as individuals. (69)

In the case examples, Gene Gavin led healing the Department of Revenue Services from its own perception of ineffectiveness. He not only worked with individuals to help them articulate their feelings about the organization and themselves, but he also enabled them to see that they could change the perception. Once they saw themselves as empowered to create changes in services they provided, they developed enthusiasm for their roles and, as an outcome, began innovative ways to improve client relationships.

Redefining Central Mission

One of the most common themes was redefining *customer* and *service*. In the Town of Wethersfield, "customer" meant someone who demanded service. The change agents, such as Lee Erdmann, helped employees redefine or reconceptualize the customer. The new paradigm that emerged from Erdmann's vision, manager and employee dialogues, and training programs was that of partnership. With a change in terms came a change in the *way* employees treated constituents. The interactions centered on mutual problem solving, shared commitment, and focus on common goals.

In a similar way, Gene Gavin's "comment cards" redefined the customer relationship in terms of accountability. Knowing customers assessed the quality of work relationships and services sharpened employees' motivation to contribute their best efforts.

Redefining relationships through using different symbolic meanings illustrates the idea that language itself influences behavior (Hayakawa, 1978; Sapir, 1949). In using word meanings to spark action, change agents helped others react to "real" situations and accomplish desired outcomes. Redefining is a matter of reframing and leads to realigning the meaning of work and organization missions.

Removing Obstacles

Change agents contended with a variety of resistances. Chief were obstacles such as differences in values, beliefs, and practices, within individuals and groups. The blockages appeared tangibly in coalitions that exerted power and influence contrary to the direction of change and in closed cultures and hostile climates. To meet and overcome the opposition, change agents used several techniques. Some central ones included training, feedback and coaching, and expanding informational support bases.

Training in New Values and Behaviors. Thinking of customers as "partners" required changing the values people held to cooperation. Lee Erdmann and Al Ilg pointed out that many town employees felt they could not provide cooperative service because laws and regulations demanded neutral judgment. In addition, the fixed financial, staff, material, and technological resources allocated through the legislature left employees with having to exclude some eligible "customers" from receiving services. Erdmann and Ilg provided training in creating novel solutions to such problems, however, through involving customers in decisions. In Wethersfield, for instance, citizen suggestions for redesigning a busy and dangerous street intersection saved not only administrative time but also construction costs.

Providing Feedback and Coaching. To help individuals overcome particular obstacles, change agents worked with clients privately and informally. Sharon Garrett, for instance, helped Dr. Overby improve his interpersonal relationships, and Terry Parker encouraged a subordinate to move into another career field. Gibb (1982, 48) points out that feedback and coaching can produce change when individuals realize interdependence: joint determination of goals, real communication in depth, and reciprocal trust.

Using Positional Power and Influence. In the case of Gene Gavin, positional power played an important role in introducing change from the top down; yet Gavin used a great deal of persuasive power to encourage employees to adapt change strategies to their own situations. Al Ilg and Lee Erdmann used persuasion as well as personal examples in their roles as change agents. They augmented their approaches by using training programs and, like Gavin, modeled the behaviors they expected employees to emulate. Ruth Crone used persuasiveness as well as information to generate support for change. Like Ilg and Erdmann, her role extended outside the organization in cultivating external stakeholder support and brokering services, but it was more prevalent.

Expanding Support Bases. Change agents as individuals may have had dreams of a desirable future state; but to translate those dreams into action, they had to garner support from a broad base of interests. Change agents, such as Ruth Crone and Lee Erdmann, formed alliances of business, civic, and other government organizations to accomplish objectives that benefited the community as a whole. They also created internal task force teams, such as in the town of Windsor and at the Department of Revenue Services, to simplify bureaucratic procedures.

Using expanded support bases to achieve shared goals involved what Frost and Egri (1991, 281) saw as the "will, skill and power of change agents and the availability of certain resource strategies." To overcome political obstacles, change agents had to appeal to the needs of a wider constituency. In bringing diverse interests to bear, change agents create a framework of mutual support. Each player needs to use the resources of others to accomplish an objective, but choices for taking over the change process are limited because of the fragile nature of the alliance.

Recommitting Purpose through Participation

One of the most striking features of the change examples was widespread managerial, employee, and external stakeholder involvement in problem solving. By contributing knowledge and skills from diverse viewpoints and interests, participants increased their competence, obtained creative results, and attained a high level of esprit de corps. R. B. Denhardt (1993) points out that teams in government allow shared power and enhanced commitment to overall mission within an increasingly pluralistic, decentralized environment. Change agents provided people opportunities to share power through working together on common problems and issues.

Participation produced several observable outcomes in decision making:

Trust. Each change agent acted on the assumption that building trust in human relationships is the basis for building effective structures (DePree, 1989). Trust was the basis of participation and satisfaction. In examining numerous encounters between bureaucrats and clientele, Danet (1981) observed that clients report more positive outcomes with bureaucratic organizations when they transacted business using mutual resources, when officials explained procedures and followed them fairly, and when bureaucrats showed warm interpersonal communications styles.

Shared Responsibility. Change agents worked toward the goal of helping individuals and departments assume responsibility for initiating and carrying out change. The use of "small wins" in the Town of Wethersfield and at the Department of Revenue Services was particularly useful in achieving this aim.

Creativity. Involving diverse interests generated a variety of creative solutions to problems. The Washington area COG's "Wednesday's Child" is typical. In tackling the problem of a large number of children needing foster care and adoptive homes, the agency created a forum that brought together experts in child welfare, potential foster parents, and the media. Discussions of challenges, needs, resources, and opportunities among forum participants introduced several ways to find children homes.

Personal Control of Goals. Participation enabled people to define goals in relation to a clear-cut, unifying objective. The tax simplification booklets put out by the Department of Revenue Services volunteers exemplified this. Volunteers rewrote the legalese into language that public users could comprehend easily. This not only cheered the customers but also pleased employees. Satisfaction and productivity rest on the ability of people to participate fully in their work (Miller and Monge, 1989).

Enthusiasm. In Erdmann's case, the program of small wins was the stepping stone for the man the town had once called "Roadkill Bob." Roadkill Bob was the person who picked up dead animals that vehicles had killed on town streets. Roadkill Bob had performed this mundane job for over 20 years. While it was a steady income, it certainly was not much to feel self-actualized about. When Roadkill Bob took training in implementing small wins, however, something inside burst into being. He became so involved in his job that he not only enthusiastically removed Wethersfield's roadkill but also much of that in neighboring communities. He received several commendations from the town and from many private organizations and citizens as well.

In summary, participation in each case example bore the kind of fruit Dinkmeyer and Eckstein (1996, 183) describe:

1. Ownership thinking takes place at all organizational levels;

2. Trust and respect prevail at all levels;

3. Employee goals are discovered and aligned with organizational ones;

4. All employees take full responsibility for actions and results;

5. The atmosphere is characterized by courage. People believe in themselves, are confident, and willing to take risks;

6. Leaders foster open discussion of ideas;

7. Leaders provide involvement and feedback;

8. Leaders don't feel threatened by staff participation and open decisions to scrutiny; and

9. People regard problems and changes as opportunities to apply expertise and grow and develop.

Reengineering Bureaucratic Structures

Each change agent adopted a team-based approach to leading change, but the structure, composition, and purpose varied. In the Town of Wethersfield, as in the Department of Revenue Services and the Metropolitan Council of Governments, the leader integrated public employee functions with private, nonprofit, and other governmental organizations. Each integrated team worked on specific problems or concerns on an ad hoc basis. Each team, moreover, retained the accountability relationship to the head of the agency or department.

In the Town of Windsor, however, the teams had a self-managed structure. There were no managers, and functions were permanent. When problems or issues in other departments crossed the functional boundaries, however, the self-managed teams sent representatives to help solve the problem. The cases illustrate that bureaucracies per se need not obstruct change.

Heckscher, Eisenstat, and Rice (1994) identify these two forms of organizational change as "cascading" and "empowered team," respectively. *Cascading* is a top-down approach in which executives share their visions and values for change with employees at lower echelons. Managers and supervisors, such as those in the Department of Revenue Services and in the Town of Wethersfield, adapt the visions and develop their own strategies for change. Ilg's "empowered teams" used liaisons to coordinate accountability for the team's contributions to the overall organization's mission. Both organizational forms, as used by the change agents, achieved expected outcomes.

Reskilling for Continuous Learning and Change

Like many private sector organizations, government agencies are undergoing rapid change. Learning is a means not only to keep abreast of the changes but also to outdistance competition. Public organizations, of course, have no comparable market share; but their products and services have undergone reinvention as a result of various forms of privatization. Private subcontractors have taken over many routine and administrative services that government agencies provided through in-house staff. Training in the most economically efficient techniques has become imperative for job security in the public sector.

In the case examples, learning helped public organizations to cultivate customer satisfaction and reduce operating costs as well as produce innovative approaches to service that increased motivation. Training followed by applications projects perhaps exemplified this best. In the towns of Wethersfield and Windsor, and in the Department of Revenue Services, employees developed creative, customer-focused solutions to many of the problems they encountered. By implementing small wins solutions with the input of customers, employees found that learning produced changes in work conditions, customer relationships, and attitudes they themselves had about their jobs. Learning fostered feelings of greater autonomy in deciding *how* jobs were done and also greater satisfaction in work processes and results.

R. B. Denhardt (1993, 259) emphasizes the importance of using education to bring about change. Change agents "create settings in which people are stimulated to learn, settings in which learning is the norm, and settings in which learning is valued above all else," he notes. Training people to assume such responsibility not only encourages innovation but also inhibits dependency in relationships. Dependency can produce many ethical dilemmas in change as well as destroy future initiative.

Reenergizing through Self-Awareness and Action

Change agents used themselves as instruments of change. They analyzed their own desires for their organizations, developed ways to communicate goals, used abilities to influence, and involved others in creating a human touch to change.

They also viewed organizations holistically. They realized that their strategies for changing organizations would affect both internal as well as external stakeholders. To plan and carry out changes, change agents worked in concert with those whom the strategies affected and used their information as guidelines. By involving others, change agents developed a realistic understanding of organizational problems and issues as well as potential strategies for intervention.

Change agents also examined their own motives for change. In each case, change agents identified a desire to create organizations that would improve promptness and efficiency of services, solve problems proactively and with reference to constituent needs, create greater commitment to the organization, feel pride and satisfaction in day-to-day work, and experience greater autonomy and personal growth through work experiences. Their motives rested on their visions, belief in people's abilities to change through commitment, and the longing to build a better organizational future.

USING QUESTIONS AS GUIDES TO CREATING INTEGRITY

In orchestrating change, the agents built collective social responsibility. Integrity of beliefs and actions among pluralistic interests involved fundamental transformation of individualistic values, beliefs, and actions to more inclusive ones. In the cases studied, change agents suspended their personal ideas of what ought to be and focused on how team members depicted it. In doing so, they used such techniques as critical thinking, questioning, reflecting, and dialogue. In changing organizations, agents must try to see how the problems and issues evolved from the participants' viewpoints. Suspending judgment can occur if the change agent adopts a strategy of curiosity and continuous inquiry. As guides, the change agent might consider these questions:

1. Where are the problems? How did they come about? How are they interrelated?

2. Who owns the problems? What is their level of commitment to change? What is my/our relationship to them?

3. How can others participate in change? What are the processes by which participation can come about? How can external stakeholders, in particular, be involved?

4. What are the common values that need to be addressed? How can we translate these into purposes and action steps?

5. How can we create dialogue? What common symbols and actions need to be included?

6. What tools and resources do we need to accomplish our goals? How can we get or develop them?

7. What are some likely types of resistance? How can we manage them?

8. What contingency plans do we have? How flexible are they?

9. What are our operating principles? Do they match our values? How do we close gaps?

10. What outcomes have we accomplished? How do they affect other systems?

11. What continuing roles do we need to carry out? How do we prepare others to assume responsibility for managing change processes?

12. What insights did we learn? About ourselves? About change? About the organization as a holistic system? How might we integrate the insights into our own individual lives? How might this benefit the organizational community?

CONCLUSION

When individuals accept responsibility for aligning beliefs with actions, they experience integrity. Covey (1991) suggests that such integrity can also result from giving of oneself in service to others:

Until people have the spirit of service, they might say they love a companion, company, or cause, but they often despise the demands these make on their lives. Double-mindedness, having two conflicting motives or interests, inevitably sets us at war with ourselves, and an internal civil war often breaks out into war with others. The opposite of double-mindedness is self-unity or integrity. We achieve integrity through the dedication of ourselves to selfless service of others. (54)

There is no journey backward. The internal and external demands for change impel moving forward. The task is to create government structures that embrace plurality, weld common visions, and create systems that adapt incrementally to particular situations.

In healing interpersonal wounds and showing others how to build relationships of trust, change agents help people identify and use others' strengths, talents, and abilities. To do so, the change agent establishes a climate of optimism, courage, and inquiry. Change agents accomplish this through training as well as through modeling skills, attitudes, and behaviors. Change agents encourage people to value each other as resources in building a workplace that gives each person meaning, growth, and dignity.

Government organizations are undergoing great change. To facilitate transformation so that people themselves take control requires the competencies of change agents. Change agents define direction, commit themselves to care, create community, and foster integrity of servanthood. Change agents, in short, are persons of conscientiousness who act on the basis of higher principles. Through them, they define and carry out the shared goals of serving the greater public good effectively, efficiently, and humanely.

REFERENCES

Cooper, T. L. (1991). *An ethic of citizenship for public administration.* Englewood Cliffs, NJ: Prentice-Hall.

Covey, S. (1991). *Principle-centered leadership.* New York: Simon and Schuster.

Danet, B. (1981). Client-organization relationships. In P. C. Nystrom and W. H. Starbuck (Eds.), *Handbook of organization design* (Vol. 2, 382–428). London: Oxford University Press.

Denhardt, R. B. (1993). *The pursuit of significance.* Belmont, CA: Wadsworth.

DePree, M. (1989). *Leadership as an art.* New York: Dell.

Dinkmeyer, D., and Eckstein, D. (1996). *Leadership by encouragement.* Delray Beach, FL: St. Lucie Press.

Frederickson, H. G. (1997). *The spirit of public administration.* San Francisco: Jossey-Bass.

Frost, P. J. and Egri, C. P. (1991). The political process of innovation. In *Research in organizational behavior* (Vol. 13, 229–295). Greenwich, CT: JAI Press.

Gibb, J. (1982). Is it helpful? In L. Porter and B. Mohr (Eds.), *Reading book for human relations training* (7th ed., 46–51). Arlington, VA: NTL Institute.

Greenleaf, R. K. (1966). *Servant responsibility in a bureaucratic society.* Commencement speech presented at Redlands College, Redlands, CA.

Hayakawa, S. I. (1978). *Language in thought and action.* New York: Harcourt, Brace & Co.

Heckscher, C., Eisenstat, R. A., and Rice, T. J. (1994). Transformational processes. In C. Heckscher and A. Donnellon (Eds.), *The post-bureaucratic organization: New perspectives on organizational change* (129–177). Newbury Park, CA: Sage.

May, L. (1996). *The socially responsive self: Social theory and professional ethics.* Chicago: The University of Chicago Press.

Merton, R. K. (1940). Bureaucratic structure and personality. *Social Forces, 18,* 560–568.

Miller, K. I., and Monge, P. K. (1988). Participation, satisfaction, and productivity: A meta-analytic review. *Academy of Management Journal, 29*(4), 727–753.

Sapir, E. (1949). *Language: An introduction to the study of speech.* New York: Harcourt, Brace and World, Inc.

Scott, W. G., and Mitchell, T. R. (1988). The problem or mystery of evil and virtue in organizations. In K. Kolenda (Ed.), *Organizations and ethical individualism* (47–72). New York: Praeger.

Stivers, C. (1993). *Gender images in public administration: Legitimacy and the administrative state.* Newbury Park, CA: Sage.

Selected Bibliography

Arendt, H. (1964). *Eichmann in Jerusalem* (Rev. ed.). New York: Viking Press.

Argyris, C. (1970). *Intervention theory and method: A behavioral science view.* Reading, MA: Addison-Wesley.

Argyris, C., and Schon, D. A. (1978). *Organizational learning.* Reading, MA: Addison-Wesley.

Averill, J. R., Catlin, G., and Chon, K. K. (1990). *Rules of hope.* New York: Springer-Verlag.

Baird, C. W. (1994, Fall). The Dunlop Commission report: Friends of unions. *Government Union Review* 6, 1–42.

Barnard, C. (1938). *The functions of the executive.* Cambridge, MA: Harvard University Press.

Bass, B. M. (1990). *Bass and Stogdill's handbook of leadership: Theory, research and managerial applications* (3rd ed.). New York: Free Press.

Billig, M. (1976). *The social psychology of intergroup relations.* New York: Academic Press.

Block, P. (1981). *Flawless consulting: A guide to getting your expertise used.* San Diego, CA: University Associates.

Bogdan, R., and Taylor, S. J. (1975). *Introduction to qualitative research methods.* New York: John Wiley.

Brink, D. O. (1989). *Moral realism and the foundations of ethics.* New York: Cambridge University Press.

Broad, M. L. and Newstrom, J. W. (1992). *Transfer of training.* Reading, MA: Addison-Wesley.

Brueggemann, W. (1979). *Hope within history.* Atlanta: John Knox Press.

Bryson, J. M., and Crosby, B. C. (1992). *Leadership for the common good: Tackling public problems in a shared power world.* San Francisco: Jossey-Bass.

Buber, M. (1958). *I and thou.* New York: Charles Scribner's Sons.

Buchwald, A. (1983). *While Reagan slept.* G. P. New York: G. P. Putnam's Sons.

Burke, W. W. (1987). *Organization development: A normative view.* Reading, MA: Addison-Wesley.

Carr, D. K., and Littman, J. D. (1980). *Excellence in government.* Arlington, VA: Coopers & Lybrand.

Children's Defense Fund. (1995). *The state of America's children yearbook 1995.* Washington D.C.

Clegg, S. R. (1975). *Power, rule and domination.* London and Boston: Routledge & Kegan Paul.

Cohen-Rosenthal, E. (1985, Autumn). Orienting labor-management cooperation toward revenue and growth: Employee involvement programs stressing revenue generation have greater potential than those emphasizing cost containment. *National Productivity Review, 4,* 385–396.

Combs, A. W., Avila, D. L., and Purkey, W. W. (1971). *Helping relationships: Basic concepts for the helping professions.* Boston: Allyn and Bacon.

Cooper, T. L. (1991). *An ethic of citizenship for public administration.* Englewood Cliffs, NJ: Prentice-Hall.

Cooperrider, D. (1990). Positive image, positive action: The affirmative basis of organizing. In S. Srivastva and D. L. Cooperrider (Eds.), *Appreciative management and leadership: The power of positive thought and action in organizations* (91–125). San Francisco: Jossey-Bass.

Covey, S. R. (1991). *Principle-centered leadership.* New York: Simon and Schuster.

Crosby, P. B. (1979). *Quality is free.* New York: New American Library.

Cutcher-Gershenfeld, J. (1984, May). Labor-management cooperation in American communities: What's in it for the unions? *Annals of the American Academy of Political and Social Science, 473,* 76–87.

Czarniawska-Joerges, B. (1992). *Exploring complex organizations.* Newbury Park, CA: Sage.

D'Andrade, R. G. (1984). Cultural meaning systems. In R. A. Shweder and R. A. LeVine (Eds.), *Culture theory.* Cambridge: Cambridge University Press.

Danet, B. (1981). Client-organization relationships. In P. C. Nystrom and W. H. Starbuck (Eds.), *Handbook of organization design* (Vol. 2, 382–428). London: Oxford University Press.

Delbeq, A. L., Van de Ven, A. H., and Gustafson, D. H. (1975). *Group techniques for program planning: A guide to Nominal and Delphi processes.* Glenview, IL: Scott, Foresman.

Deming, W. E. (1982). *Quality, productivity, and competitive position.* Cambridge, MA: MIT Press.

Denhardt, K. G. (1988). *The ethics of public service.* Westport, CT: Greenwood Press.

Denhardt, R. B. (1993). *The pursuit of significance.* Belmont, CA: Wadsworth.

DePree, M. (1989). *Leadership as an art.* New York: Dell.

Desroche, H. (1979). *The sociology of hope.* London: Routledge & Kegan Paul.

Dinkmeyer, D., and Losoncy, L. (1980). *The encouragement book: Becoming a positive person.* New York: Prentice-Hall.

Dinkmeyer, D., and Eckstein, D. (1996). *Leadership by encouragement.* Delray Beach, FL: St. Lucie Press.

Douglas, M. (1986). *How institutions think*. Syracuse, NY: Syracuse University Press.

Dreikurs, R. (1950). *Fundamentals of Adlerian psychology*. New York: Greenberg.

Eaton, A. E. (1994, April). The survival of employee participation programs in unionized settings. *Industrial and Labor Relations Review, 47*(3), 371–389.

Eaton, A. E. and Voos, P. B. (1992). The ability of unions to adapt to innovative workplace arrangements. *American Economic Review, 79*(2), 72–76.

Elden, M., and Levin, M. (1991). Cogenerative learning: Bringing participation into action research. In W. F. Whyte (Ed.), *Participatory action research* (127–142). Newbury Park, CA: Sage.

Ellul, J. (1973). *Hope in time of abandonment*. New York: Seabury Press.

Erez, M., and Arad, R. (1986, November). Participative goal setting: Social-motivational and cognitive factors. *Journal of Applied Psychology, 71*, 591–597.

Etzioni, A. (1961). *A comparative analysis of complex organizations*. New York: Free Press.

Fairholm, G. W. (1993). *Organizational power politics: Tactics in organizational leadership*. Westport, CT: Praeger.

Ferguson, K. E. (1984). *The feminist case against bureaucracy*. Philadelphia: Temple University Press.

Filley, A. C., House, R. J., and Kerr, S. (1976). *Managerial process and organizational behavior* (2nd ed.). Glenview, IL: Scott, Foresman.

Fisher, R., and Ury, W. (1981) *Getting to yes: Negotiating agreement without giving in*. Boston: Houghton Mifflin.

Follett, M. P. (1926). The giving of orders. In H. C. Metcalf (Ed.), *Scientific Foundations of Business Administration*. Baltimore, MD: Williams & Wilkins Co.

Fox, M. (1979). *A spirituality named compassion*. San Francisco: HarperCollins.

Fox, M. (1994). *The reinvention of work: A new vision of livelihood for our time*. New York: HarperCollins.

Frederickson, H. G. (1997). *The spirit of public administration*. San Francisco: Jossey-Bass.

Freire, P. (1990). *Pedagogy of the oppressed*. New York: Continuum Press.

French, W. L., and Bell, C. H., Jr. (1990). *Organization development* (4th ed.). Englewood Cliffs, NJ: Prentice-Hall.

Fromm, E. (1941). *Escape from freedom*. New York: Farrar and Rinehart.

Frost, P., and Egri, C. (1990). Appreciating executive action. In S. Srivastva and D. L. Cooperrider (Eds.), *Appreciative management and leadership: The power of positive thought and action in organizations* (289–322). San Francisco: Jossey-Bass.

Frost, P. J., and Egri, C. P. (1991). The political process of innovation. In *Research in organizational behavior* (Vol. 13, 229–295). Greenwich, CT: JAI Press.

Fuller, A. (1990). *Insight into value*. Albany: State University of New York Press.

Gardner, J. (1976). *No easy victories*. New York: Harper and Row.

Gardner, J. W. (1991). *Building community*. Washington, D.C.: Independent Sector.

Geertz, C. (1973). *The interpretation of cultures*. New York: Basic Books.

Geertz, C. (1983). *Local knowledge*. New York: Basic Books.

Gendlin, E. T. (1962). *Experiencing the creation of meaning*. New York: Free Press.

Gerth, M., and Mills, C. W. (1946). *From Max Weber: Essays in sociology*. New York: Oxford University Press.

Gibb, J. (1982). Is it helpful? In L. Porter and B. Mohr (Eds.), *Reading book for human relations training* (7th ed., 46–51). Arlington, VA: NTL Institute.

Gibb, J. (1994). *Trust*. North Hollywood, CA: Newcastle Publishing Co., Inc.

Gibran, K. (1966). *The prophet*. New York: Alfred A. Knopf.

Glaser, B. G., and Strauss, A. L. (1967). *The discovery of grounded theory*. Chicago: Aldine.

Gold, C. (1986). *Labor-management committees: Confrontation, cooptation, or cooperation*. Ithaca, NY: Cornell University Press.

Goldstein, I. L. (1993). *Training in organizations* (3rd ed.). Pacific Grove, CA: Brooks/Cole.

Goyer, K. S. (1970, March). Communication, communicative processes, and meaning: Toward a unified theory. *Journal of Communications, 20*, 1–46.

Gray, B. (1989). *Collaborating: Finding common ground for multiparty problems*. San Francisco: Jossey-Bass.

Greenleaf, R. K. (1966). *Servant responsibility in a bureaucratic society*. Commencement Speech presented at Redlands College, Redlands, CA.

Greenleaf, R. K. (1977). *Servant leadership*. New York: Paulist Press.

Guba, E. G. and Lincoln, Y. S. (1981). *Effective evaluation*. San Francisco: Jossey-Bass.

Guyot, J. F. (1962). Government bureaucrats are different. *Public Administration Review, 22*, 195–202.

Hackman, J. R. and Oldham, G. (1980). *Work redesign*. Reading, MA: Addison-Wesley.

Harrison, M. I. (1970). Choosing the depth of organizational intervention. *Journal of Applied Behavioral Science, 6*, 181–202.

Hart, S., Boroush, M., Enk, G., and Hornick, W. (1985). Managing complexity through consensus mapping: Technology for the structuring of small group decisions. *Academy of Management Review, 10*, 587–600.

Hayakawa, S. I. (1978). *Language in thought and action*. New York: Harcourt, Brace and Co.

Hecker, S., and Hallock, M. (Eds.). (1991). *Labor in a global economy: Perspectives from the U.S. and Canada*. Eugene, OR: University of Oregon Books.

Heckscher, C., Eisenstat, R. A., and Rice, T. J. (1994). Transformational processes. In C. Heckscher and A. Donnellon (Eds.), *The post-bureaucratic organization: New perspectives on organizational change* (129–177). Newbury Park, CA: Sage.

Herzberg, F. (1983). One more time: How do you motivate employees? *Harvard Business Review, 46*(1), 53–62.

Hirschorn, L. (1991). *Managing in the new team environment: Skills, tools, and methods*. Reading, MA: Addison-Wesley.

Hofstede, G. (1980). *Culture's consequences: International differences in work-related values*. Beverly Hills, CA: Sage.

Hofstede, G. (1991). *Cultures and organizations: Software of the mind*. London: McGraw-Hill.

House, R. J. (1974). Path-goal theory of leadership. *Journal of Contemporary Business, 3*, 81–97.

Husserl, E. (1983). *Ideas pertaining to a pure phenomenology and to a phenomenological philosophy* (F. Kersten, Trans.). The Hague: M. Nijhoff.

Hyde, R. B. (1994). Listening authentically: A Heideggerian perspective on interpersonal communication. In K. C. Carter and M. Presnell (Eds.), *Interpretive approaches to interpersonal communication* (179–195). Albany: State University of New York Press.

Ichniowski, C. (1984, June). *Ruling out productivity? Labor contract pages and plant economic performance* (Working Paper No. 1967). Cambridge, MA: National Bureau of Economic Research.

Israel, B. A., House, J. A., Schurman, S. J., Heany, C. A., and Mero, R. P. (1989). The relation of personal resources, participation, influence, interpersonal relationships, and coping strategies to occupational stress, job strains and health: A multivariate analysis. *Work and Stress, 23*(2), 163–194.

Jackson, S. E. (1983). Participation in decision making as a strategy for reducing job-related strain. *Journal of Applied Psychology, 68*(1), 3–19.

James, W. (1890). *The Principles of Psychology.* New York: Holt.

Janis, I. L. (1972). *Victims of groupthink.* Boston: Houghton Mifflin.

Jennings, K. M., Smith, J. A., and Traynhem, E. C. (1986). *Labor-management cooperation in a public service industry.* New York: Praeger.

Juran, J. M. (1989). *Juran on leadership for quality: An executive handbook.* New York: Free Press.

Karier, T. (1985, February). Unions and monopoly profits. *Review of Economics and Statistics, 62*(1), 34–42.

Keehley, P. (1992, August). TQM for local governments: The principles and prospects. *Public Management, 74*, 10–16.

Killian, R. A. (1976). *Managing human resources: An ROI approach.* New York: Amacom.

Kierkegaard, S. (1966). *Works of love.* New York: Harper.

Kochan, T. A., Katz, H. C., and Mower, N. R. (1985). *Worker participation and American unions: Threat or opportunity?* Kalamazoo, MI: Upjohn Institute for Employment Research.

Kram, K. (1983). Phases of the mentor relationship. *Academy of Management Journal, 26*(4), 608–624.

Lawson, D. M. (1991, December). Language for change. *Individual Psychology, 47* (4), 456–463.

Leana, C. (1983). *The effects of group cohesiveness and leader behavior on defective decision processes: A test of Janis' "Groupthink" model.* Paper presented at a meeting of the Academy of Management, Dallas, TX.

Levine, M. J.(1991, February). Legal obstacles to union-management cooperation in the federal service. *Labor Law Journal, 42*, 103–110.

Lewin, K. (1945). Research center for group dynamics. *Sociometry, 8*(2), 9.

Lewin, K. (1951). *Field theory in social science.* New York: Harper and Row.

Lincoln, Y. S., and Guba, E. G. (1985). *Naturalistic inquiry.* Beverly Hills, CA: Sage.

Lippitt, G. (1979). The trainer's role as an internal consultant. In C. R. Bell and L.

Nadler (Eds.), *The client-consultant handbook* (56–66). Houston, TX: Gulf Publishing Company.

Lippitt, G., and Lippitt, R. (1986). *The consulting process in action* (2nd ed.). San Diego, CA: University Associates.

Lippitt, G. L. (1982). *Organizational renewal* (2nd ed.). Englewood Cliffs, NJ: Prentice-Hall.

Lipsky, M. (1980). *Street-level bureaucracy*. New York: Russell Sage.

Luft, J. (1984). *Group process: An introduction to group dynamics* (3rd ed.). Palo Alto, CA: Mayfield.

Maccoby, M. (1977). *The gamesman: The new corporate leaders*. New York: Simon and Schuster.

Mackie, J. L. (1990). *Ethics: Inventing right and wrong*. London: Penguin Books.

Manchester, W. (1983). *One brief shining moment*. Boston: Little, Brown and Company.

Mangum, G. L., and Mangum, S. L. (1993, July–August). Assessing alternative employment relations systems. *Challenge, 36:* 29–37.

Margulies, N., and Wallace, J. (1973). *Organizational change: Techniques and applications*. Glenview, IL: Scott, Foresman.

Maslow, A. H. (1987). *Motivation and personality*. (3rd ed.). New York: Harper and Row.

May, L. (1996). *The socially responsive self: Social theory and professional ethics*. Chicago: The University of Chicago Press.

Merriam, S. B., and Caffarella, R. S. (1991). *Learning in adulthood: A comprehensive guide*. San Francisco: Jossey-Bass.

Merton, R. K. (1940). Bureaucratic structure and personality. *Social Forces, 18,* 560–568.

Mezirow, J., and Associates (1990). *Fostering critical reflection in adulthood*. San Francisco: Jossey-Bass.

Miles, M. B. and Huberman, A. M. (1984). *Qualitative data analysis: A sourcebook of new methods*. Beverly Hills, CA: Sage.

Miles, M. B., and Huberman, A. M. (1994). Data management and analysis methods. In N. K. Denzin and Y. S. Lincoln (Eds.), *Handbook of qualitative research* (428–444). Thousand Oaks, CA: Sage.

Miller, K. I., and Monge, P. K. (1988). Participation, satisfaction, and productivity: A meta-analytic review. *Academy of Management Journal, 29*(4), 727–753.

Moltmann, J. (1983). *Theology of hope*. Minneapolis: Fortress Press.

Morrison, A. (1987). *Breaking the glass ceiling: Can women reach the top of America's largest corporations?* Reading, MA: Addison-Wesley.

Mosher, F. (1982). *Democracy and the public service*. New York: Oxford University Press.

Muyskens, J. L. (1979). *The sufficiency of hope*. Philadelphia, PA: Temple University Press.

Myers, K., and Killeen, B. (1994, April). Building union-management partnerships. *Quality Progress, 27*(4), 95–97.

Norsworthy, J. R., and Zabala, C. A. (1985, July). Worker attitudes, worker behavior, and productivity in the U.S. automobile industry. *Industrial and Labor Relations Review, 38,* 544–557.

Patton, M. Q. (1980). *Qualitative evaluation methods.* Beverly Hills, CA: Sage.

Patton, M. Q. (1990). *Qualitative evaluation and research methodology.* Newbury Park, CA: Sage.

Peck, M. S. (1987). *The different drum: Community making and peace.* New York: Simon & Schuster.

People and partnerships: Metropolitan Washington Council of Governments 1995 Annual Report. (1995). Washington, D.C.: Metropolitan Washington Council of Governments.

Perline, M. M., and Sexton, E. A. (1994, July). Managerial perceptions of labor-management cooperation. *Industrial Relations, 33*(1), 377–385.

Perrow, C. (1986). *Complex organizations: A critical essay* (3rd ed.). New York: Random House.

Polanyi, M., and Prosch, H. (1975). *Meaning.* Chicago: University of Chicago Press.

Poole, M. S., and McPhee, R. D. (1983). A structural analysis of organizational climate. In L. L. Putnam and M. E. Pacanowsky (Eds.), *Communication and organizations* (195–219). Beverly Hills, CA: Sage.

Porter, L. W., and Mitchell, V. F. (1967). Comparative study of need satisfaction in military and business hierarchies. *Journal of Applied Psychology, 51,* 139–144.

Powell, J. (1976). *Fully human, fully alive.* Allen, TX: Argus Communications.

Rainey, H. G. (1987). Reward expectancies, role perceptions, and job satisfaction among government and business managers: Indications of commonalities and differences. *Proceedings of the Academy of Management* (Atlanta, GA), 357–361.

Rainey, H. G. (1997). *Understanding and managing public organizations* (2nd ed.). San Francisco: Jossey-Bass.

Rehfuss, J. (1979, May–June). Managing the consultantship process. *Public Administration Review, 39*(3), 211–214.

Reisman, B., and Compa, L. (1985, May–June). The case for adversarial unions: A traditional labor-management relationship, rather than one based on concessions and cooperation is best for both sides. *Harvard Business Review, 63,* 22–24.

Rist, R. C. (1994). Influencing the policy process with qualitative research. In N. K. Denzin and Y. S. Lincoln (Eds.), *Handbook of qualitative research* (545–557). Thousand Oaks, CA: Sage.

Rogers, C. R. (1961). *On becoming a person.* Boston: Houghton Mifflin.

Rogers, C. (1977). *Carl Rogers on personal power.* New York: Delacorte Press.

Rogers, C., and Stevens, B. (1967). *Person to person: The problem of being human.* Walnut Creek, CA: Real People Press.

Sapir, E. (1949). *Language: An introduction to the study of speech.* New York: Harcourt, Brace and World, Inc.

Schein, E. H. (1978). *Career dynamics: Matching individual and organizational needs.* Reading, MA: Addison-Wesley.

Schein, E. H. (1985). *Organizational culture and leadership.* San Francisco: Jossey-Bass.

Schein, E. H. (1992). *Organizational culture and leadership* (2nd ed.). San Francisco: Jossey-Bass.

Schon, D. A. (1987). *Educating the reflective practitioner*. San Francisco: Jossey-Bass.

Schutz, A. (1970). *On phenomenology and social relations* (H. R. Wagner, Trans.). Chicago: University of Chicago Press.

Scott, W. G., and Mitchell, T. R. (1988). The problem or mystery of evil and virtue in organizations. In K. Kolenda (Ed.), *Organizations and ethical individualism* (47–72). New York: Praeger.

Scriven, M. (1991). Beyond formative and summative evaluations. In M. W. McLaughlin and D. C. Phillips (Eds.), *Evaluation and education: At quarter century* (19–64). Chicago: University of Chicago Press.

Senge, P. (1990). *The fifth discipline: The art and practice of the learning organization*. New York: Doubleday/Currency.

Simon, H. A. (1947). *Administrative behavior*. New York: Macmillan.

Spradley, J. P. (1979). *The ethnographic interview*. New York: Holt, Rinehart and Winston.

Stillman, R. J., II (1988). *Public administration: Concepts and cases* (4th ed.). Boston: Houghton Mifflin.

Stillman, R. J., II. (1991). *Preface to public administration: A search for themes and direction*. New York: St. Martin's Press.

Stivers, C. (1993). *Gender images in public administration: Legitimacy and the administrative state*. Newbury Park, CA: Sage.

Sulzner, G. T. (1982). The impact of labor-management cooperation committees on personnel policies and practices at twenty federal bargaining units. *Journal of Collective Negotiations, 11*(4), 37–45.

Swift, M. (1991, November 17). A quarter century of Ilg. *Hartford Courant.*

Tillich, P. (1955). *The new being*. New York: Scribner.

Ulanov, A., and Ulanov, B. (1991). *The healing imagination*. Mahwah, NJ: Paulist Press.

Vaill, P. B. (1996). *Learning as a way of being*. San Francisco: Jossey-Bass.

Van Gundy, A. B. (1984). *Managing group creativity: A modular approach to problem solving*. New York: AMACOM.

Van Manen, M. (1990). *Researching lived experience*. London, OT: The University of Western Ontario Press.

Waldo, D. (1980). *The enterprise of public administration*. Novato, CA: Chandler and Sharp.

Webster, M., and Sobieszek, B. I. (1974). *Sources of self-evaluation: A formal theory of significant others and social influence*. New York: Wiley Interscience.

Weick, K. E. (1995). *Sensemaking in organizations*. Newbury Park, CA: Sage.

Weisbord, M. (1976). Organizational diagnosis: Six places to look for trouble with or without a theory. *Group and Organizational Studies, 1*(4), 430–447.

Weisbord, M. R. (1991). *Organizational diagnosis: A workbook of theory and practice*. Reading, MA: Addison-Wesley.

Weiss, C. H. (1970). The politicization of evaluation research. *Journal of Social Issues, 26*, 57–68.

Weiss, C. H. (Ed.). (1972). *Using social research in public policy making*. Lexington, MA: Lexington Press.

Weitman, S. (1978). Prosocial behavior and its discontent. In L. Wispe (Ed.), *Altruism, sympathy, and helping: Psychological and sociological principles* (239–246). New York: Academic Press.

Wellins, R. S., Byham, R. C., and Wilson, J. M. (1981). *Empowered teams.* San Francisco: Jossey-Bass.

White, K. W. (1994). Hans-Georg Gadamer's philosophy of language: A constitutive-dialogic approach to interpersonal understanding. In K. C. Carter and M. Presnell (Eds.), *Interpretive approaches to interpersonal communications* (83–114). Albany: State University of New York Press.

White, L. P., and Wooten, K. C. (1986). *Professional ethics and practice in organizational development.* New York: Praeger.

Wholey, J. S. (1979). *Evaluation: Promise and performance.* Washington, D.C.: Urban Institute.

Yin, R. K. (1984). *Case study research: Design and methods.* Beverly Hills, CA: Sage.

Index

About the Author

A. CAROL RUSAW is an Associate Extension Professor at the Institute of Public Service, University of Connecticut, and has over 15 years experience as an adult educator and change agent in government. She provides management training and organizational consulting to state and local governments and teaches organizational behavior and management, leadership, and organizational theory in the Master's of Public Affairs program at the University of Connecticut.